CW01263445

Principles for Building Resilience
Sustaining Ecosystem Services in Social–Ecological Systems

As both the societies and the world in which we live face increasingly rapid and turbulent changes, the concept of resilience has become an active and important research area. Reflecting the very latest research, this book provides a critical review of the ways in which the resilience of social–ecological systems, and the ecosystem services they provide, can be enhanced.

With contributions from leaders in the field, the chapters are structured around seven key principles for building resilience: maintain diversity and redundancy; manage connectivity; manage slow variables and feedbacks; foster complex adaptive systems thinking; encourage learning; broaden participation; and promote polycentric governance. The authors assess the evidence in support of these principles, discussing their practical application and outlining further research needs. Intended for researchers, practitioners and graduate students, this is an ideal resource for anyone working in resilience science and for those in the broader fields of sustainability science, environmental management and governance.

REINETTE (OONSIE) BIGGS is a researcher at the Stockholm Resilience Centre (SRC), Stockholm University, Sweden, and a research associate at the Centre for Studies in Complexity, Stellenbosch University, South Africa.

MAJA SCHLÜTER is a researcher at the SRC, Stockholm University, Sweden, and head of the research group SES-LINK.

MICHAEL L. SCHOON is an assistant professor at the School of Sustainability, Arizona State University, USA.

Principles for Building Resilience

Sustaining Ecosystem Services in Social–Ecological Systems

Edited by

REINETTE BIGGS
Stockholm Resilience Centre, Stockholm University, Sweden;
and the Centre for Studies in Complexity, Stellenbosch University, South Africa

MAJA SCHLÜTER
Stockholm Resilience Centre, Stockholm University, Sweden

MICHAEL L. SCHOON
School of Sustainability, Arizona State University, USA

CAMBRIDGE UNIVERSITY PRESS

CAMBRIDGE
UNIVERSITY PRESS

University Printing House, Cambridge CB2 8BS, United Kingdom

One Liberty Plaza, 20th Floor, New York, NY 10006, USA

477 Williamstown Road, Port Melbourne, VIC 3207, Australia

314-321, 3rd Floor, Plot 3, Splendor Forum, Jasola District Centre, New Delhi - 110025, India

79 Anson Road, #06-04/06, Singapore 079906

Cambridge University Press is part of the University of Cambridge.

It furthers the University's mission by disseminating knowledge in the pursuit of education, learning and research at the highest international levels of excellence.

www.cambridge.org
Information on this title: www.cambridge.org/9781107082656

© Cambridge University Press 2015

This publication is in copyright. Subject to statutory exception and to the provisions of relevant collective licensing agreements, no reproduction of any part may take place without the written permission of Cambridge University Press.

First published 2015
4th printing 2016

A catalogue record for this publication is available from the British Library

ISBN 978-1-107-08265-6 Hardback

Cambridge University Press has no responsibility for the persistence or accuracy of URLs for external or third-party internet websites referred to in this publication, and does not guarantee that any content on such websites is, or will remain, accurate or appropriate.

To the legendary Ralf Yorque Jr for her ability to inspire us during the many surprises and ongoing development and change that such a project – and the world around us – inevitably entails.

Contents

Acknowledgements	*page* xii
Foreword	xix
CARL FOLKE	
List of contributors	xxiii

1 An introduction to the resilience approach and principles to sustain ecosystem services in social–ecological systems   1
   REINETTE BIGGS, MAJA SCHLÜTER AND MICHAEL L. SCHOON
   1.1. Challenges of a rapidly changing world   2
   1.2. The resilience approach   7
   1.3. Ecosystem services as features of social–ecological systems   13
   1.4. Identifying principles for building resilience   18
   1.5. Objectives and organization of the book   23

2 Politics and the resilience of ecosystem services   32
   MICHAEL L. SCHOON, MARTIN D. ROBARDS, KATRINA BROWN, NATHAN ENGLE, CHANDA L. MEEK AND REINETTE BIGGS
   2.1. Introduction   33
   2.2. The trade-offs of selecting between bundles of ecosystem services   35
   2.3. The challenges of distribution   40
   2.4. Responding to emergent asymmetries   42
   2.5. The benefits of wider deliberation   43
   2.6. Conclusion   45

viii CONTENTS

3 Principle 1 – Maintain diversity and redundancy ... 50
KAREN KOTSCHY, REINETTE BIGGS, TIM DAW,
CARL FOLKE AND PAUL C. WEST
   3.1. Introduction ... 51
   3.2. What do we mean by diversity and redundancy? ... 52
   3.3. How does maintaining diversity and redundancy enhance the resilience of ecosystem services? ... 54
   3.4. Under what conditions may resilience of ecosystem services be compromised? ... 59
   3.5. How can the principle of maintaining diversity and redundancy be operationalized and applied? ... 63
   3.6. Key research and application gaps ... 66

4 Principle 2 – Manage connectivity ... 80
VASILIS DAKOS, ALLYSON QUINLAN, JACOPO
A. BAGGIO, ELENA BENNETT, ÖRJAN BODIN
AND SHAUNA BURNSILVER
   4.1. Introduction ... 81
   4.2. What do we mean by connectivity? ... 81
   4.3. How does connectivity enhance the resilience of ecosystem services? ... 83
   4.4. Under what conditions may resilience of ecosystem services be compromised? ... 89
   4.5. How can the principle of connectivity be operationalized and applied? ... 95
   4.6. Key research and application gaps ... 98

5 Principle 3 – Manage slow variables and feedbacks ... 105
REINETTE BIGGS, LINE GORDON, CIARA
RAUDSEPP-HEARNE, MAJA SCHLÜTER
AND BRIAN WALKER
   5.1. Introduction ... 106
   5.2. What do we mean by slow variables and feedbacks? ... 109

	5.3.	How do slow variables and feedbacks enhance the resilience of ecosystem services?	110
	5.4.	Under what conditions may resilience of ecosystem services be compromised?	120
	5.5.	How can the principle of managing slow variables and feedbacks be operationalized and applied?	127
	5.6.	Key research and application gaps	131
6	Principle 4 – Foster complex adaptive systems thinking	142
	ERIN L. BOHENSKY, LOUISA S. EVANS, JOHN M. ANDERIES, DUAN BIGGS AND CHRISTO FABRICIUS	
	6.1.	Introduction	143
	6.2.	What do we mean by fostering CAS thinking?	145
	6.3.	How does CAS thinking enhance the resilience of ecosystem services?	148
	6.4.	Under what conditions may resilience of ecosystem services be compromised?	156
	6.5.	How can CAS thinking be operationalized and applied?	158
	6.6.	Key research and application gaps	165
7	Principle 5 – Encourage learning	174
	GEORGINA CUNDILL, ANNE M. LEITCH, LISEN SCHULTZ, DEREK ARMITAGE AND GARRY PETERSON	
	7.1.	Introduction	175
	7.2.	What do we mean by 'learning'?	178
	7.3.	How does learning enhance the resilience of ecosystem services?	179
	7.4.	Under what conditions may resilience of ecosystem services be compromised?	186
	7.5.	How can the principle of learning be operationalized and applied?	190
	7.6.	Key research and application gaps	192

8 Principle 6 – Broaden participation   201
   ANNE M. LEITCH, GEORGINA CUNDILL,
   LISEN SCHULTZ AND CHANDA L. MEEK
   8.1. Introduction   202
   8.2. What do we mean by participation?   203
   8.3. How does participation enhance the resilience
         of ecosystem services?   204
   8.4. Under what conditions may resilience of ecosystem
         services be compromised?   211
   8.5. How can the principle of participation be
         operationalized and applied?   214
   8.6. Key research and application gaps   218

9 Principle 7 – Promote polycentric governance
   systems   226
   MICHAEL L. SCHOON, MARTIN D. ROBARDS,
   CHANDA L. MEEK AND VICTOR GALAZ
   9.1. Introduction   227
   9.2. What do we mean by polycentricity?   228
   9.3. How does polycentricity enhance the resilience of
         ecosystem services?   231
   9.4. Under what conditions may resilience of ecosystem
         services be compromised?   235
   9.5. How can the principle of polycentricity be
         operationalized and applied?   239
   9.6. Key research and application gaps   241

10 Reflections on building resilience – interactions
   among principles and implications for governance   251
   MAJA SCHLÜTER, REINETTE BIGGS, MICHAEL
   L. SCHOON, MARTIN D. ROBARDS AND JOHN
   M. ANDERIES
   10.1. Introduction   252

10.2.	Key insights from the individual principles	254
10.3.	Interactions amongst the principles	259
10.4.	Evidence for the different principles	263
10.5.	Implications for management and governance of social–ecological systems	265
10.6.	Future research needs	273
10.7.	Conclusions	277

Index   283

Acknowledgements

This book is the product of a long-standing and rewarding collaboration among a group of young scholars who first connected in 2007 to form the Resilience Alliance Young Scholars (RAYS) network. The RAYS was initiated by the Resilience Alliance (RA, http://www.resalliance.org) to provide a space for young resilience scholars linked to the RA and other resilience research nodes around the world to come together and share ideas, and develop a next generation of internationally networked resilience scientists. At the time the first RAYS group was initiated, most of us were PhD students or just starting postdocs. Ultimately, this book and the opportunity to develop the RAYS would not have been possible without the foresight and support of the RA in creating this space, and co-funding a series of workshops at which we met, formed some wonderful friendships and had a fantastic lot of fun!

The RAYS first met face to face at the first ever Resilience conference held in Stockholm in April 2008: Resilience 2008 – Resilience, Adaptation and Transformation in Turbulent Times, hosted by the newly established Stockholm Resilience Centre in Sweden. At this workshop we agreed that we wanted to become 'guerrilla researchers' that took on big ideas and challenged established 'truths' in the social–ecological resilience field. This sentiment laid the foundation for a series of collaborative projects, including the one that eventually morphed into this book. Our appreciation goes to all the RAYS and senior RA members that were part of this first meeting, and provided the original inspiration for this book. A special thank you also to the Resilience Alliance Surprises Group (Steve Carpenter, Marten Scheffer, Frances Westley and Carl Folke) who provided further inspiration for this project through discussions at a meeting in Uruguay in January 2009, which Reinette (Oonsie) Biggs attended.

The project first got underway through an online discussion amongst the RAYS following the 2008 meeting, which led to an idea for a paper that would critically review various 'propositions' (some of which had arguably attained a somewhat myth-like status) that have been put forward as important factors for enhancing resilience in social–ecological systems. Our idea was to dig in and find out just how important were factors like diversity and participation in building resilience. How much evidence was there really for these propositions? When and where, and in what forms did they really matter? We wanted to write the paper we wish we could have read when we entered graduate school, and hopefully help future students (including our own students!) get their heads around the huge cross-disciplinary and sometimes bewildering resilience literature.

A landmark event in the development of the paper, which was eventually published in *Annual Review of Environment and Resources* in November 2012, was a two-and-a-half-day 'mock-court' workshop that was held on Gabriola Island, Canada in September 2009 in conjunction with an RA science meeting. At that time we had ten draft principles, and a small team of authors were tasked with developing and presenting the 'defence case' for each principle. This 'testimony' by the RAYS 'expert witnesses' for each principle was then cross-examined at length by a senior member of the RA. Subsequently, the floor was opened to all participants for questioning, several of whom had been specifically appointed to act as 'devil's advocates' for the different principles. The feedback and input from those who acted as cross-examiners and devil's advocates was hugely valuable in refining the set of principles and providing a balanced, critical review of each, laying the foundation for both the paper and this book. We also thank all the RA and RAYS participants at the main RA science meeting who participated in the Delphi-like survey process we ran directly after the mock-court workshop to refine the set of principles we had presented. Together, these two processes were key to settling on the seven principles presented in the paper and this book. A special and big thank you for the insights, time and effort contributed by the cross-examiners: Elinor Ostrom, Katrina Brown, Frances Westley, Per Olsson, Mike Jones, Line Gordon, Marty Anderies and Christo Fabricius. We also greatly appreciate the input of the RAYS members who acted as devil's advocates and discussants at this workshop (and provided some very good entertainment): Victor Galaz, Terry Iverson, John Parker, Beatrice Crona and Jacopo Baggio. Although none of the cross-examiners or devil's advocates were involved in the further development of the paper, many of these people were subsequently re-engaged in the process of developing this book. In fact, several of these folks already suggested at that time that the scope of the topic we are tackling is so huge that we should consider a book rather than a paper; however, we found this prospect much too intimidating to contemplate at that stage!

A second important point of feedback and critique on the paper was provided during a 1.5-hour session we ran at the Resilience 2011 conference, entitled Resilience Propositions on Trial. This session was modelled on the mock-court process we ran in Canada, but focused on just two principles: diversity and redundancy, and learning and experimentation. This time round we decided to go for more of a mix of RAYS and senior RA scholars on the defence and cross-examination teams. A special thank you to everyone who participated in this session, which evoked a great deal of laughter, and some wonderful play-acting! The cross-examiners included Graeme Cumming, Elinor Ostrom, Vasilis Dakos, Duan Biggs, Claudia Pahl-Wostl, Sander van der Leeuw, Mike Schoon and Maja Schlüter; the defence team members were Brian Walker, Garry Peterson, Karen Kotschy, Shauna BurnSilver, Reinette (Oonsie) Biggs, Paul West, Frances Westley, Katrina Brown, Anne Leitch, Louisa Evans, Samantha Stone-Jovicich and Lisen Schultz; and the devil's advocates included Terry Iverson and Chanda Meek. Serendipitously, this session was attended by one of the conference's keynote speakers, Professor William Clark of Harvard University, USA. He was very supportive of the more reflective, critical stance adopted in our project, and invited us to submit a proposal to *Annual Review in Environment and Resources*, which a small team of us cobbled together there and then. After which started the hard work – and many fun exchanges – to whittle down what had become a short monograph on each principle into a coherent paper.

By the time we submitted the paper, we had come to the realization that a book was not such a bad idea after all, and that in fact we already had much of the material for it. More importantly, in the course of developing the paper, we had fleshed out a shared conceptual framework and approach that could make for a really coherent, integrated, multi-author book. We also realized that developing such a product could provide a valuable opportunity for facilitating more interaction between the RAYS and the RA. We therefore invited a number of additional folks as authors on the book to help further broaden and solidify our review. That is the product you now hold in your hands. A big thank you to Dominic Lewis, Megan Waddington and Renee Duncan-Mestel at Cambridge University Press for guiding us through this process. Much thanks and appreciation also to Linda Luvuno for helping ensure that all the chapters and references were consistently formatted, and lending a friendly helping hand with many aspects of the final manuscript preparation. A big thanks to Jerker Lokrantz at Azote Images for so beautifully preparing all the figures for the book. Many authors also put effort into providing detailed review comments; the contribution of this to the internal consistency and quality of the book are much appreciated. In particular we thank Duan Biggs, Line Gordon and Louisa Evans for comments on Chapter 2, Ciara Raudsepp-Hearne, Victor Galaz and Shauna BurnSilver (Chapter 3), Karen Kotschy, Paul West and Marty Anderies (Chapter 4), Karen Kotschy, Vasilis Dakos and Garry Peterson (Chapter 5), Line Gordon, Jacopo Baggio, Anne Leitch and two external reviewers from CSIRO in Australia, Elizabeth Hobman and Rod McCrea (Chapter 6), Duan Biggs and Allyson Quinlan (Chapter 7), Örjan Bodin and Mark Reed (Chapter 8), Marty Anderies,

Shauna BurnSilver and Lisen Schultz (Chapter 9). Sturle Hauge Simonsen, Fredrik Moberg and the team at Azote and Matador Kommunikation are much thanked for their professional and very speedy preparation of a layman's summary of the book in the form of the brochure *Applying resilience thinking: seven principles for building resilience in social–ecological systems*. This brochure was distributed at a session (which we believe will be the final Resilience conference session on this project!) we organized at the Resilience 2014: Resilience and Development – Mobilizing for Transformation conference in Montpellier in May 2014.

Given the large number of authors involved and the early phases of many of their careers, a large variety of funding streams supported the development of this book. Without this support, and the freedom it gave us to pursue ambitious guerrilla-type research topics, this book would not have materialized. Reinette (Oonsie) Biggs was supported through a Centre of Excellence grant by the Swedish Research Council Formas, a Branco Weiss Society in Science fellowship and a fellowship from the Stellenbosch Institute for Advanced Study (STIAS) during the course of coordinating the paper and this book. Maja Schlüter was supported by a Branco Weiss Society in Science fellowship and acknowledges the Project Besatzfisch funded by the German Ministry of Education and Research in the Program for Social–Ecological Research (grant 01UU0907), and a grant by the European Research Council under the EU FP7 (FP/2007–2013)/ERC grant agreement no. 283950 SES-LINK. J. Marty Anderies gratefully acknowledges support from the US National Science Foundation grant numbers SES-0645789 and GEO-1115054. Derek Armitage's research is supported by ArcticNet and by the Social Science and Humanities Research Council of Canada. Jacopo A. Baggio acknowledges a postdoctoral fellowship from the Center for the Study of Institutional Diversity at Arizona State University and support from NSF grant GEO-1115054. Elena Bennett was supported by the National Science and Engineering Research Council (NSERC) Discovery. Örjan Bodin acknowledges support from the strategic research programme Ekoklim at Stockholm

University, Sweden. Georgina Cundill acknowledges a Rhodes University postdoctoral fellowship. Vasilis Dakos was supported by a Dutch Rubicon and an EU Marie Curie fellowship. Christo Fabricius is grateful to the National Research Foundation for its ongoing support of the Southern African node of the Resilience Alliance and his research. Anne Leitch gratefully acknowledges a postgraduate scholarship from James Cook University, Australia. Lisen Schultz and Line Gordon thank Ebba and Sven Schwartz Stiftelse for support. The support of Mistra through a core grant to the Stockholm Resilience Centre is acknowledged for support of staff from the Resilience Centre and the production costs of the brochure.

Lastly, a big thank you to all our readers – including graduate students, fellow researchers and practitioners. Ultimately, it was the idea that you might find a synthesis like this useful and insightful in helping guide actions towards building a better world that gave us the inspiration and energy to put this book together. We hope it lives up to this!

Foreword

Why should we care at all about resilience? The biosphere – the sphere of life – is the living part of the outermost layer of our rocky planet, the part of the Earth's crust, waters and atmosphere where life dwells. It is the global ecological system integrating all living beings and their relationships. Humans are embedded parts of the biosphere and shape it, from local to global scales, from the past to the future. At the same time humans are fundamentally dependent on the capacity of the biosphere to sustain development. Humanity is indeed an embedded part of the biosphere shaping and reshaping its environment. In this sense humanity co-evolves with the planet and our beliefs, perceptions, choices and actions shape our future in the biosphere. Fundamental issues for humanity like democracy, health, poverty, inequality, power, human rights, security and peace all rest on the life-support capacity and resilience of the biosphere.

The situation of the Anthropocene – where the biosphere is shaped by humanity from local to global levels – reinforces that there are no ecosystems without people and no human development without support from the biosphere, hence, social–ecological systems. Humans and nature are truly intertwined and ecosystem services are critical for well-being. Analysing the world from historical, economic, geographical, ecological or other disciplinary approaches will provide bits of the puzzle. But, in the Anthropocene, the scale, speed and connectivity of human actions interact with the dynamics of the Earth system in new ways, which call for new understanding, new integrated approaches and collaborations across disciplines. Analysing situations of incremental change and assuming a stable environment is no longer the most fruitful way to understand the world and improve the human predicament. Viewing the world as a complex system is a more recent and promising approach that is emerging across the disciplines, including social and natural sciences as well as the humanities, and also the foundation of this book.

Reinette (Oonsie) Biggs, Maja Schlüter and Michael Schoon have done an excellent job pushing the frontier of sustainability science and resilience thinking by orchestrating the inspiring chapters of *Principles for Building Resilience: Sustaining Ecosystem Services in Social–Ecological Systems* into a coherent and significant book. The book has the biosphere and a complex systems approach as the foundation for understanding social–ecological systems and resilience.

Resilience as used here is about having the ability to live with change, and develop with it. It is about cultivating the capacity to sustain development in the face of change, incremental and abrupt, expected and surprising. Resilience is about persisting with change on the current path of development, improving and innovating on that path. Sometimes actions lead to path dependency and to traps that are difficult to get out of. The resilience of the system has become too robust and too rigid. In such situations the challenge is to reduce resilience and try to shift away from the current path into new ones. Sometimes those shifts may be smooth, other times revolutionary.

Shifts between states and development pathways are at the core of resilience research. In research on social–ecological systems and resilience, adaptation refers to human actions that sustain development on the current pathway, while transformation is about shifting development into new pathways and even creating new pathways. Deliberate transformation involves breaking down the resilience of the old and building the resilience of the new. A shifting pathway does not take place in a vacuum. It draws on resilience from multiple scales and diverse sources, making use of crises as windows of opportunity, recombining experience and knowledge, learning with change, and governing transformations for innovative pathways in tune with the resilience of the biosphere.

This is the very focus of *Principles for Building Resilience: Sustaining Ecosystem Services in Social–Ecological Systems*. The book investigates a set of propositions for general features of resilience in relation to uncertainty. It is about how to deal with an uncertain future in relation to diverse pathways, and thresholds and tipping points between them. The authors expand on the significant paper 'Toward principles for enhancing the resilience of ecosystem services', which was published in *Annual Review of Environment and Resources* in 2012, led by Reinette (Oonsie) Biggs and Maja Schlüter. The paper identified seven generic principles for enhancing the capacity of social–ecological systems to continue delivering desired sets of ecosystem services in the face of disturbance and ongoing change:

- maintain diversity and redundancy;
- manage connectivity;
- manage slow variables and feedbacks;
- foster an understanding of social–ecological systems as complex adaptive systems;
- encourage learning and experimentation;
- broaden participation; and
- promote polycentric governance systems.

It then critically reviewed evidence in support of each of these principles. In doing so, the paper attempted to bring together some very different strands of resilience research, specifically in relation to the implications of the findings for managing ecosystem services.

The book is a major and comprehensive extension of the insights and findings of the general resilience principles paper. It brings together different disciplinary traditions and strands of resilience work in an interdisciplinary and coherent way. The authors, engaged with research groups, centres and institutes of the Resilience Alliance, have operated as a team, developing a common conceptual framework and approach to a deep investigation of the principles.

Work on resilience has exploded in the last decade. Resilience is used in many different areas and disciplines and sometimes interpreted in ways to fit old paradigms and discourses. In contrast, what is beautiful here is that the foundation of this book recognizes that humanity is an embedded part of the biosphere and is dependent on its life-supporting environment generating essential ecosystem services as a precondition for societal development and progress. It is explicit about the challenges of the Anthropocene, with human well-being and ecosystem service trade-offs occurring across spatial and temporal scales, being co-produced by social–ecological systems, and accounting for issues of power and equity in this context. In particular, given the proliferation of resilience-related research the attempt to systematically assess and critically evaluate empirical evidence in support of the seven propositions and claims that have been put forward as underlying principles for building resilience in social–ecological systems is of great value.

The turbulent times in which we live open up space for new ways of thinking and action that take complexity seriously. This book is a manifestation of the situation, with authors collaborating in and integrating diverse disciplines and knowledge systems, and taking on the search for understanding the complexity and dynamics of social–ecological systems together with the challenges of biosphere stewardship. The book provides an exciting, coherent and in-depth review of the state of understanding on how different key factors affect the resilience of social–ecological systems. It nicely discusses the practical application of these principles and lays out further research needs in relation to managing and governing ecosystem services for human well-being. It is an excellent contribution to the frontier of resilience research and sustainability science. Every chapter is worth diving deep into, reflecting upon and rethinking. The book will no doubt be a source of inspiration for many.

Carl Folke
Director of the Beijer Institute, Royal Swedish
Academy of Sciences; Founder and Science
Director of the Stockholm Resilience Centre,
Stockholm University

Contributors

John M. Anderies: School of Human Evolution and Social Change, Arizona State University, Tempe, Arizona, USA

Derek Armitage: Environmental Change and Governance Group and the Department of Environment and Resource Studies, University of Waterloo, Ontario, Canada

Jacopo A. Baggio: Center for the Study of Institutional Diversity, School of Human Evolution and Social Change, Arizona State University, Tempe, Arizona, USA

Elena Bennett: Department of Natural Resource Sciences and School of Environment, McGill University, Montreal, Quebec, Canada

Duan Biggs: Centre of Excellence for Environmental Decisions, School of Biological Sciences, University of Queensland, Brisbane and Australian Research Council Centre of Excellence for Coral Reef Studies, James Cook University, Townsville, Queensland, Australia; and Scientific Services, South African National Parks, Skukuza, South Africa

Reinette (Oonsie) Biggs: Stockholm Resilience Centre, Stockholm University, Sweden and Centre for Studies in Complexity, Stellenbosch University, South Africa

Örjan Bodin: Stockholm Resilience Centre, Stockholm University, Sweden

Erin L. Bohensky: CSIRO Ecosystem Sciences, ATSIP, James Cook University, Townsville, Queensland, Australia

Katrina Brown: Environment and Sustainability Institute, University of Exeter, Penryn Campus, Cornwall, UK

Shauna BurnSilver: School of Human Evolution and Social Change, Arizona State University, Tempe, Arizona, USA

Georgina Cundill: Department of Environmental Science, Rhodes University, Grahamstown, South Africa

Vasilis Dakos: Integrative Ecology Group, Bascompte Lab, Estación Biológica de Doñana, CSIC, Sevilla, Spain

Tim Daw: Stockholm Resilience Centre, Stockholm University, Sweden and School of International Development, University of East Anglia, Norwich, UK

Nathan Engle: The World Bank, Washington, DC, USA

Louisa S. Evans: Geography, College of Life and Environmental Sciences, University of Exeter, UK and Australian Research Council Centre of Excellence for Coral Reef Studies, James Cook University, Townsville, Queensland, Australia

Christo Fabricius: Sustainability Research Unit, Nelson Mandela Metropolitan University, George, South Africa

Carl Folke: Stockholm Resilience Centre, Stockholm University and Beijer Institute of Ecological Economics, The Royal Swedish Academy of Sciences, Stockholm, Sweden

Victor Galaz: Stockholm Resilience Centre, Stockholm University, Sweden

Line Gordon: Stockholm Resilience Centre, Stockholm University, Sweden

Karen Kotschy: Centre for Water in the Environment, University of the Witwatersrand, Johannesburg, South Africa

Anne M. Leitch: Australian Research Council Centre of Excellence for Coral Reef Studies, James Cook University, Townsville, Queensland, Australia

Chanda L. Meek: Department of Political Science, University of Alaska, Fairbanks, USA

Garry Peterson: Stockholm Resilience Centre, Stockholm University, Sweden

Allyson Quinlan: Resilience Alliance, Department of Biology, Acadia University Wolfville, Nova Scotia, Canada

Ciara Raudsepp-Hearne: Independent researcher – Montreal, Canada

Martin D. Robards: Wildlife Conservation Society, Fairbanks, Alaska, USA

Maja Schlüter: Stockholm Resilience Centre, Stockholm University, Sweden

Michael L. Schoon: School of Sustainability, Arizona State University, Tempe, Arizona, USA

Lisen Schultz: Stockholm Resilience Centre, Stockholm University, Sweden

Brian Walker: Ecosystem Sciences, CSIRO, Canberra, A.C.T., Australia

Paul C. West: Institute of the Environment, University of Minnesota, St. Paul, Minnesota, USA

1 An introduction to the resilience approach and principles to sustain ecosystem services in social–ecological systems

Reinette Biggs, Maja Schlüter and Michael L. Schoon

SUMMARY

A major challenge of the twenty-first century is ensuring an adequate and reliable flow of essential ecosystem services to meet the needs of the world's burgeoning and increasingly wealthy population. This challenge needs to be addressed in the face of rapidly changing social, technological and environmental conditions that characterize the world today. Social–ecological resilience is one fast-growing approach that attempts to inform this challenge and provide practical guidance to decision-makers and practitioners. The resilience approach views humans as part of the biosphere, and assumes that the resulting intertwined social–ecological systems behave as complex adaptive systems – i.e. they have the capacity to self-organize and adapt based on past experience, and are characterized by emergent and non-linear behaviour and inherent uncertainty. A rapidly growing body of research on resilience in social–ecological systems has proposed a variety of attributes that are important for enhancing resilience. This book aims to critically assess and synthesize this literature. In this chapter we introduce the resilience approach and the process by which we identified seven

Principles for Building Resilience: Sustaining Ecosystem Services in Social–Ecological Systems, eds R. Biggs, M. Schlüter and M. L. Schoon. Published by Cambridge University Press. © Cambridge University Press 2015.

generic principles for enhancing the capacity of social–ecological systems to produce desired sets of ecosystem services in the face of disturbance and change.

1.1 CHALLENGES OF A RAPIDLY CHANGING WORLD

We live in an era of rapid and unprecedented change. The past century has seen the mass production and adoption of motor cars and telephones, a 15-fold increase in the global economy, large-scale conversion of land to agriculture and an increase in the global population from 1.6 billion people in 1900 to over 7 billion in 2011 (MA 2005a; Steffen *et al.* 2007) (Fig. 1.1). Despite ongoing challenges with addressing poverty, these rapid changes have brought huge benefits and dramatic improvements to many people's lives, particularly since the end of the Second World War in 1945 (MA 2005a; Steffen *et al.* 2007). Tellingly, for most of human history the average life expectancy was 20–30 years, reflecting the combined effects of poor nutrition, disease and warfare, especially on infant survival (Lancaster 1990). In 1900, the average global life expectancy still stood at 31 years, but by 2010 it had reached 67 years (CIA 2013), and is predicted to continue increasing and level off somewhere below 100 years (UN 2004). Millions of people today have access to a huge variety of goods, health, mobility and comforts that even kings and queens could not have dreamed of just a century ago.

However, there are growing concerns about whether these massive strides in human well-being can be sustained, and particularly whether substantially improving the lives of the 2.4 billion people who still live in poverty (World Bank 2014), as well as meeting the needs of the additional 1.5–2.5 billion people that are expected to join us on the planet by 2050 (UN 2013), is possible given the current trends of environmental degradation and change (MA 2005a; Intergovernmental Panel on Climate Change (IPCC) 2014). Despite huge technological advances, people still ultimately depend largely on nature for a variety of essential needs, including fresh air, clean water and food, protection from hazards such as droughts and storms, and a wide variety of cultural, spiritual and recreational needs that play a

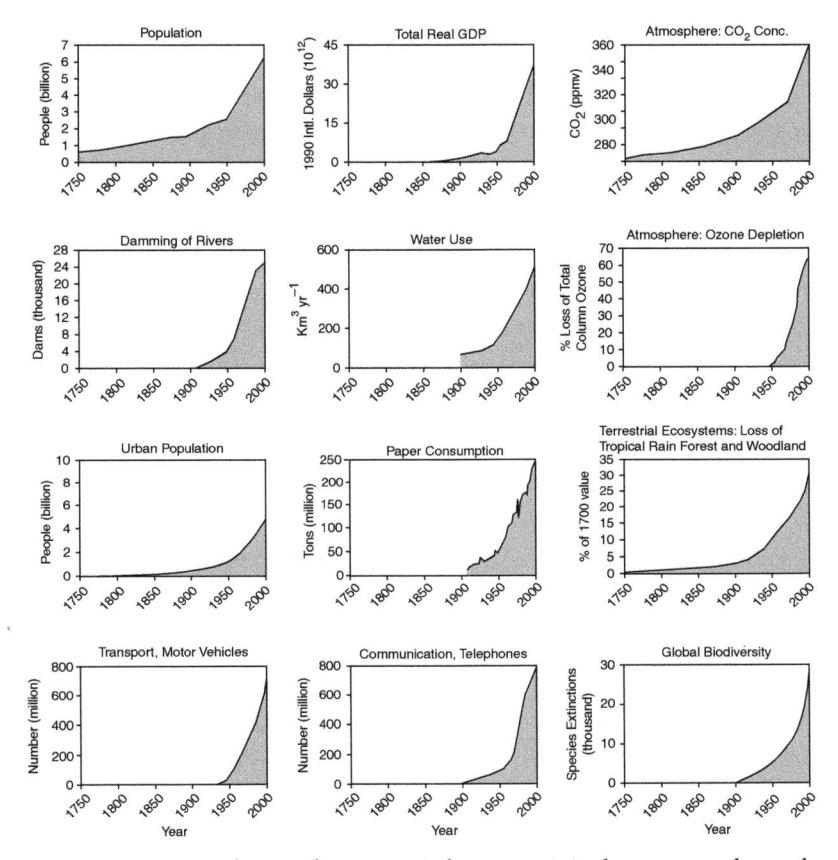

FIG. 1.1 Substantial increases in human activity have occurred over the past century, particularly since the end of the Second World War in 1945, with substantial impacts on the Earth's environment and functioning. These changes and impacts have often been even more pronounced in particular places and regions. From Steffen *et al.* (2011).

key role in human well-being (MA 2005a). Such benefits derived from the interaction of people with nature are known as ecosystem services (Ernstson 2013; Reyers *et al.* 2013; Huntsinger and Oviedo 2014).

There is growing evidence that the massive scale and extent of human activities such as agriculture, transport and release of novel chemicals are undermining the capacity of nature to generate key ecosystem services on which we depend (MA 2005a; IPCC 2014). For example, more than 50% of inland waters (excluding lakes and rivers) have been lost in parts of North America, Europe and Australia due to changes in land cover, drainage, infilling, invasive species and the effects of pollution, salinization and eutrophication (Finlayson *et al.* 2005). The cumulative impact of such activities on the biosphere – the thin layer of the Earth's surface and atmosphere that supports all life on Earth – is affecting the functioning of the planet, not just at local and regional scales, but at global scales (Steffen *et al.* 2004). Climate change provides a premier example. It is now well established scientifically that rising atmospheric carbon dioxide levels resulting from anthropogenic fossil-fuel combustion and land clearing are changing rainfall and temperature patterns around the world and leading to an increased incidence of extreme events such as droughts and storms (IPCC 2014). These changes are impacting food security, disease prevalence and infrastructure, as well as impacting traditional lifestyles and cultural practices that shape people's identity. They therefore pose direct threats to human security and well-being (IPCC 2014).

The profound shift to today's situation where human activities fundamentally shape the functioning of the planet, not just at local and regional scales but globally, has been suggested to mark a new geological era in the history of the Earth: the Anthropocene (Crutzen and Stoermer 2000). For most of human history, people had limited and localized impacts on the Earth's environment. If the environment became too degraded to support a community, people could usually move elsewhere (Diamond 2004). This started to change, however, with the onset of the industrial era in the 1800s. Particularly since the 1950s, human activities have been substantially impacting not just local and regional environments, but planetary functioning at a global scale (Steffen *et al.* 2007). This scaling up of the impact of human activities and the consequent changes to the functioning of the Earth system potentially have far-reaching and substantial consequences for the provision of key ecosystem services on which humanity depends.

A variety of novel and unpredictable effects that are difficult for society to cope with are of particular concern. Effects such as climate change, biodiversity loss, and changes in nutrient cycles are increasing the incidence of highly disruptive and unpredictable shocks such as large storms and disease outbreaks (MA 2005a; IPCC 2014). Human-induced changes to the environment are also increasing the potential for crossing critical thresholds or tipping points that could lead to large, non-linear and potentially irreversible changes at local through global scales, such as the death of coral reefs, shifts in regional monsoon rainfall patterns or collapse of the Greenland ice sheet (MA 2005a; Rockström *et al.* 2009; Barnosky *et al.* 2012). Beyond these somewhat known effects, our impacts on the environment are leading to completely novel changes that are very difficult to anticipate, and could have dramatic impacts on a variety of ecosystem services. The use of chlorofluorocarbons (CFCs) in refrigerators that led to the creation of the ozone hole is one example (Farman *et al.* 1985). Other examples include the potential emergence and spread of new diseases such as severe acute respiratory syndrome (SARS), or the potential consequences of nuclear proliferation and massively increased global connectivity and trade on the environment (Martin 2007).

The challenge of ensuring human well-being in the face of these rapid, ongoing changes to the environment and human society, and the substantial uncertainties they are generating, has given rise to a variety of new approaches and types of science (Gibbons *et al.* 1994; Funtowicz *et al.* 1999). One of these is the resilience approach (Walker and Salt 2006; Folke *et al.* 2010), which falls within the broad emerging field of sustainability science, a new research area that seeks to understand the interactions between nature and society in order to inform pressing sustainability challenges (Kates *et al.* 2001; Clark and Dickson 2003). Fundamental to the resilience approach is the assumption that people are embedded in the biosphere at local to global scales, where they interact with and help shape their environment, and are intricately dependent on it for a variety of ecosystem services that underpin human well-being (Berkes and Folke 1998; Berkes *et al.* 2003; Walker and Salt 2006). Resilience studies therefore focus largely on the study of intertwined social–ecological systems

(SES). These SES are assumed to behave as complex adaptive systems (CAS), i.e. they have the capacity to self-organize and adapt based on past experience, and they are characterized by emergent and non-linear behaviour, and generate substantial and sometimes irreducible uncertainties (Norberg and Cumming 2008). The resilience approach focuses specifically on the capacity of SES to deal with change in these kinds of systems. This includes not only recovery from unexpected shocks and avoiding undesirable tipping points, but also the capacity to adapt to ongoing change and fundamentally transform SES if needed (Walker *et al.* 2004; Folke *et al.* 2010).

Over the past two decades the resilience approach has attracted increasing attention, and there has been an explosion of research into system attributes that may promote or undermine the resilience of ecological systems, social systems and SES, and the ecosystem services upon which society depends (Gunderson and Holling 2002; Berkes *et al.* 2003; Walker and Salt 2006; Chapin *et al.* 2009; Boyd and Folke 2011). Given the diversity of potential attributes that affect resilience in SES, this research has drawn on a wide range of disciplines, including the social, economic, political and ecological sciences. A variety of potential factors have been proposed as key to building resilience based on theoretical and empirical research across a range of systems and case studies (Anderies *et al.* 2006; Walker and Salt 2006; Walker *et al.* 2006; Ostrom 2009). The diversity of disciplines and strands of resilience work involved has, however, led to a somewhat dispersed and fragmented understanding of the importance of different factors in different contexts. This fragmentation is limiting a coherent understanding of what factors are likely to be important for building resilience in a particular social–ecological setting, and how these factors can be practically operationalized to better manage SES in support of human well-being and long-term social and environmental sustainability.

This book aims to address this gap and help make sense of the large and growing body of work on resilience to identify key underlying principles for building resilience, and how these may be practically applied in real-world settings to advance sustainability. The book builds directly on an earlier review paper (Biggs *et al.* 2012b) that critically evaluated empirical evidence in support of various propositions and claims of factors that promote resilience of ecosystem services. We define resilience of ecosystem services as the capacity of SES to continue providing desired sets of ecosystem services in the face of unexpected shocks as well as ongoing change and development. Based on the paper and the work in this book we identify seven general principles for enhancing resilience of ecosystem services produced by SES: (P1) maintain diversity and redundancy, (P2) manage connectivity, (P3) manage slow variables and feedbacks, (P4) foster CAS thinking, (P5) encourage learning and experimentation, (P6) broaden participation and (P7) promote polycentric governance systems. These principles form the seven core chapters of the book, and throughout we cross-reference these chapters by their principle number and name (e.g. P1 – Diversity).

The first two chapters set the stage for the book. In this chapter we introduce the resilience approach, including its underlying rationale and assumptions. We introduce the concept of ecosystem services as a critical integrator between people and nature, and a potential focus for resilience-building initiatives and SES stewardship. Finally, we describe the process by which we identified the seven principles that form the core of this book. Before discussing the individual principles, Chapter 2 considers the social and political dimensions of ecosystem services, emphasizing that before applying any of the principles it is critical to reflect on which ecosystem services are the focus for resilience-building initiatives and who benefits and loses from these choices.

1.2 THE RESILIENCE APPROACH

Resilience is a perspective for the analysis of SES that emphasizes the need to understand and manage change, particularly unexpected change. Like other approaches within the sustainability science field, resilience studies are fundamentally problem-driven and integrate a variety of disciplinary approaches and perspectives to help address the considerable sustainability challenges facing society. The human–environment interactions at the core of sustainability science studies are, however, being conceptualized in a variety of ways, ranging from relatively loose links to strong interactive feedbacks between social and ecological system components. The resilience approach falls at the latter end of this spectrum.

Fundamental to the resilience approach is the notion that human society is embedded in and part of the Earth's biosphere. In this view, humans and nature are truly intertwined and interdependent: human action shapes ecosystem dynamics from local to global scales, while human societies rely on a wide variety of ecosystem services generated by SES for their well-being, including spiritual and psychological well-being (Folke 2006; Folke *et al.* 2011). In the resilience perspective, the SES resulting from these interactions are not seen as social plus ecological systems. Instead, they are seen as cohesive systems in themselves that occur at the interface between social and ecological systems, characterized by strong interactions and feedbacks between social and ecological system components that determine the overall dynamics of the SES (Fig. 1.2) (Folke *et al.*

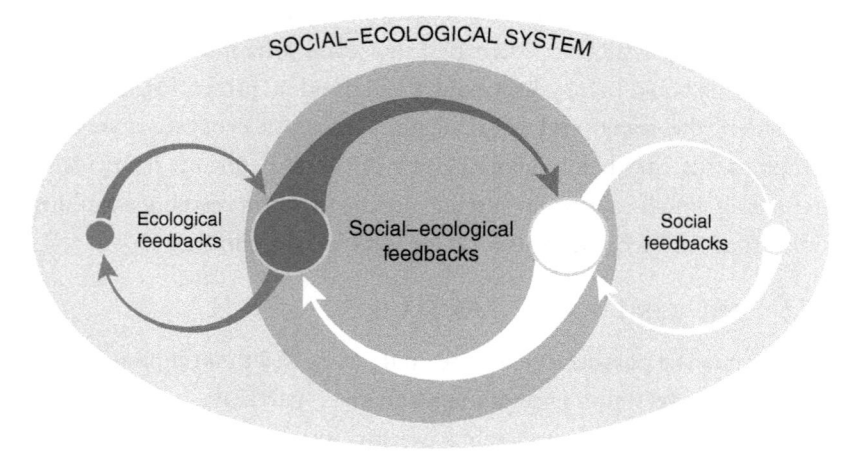

FIG. 1.2 In the resilience approach, SES are not simply seen as social plus ecological systems. Rather they are viewed as systems centred on the feedbacks between ecological (grey) and social (white) system components, which lie at the interface of social and ecological systems.

2010). A resilience approach thus moves beyond viewing humans as external drivers of ecosystem dynamics, as common in ecology or natural resource management, or natural resources as rather simple and constant inputs to production processes, as in economics. Instead it adopts an integrative analysis of complex interdependencies of actors, institutions and ecosystems across multiple scales (Gunderson and Holling 2002; Ostrom 2009; Boyd and Folke 2011).

Perhaps further setting it apart from several other approaches, the resilience perspective fundamentally assumes that SES behave as CAS (Folke 2006; Levin *et al.* 2013). In other words, SES have the capacity to self-organize and adapt or learn in response to internal or external disturbances and changing conditions, and are characterized by non-linear dynamics (Gros 2008). SES are seen as continuously evolving entities, with ongoing change arising from social–ecological interactions in the system, constrained and shaped by a given social–ecological setting (Gunderson and Holling 2002; Folke 2006). The diversity of SES components is seen as essential for this self-organizing ability as heterogeneity provides a source of variation for adaptation (P1 – Diversity) (Levin 1999). However, given the nature of SES as CAS, change is not uniform and continuous. Rather, periods of gradual change can be interrupted by rapid and sudden, often unexpected change (P3 – Slow variables and feedbacks) (Holling 2001).

From a resilience perspective, change is therefore an inherent characteristic of SES. The resilience approach views disturbance and change not necessarily as something negative that should be avoided, but as an inherent feature of SES that presents ongoing opportunities for renewal and improvement (Gunderson *et al.* 1995; Holling 2001; Gunderson and Holling 2002). Shocks, disturbance and crises are seen as particularly important in opening up opportunities for reorganization. These opportunities are shaped by the conditions and dynamics of systems at both smaller and larger scales (Gunderson *et al.* 1995; Gunderson and Holling 2002). A resilient SES is seen as a system that persists and maintains its capacity to sustain ecosystem services and human well-being in the face of disturbance, both by buffering shocks but also through adapting and reorganizing in response to change (Walker *et al.* 2004; Folke *et al.* 2010). Resilience thus deals with the tension between persistence and change, i.e. on the one hand understanding and managing the capacity to absorb shocks and maintain function, but on the other hand also to maintain the capacity for renewal, reorganization and development at a variety of scales (Folke 2006).

Changes in SES are understood to take place at a variety of interlinked organizational, spatial and temporal scales, with some changes occurring slowly and others faster. Interactions between individual SES components at lower scales or levels give rise to the macro-scale properties of the system, which are often emergent features that are not predictable from the lower-level components or interactions. For example, mechanization encouraged the cultivation of marginal land by individual farmers on the US Great Plains in the 1920s. When a severe drought struck in the 1930s, the amount of bare land was so extensive that it gave rise to massive dust storms never previously seen in the region (Peters *et al.* 2008). Such macro-scale conditions in turn affect local-level processes and actions (Gunderson and Holling 2002; Norberg and Cumming 2008). In the case of the US Dust Bowl, this led to severe soil erosion, human health impacts and the abandonment of farms by tens of thousands of families (Worster 2004). This example illustrates how processes at different scales in an SES can interact and lead to unexpected outcomes. Policies based only on local-scale dynamics can lead to wrong judgements about the macro-scale state of an SES, and inappropriate actions, and vice versa. The emergence of such macro-scale behaviour, interacting timescales and complex interactions and feedbacks across scales make the behaviour of SES inherently difficult to predict. Analysing and modelling SES with simple linear and reductionist dynamics, as has been common for example in mainstream economics, often gives a misleading representation of how SES work, with substantial implications for ecosystem management policy and practice (Levin *et al.* 2013).

In particular, interactions between SES components can cause non-linear dynamics, multiple stability domains and unexpected, rapid change. Feedbacks that lead to accelerating effects can cause a system to shift from one domain to another, undergoing a so-called regime shift (P3 – Slow variables and feedbacks). Regime shifts are large, persistent and often abrupt changes in the structure and dynamics of SES that occur when there is a reorganization of the dominant feedbacks in a system (Scheffer *et al.* 2001; Scheffer 2009). The iconic example is lakes shifting from a clear to turbid water regime, with marked impacts on ecosystem services such as drinking water and water-based recreation (Carpenter 2003). Regime shifts usually occur due to a combination of a shock (e.g. large rainstorm) and gradual changes in slow variables (e.g. nutrient accumulation) that erode the strength of the dominant feedback processes in an SES. When a critical threshold is crossed, a different set of feedbacks becomes dominant and the system reorganizes, often abruptly, into a new regime with a different structure and dynamic (Biggs *et al.* 2012a). Feedbacks can also generate traps that keep the system in an undesirable regime leading to increasing degradation of ecosystem services (Enfors 2013). For instance, feedbacks in European fisheries generated by subsidies and technological development have resulted in overcapacity and political pressure for short-term decision-making and unsustainable quotas that keep the system trapped in a cycle of overexploitation (Österblom *et al.* 2011). Ignoring non-linearities and the potential for traps and regime shifts in SES risks implementing inappropriate policies; for instance, extraction rates that are too high and lead to a regime shift (Levin *et al.* 2013).

In a globalizing world there are an increasing number of cross-scale links and feedbacks generated by flows of people, resources and information that connect distant people and places (Adger *et al.* 2009). These new interactions across multiple scales are reshaping the capacity of biophysical systems to sustain human well-being (P2 – Connectivity) (Biggs *et al.* 2011; Folke *et al.* 2011) and increasing the potential for regime shifts (MA 2005a). For example, global market demands now significantly shape local exploitation patterns (e.g. land use, water use and use of marine resources), which can lead to significant landscape-level changes such as fragmentation or degradation (Lambin *et al.* 2003; Berkes *et al.* 2006), which in turn have various non-linear effects on biodiversity and ecosystem services. The development of institutions to deal with these new connections often cannot keep pace, resulting in severe overexploitation (Walker *et al.* 2009; Galaz *et al.* 2012; Galaz 2014). Similarly, global changes such as changes in rainfall variability are leading to local changes in the frequency of natural disasters that affect food production, trade and possibly socio-political stability (Fraser and Rimas 2010).

In summary, the resilience approach assumes a strong interdependence and level of interaction between social and ecological systems, and that the resulting SES behave as CAS, which may be subject to abrupt, non-linear change. Furthermore, it acknowledges the multi-level nature of SES and the increasing interconnectedness of social and ecological processes across multiple scales. The CAS nature of SES has important implications for how SES can be analysed and managed. In particular, it is seen to lead to outcomes that are unpredictable and unexpected, and calls for governance approaches that are better able to deal with profound uncertainty. In addition, given the current unsustainable trajectory of SES at a wide range of scales, the resilience approach emphasizes that incremental change that slowly adapts SES to address the challenges society faces is not enough. Instead, there is a need to better understand how large and substantive change, i.e. transformational change, can be brought about (P4 – CAS thinking). How do features such as social learning that enable understanding and experimentation (P5 – Learning), social networks that provide trust and new ideas (P6 – Participation), bridging organizations that provide for interactions across multiple organizational levels (P7 – Polycentricity) and inspirational leadership support or prevent transformational change that can foster sustainability?

Finally, and importantly, resilience as an approach and set of assumptions for analysing, understanding and managing change in

SES (as discussed above) should be distinguished from resilience as a property of an SES. Resilience as a system property has been defined as the capacity of a specific SES, subject to ongoing change, to continually self-organize and adapt in a way that retains the same controls on system function and structure, and hence keeps the system in a particular stability domain (Holling 1973; Folke *et al.* 2010) – i.e. it can be seen as the capacity of a system to withstand a regime shift. When analysing resilience as a system property it is useful to consider, 'resilience of what to what?' (Carpenter *et al.* 2001). More normatively and operationally, in this book we define resilience of an SES as the capacity of an SES to sustain human well-being in the face of change, both by buffering shocks but also through adapting or transforming in response to change. In this book we focus specifically on generic principles that enhance the capacity of SES to continue providing key ecosystem services that underpin human well-being in the face of unexpected shocks and gradual, ongoing change.

1.3 ECOSYSTEM SERVICES AS FEATURES OF SOCIAL–ECOLOGICAL SYSTEMS

Ecosystem services can be defined as the benefits people obtain from their interaction with nature (Ernstson 2013; Reyers *et al.* 2013; Huntsinger and Oviedo 2014). These encompass a wide variety of ecosystem-based goods and functions that underpin a range of basic human needs (e.g. nutrition, health, security), as well as important cultural and spiritual meanings that people obtain from their relationship and interaction with ecosystems. The Millennium Ecosystem Assessment (MA) was ground-breaking in highlighting the large diversity of ecosystem services that influence human well-being, and identified three core categories: (i) Provisioning services, such as crops, fish, cotton or timber; (ii) Regulating services, such as regulation of pests and diseases and climate regulation; and (iii) Cultural services, such as hiking, canoeing, sacred forests with cultural significance, or natural areas used for rites of passage (Fig. 1.3) (MA 2003; MA 2005a). The MA also identified a fourth category,

ECOSYSTEM SERVICES

PROVISIONING
- Food
- Freshwater
- Wood and fibre
- Fuel
- Other

REGULATING
- Climate regulation
- Flood regulation
- Disease regulation
- Water purification
- Other

CULTURAL
- Aesthetic
- Spiritual
- Educational
- Recreational
- Other

CONSTITUENTS OF WELL-BEING

SECURITY
- Personal safety
- Secure resource access
- Security from disasters

BASIC MATERIAL FOR GOOD LIFE
- Adequate livelihoods
- Sufficient nutritious food
- Shelter
- Access to goods

HEALTH
- Strength
- Feeling well
- Access to clean air and water

GOOD SOCIAL RELATIONS
- Social cohesion
- Mutual respect
- Ability to help others

FREEDOM OF CHOICE AND ACTION

Opportunity to be able to achieve what an individual values doing and being

SOCIAL–ECOLOGICAL SYSTEMS

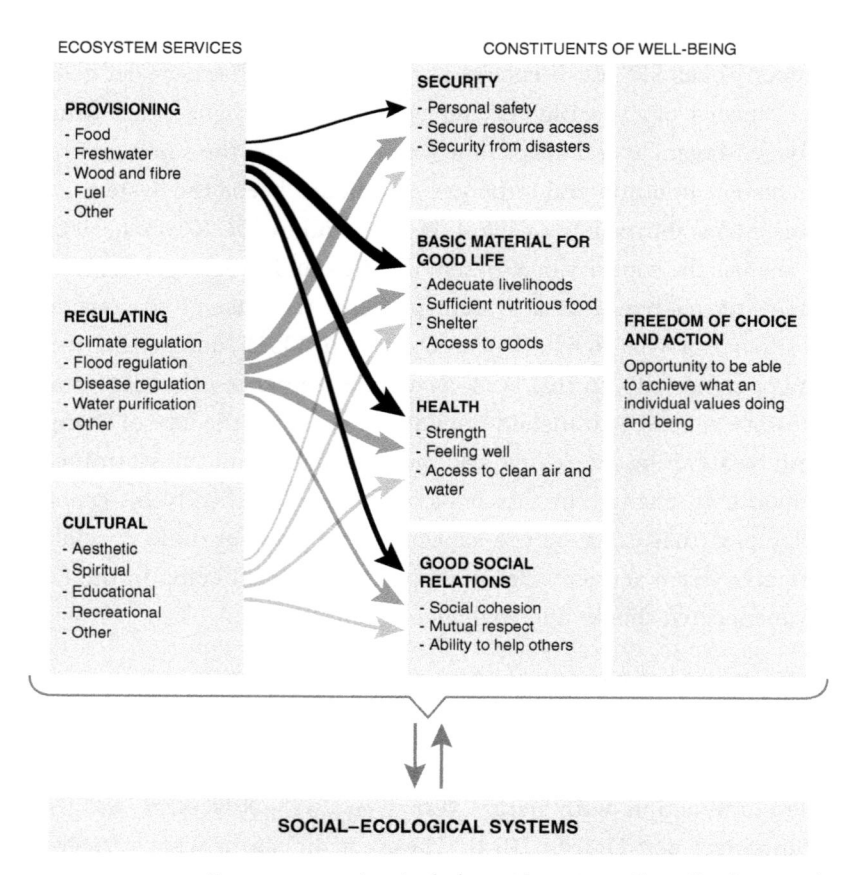

FIG. 1.3 Ecosystem services include a wide variety of benefits that people obtain from interacting with nature, including provisioning services (e.g. food), regulating services (e.g. climate regulation) and cultural services (e.g. spiritual and recreational benefits). These in turn influence a wide range of human well-being constituents, including basic needs, security, health, social relations and freedom of choice and action. In the resilience perspective, ecosystem services are seen as co-produced by ecosystems and human society, and therefore products of SES. Modified from MA (2005a).

supporting ecosystem services, which includes underlying ecosystem functions such as soil formation and nutrient cycling that underpin the other three categories. In this book we view ecosystem services as the full variety of benefits that people obtain from their interaction with nature, and focus primarily on provisioning, regulating and cultural ecosystem services.

Following a growing number of resilience studies, we view ecosystem services as a key emergent outcome of social–ecological interactions, and a central connector and mediator between social and ecological systems. Importantly, we see ecosystem services not as produced by nature alone, but rather as SES features resulting from the interplay between the capacity of an ecosystem to produce ecosystem services, and human values, technology, skills and institutions to realize these (Ernstson 2013; Reyers *et al.* 2013; Huntsinger and Oviedo 2014). A great example is crop production. Nature has provided the wild ancestors for today's major food crops, and also largely provides the temperature, rainfall, soil nutrients and pollination conditions needed to grow food. However, crop production requires that these ecological aspects be combined with a vast array of human needs, technologies, skills and institutions to actually grow crops and deliver food. Similarly, while species, ecosystems and ecological processes have intrinsic value in and of themselves, they are only an ecosystem service if they are valued by people (Spangenberg *et al.* 2014). For instance a park in a city is there because humans have invested time, labour and financial resources to establish it, and it only provides recreational ecosystem services if people have access to it.

We also highlight that while some ecosystem services can be partly valued in monetary terms, which can be very useful in informing policy choices, a large variety of ecosystem services cannot be quantified economically (MA 2003; TEEB 2010; Kareiva *et al.* 2011). This does not detract from their importance or value. In fact some of the ecosystem services that are least amenable to quantification in monetary terms may have very large impacts on human well-being through their impacts on people's sense of identity, purpose in life and psychological well-being. For instance, most traditional societies are deeply structured around their interaction with nature. Being a fishing community, a reindeer herding society or a farming community has a fundamental influence on the cultural identity of that society, the structure and roles in the community, and the traditions and festivals that bind the community together (de Groot *et al.* 2005). For many Arctic communities, such values and their whole way of life is being affected by the impacts of climate change, leading to a variety of social and psychological impacts, and arguably represent a larger threat to well-being than for instance a shortage of food (Willox *et al.* 2013). In modern developed societies, access to and interactions with nature are also highly valued, as expressed for instance in the premium placed on houses with a view or waterfront location (Bond *et al.* 2002), and in the proliferation of green spaces and parks around many developed cities (Raudsepp-Hearne *et al.* 2010; Beilin *et al.* 2014). There is also growing evidence that, for instance, more green spaces in cities are associated with lower crime rates and better educational outcomes (James *et al.* 2009), and that people in hospital rooms that look out on green vegetation recover more rapidly than those that don't (Bolund and Hunhammar 1999). Nevertheless, many ecosystem services remain undervalued and underappreciated, especially where they are produced in distant locations or where they contribute only indirectly to the benefits experienced by consumers (MA 2003; TEEB 2010).

Any SES or landscape does not only produce one ecosystem service, but a whole set or 'bundle' of interacting ecosystem services at a variety of scales (MA 2005a; Raudsepp-Hearne *et al.* 2010). For instance, a coral reef may provide a range of ecosystem services including subsistence fisheries, protection from coastal storms, as well as recreational and spiritual benefits. The sets of ecosystem services produced by a particular SES are not independent of one another, and it is not possible to maximize the production or resilience of all ecosystem services simultaneously. For instance, by its very nature, crop production has strong trade-offs with conservation of natural habitat and the ecosystem services this provides, such as pollination, regulation of soil erosion, wild foods and recreational benefits (Foley *et al.* 2005). Such trade-offs exist between ecosystem services at a particular scale, as well as between ecosystem services at different scales (Rodríguez *et al.* 2006). For example, forests can provide timber and fuelwood at a local scale, but this directly impacts the carbon-sequestration benefit that they provide at a global scale (MA 2005b).

In this book we focus on the resilience of ecosystem services – i.e. the capacity of SES to continue providing some desired set of ecosystem services in the face of unexpected shocks as well as more gradual ongoing change. We argue that addressing the resilience of ecosystem services is at least one very useful focus for assessing the resilience of SES. We fully acknowledge, however, that there are other crucial SES outcomes of importance to society, such as women's rights or education. However, many of these aspects are less directly connected to ecosystems, and the features of society that promote resilience of these aspects may differ from those that promote resilience of ecosystem services. Given the emphasis of the resilience approach on understanding dynamics and change in SES, and to keep the scope of the synthesis presented in this book manageable, we have chosen to specifically address factors that promote the resilience of ecosystem services. We do not, however, focus on any particular set of ecosystem services or make any judgement on which specific ecosystem services a particular community may or should desire. Rather we aim to discuss general principles that could be applied to build resilience of whichever set of ecosystem services a particular society values.

Decisions about which ecosystem services to sustain are inherently political as different sectors of society usually value, need and demand different ecosystem services. Any particular set of ecosystem services selected therefore requires trade-offs between different users (Robards *et al.* 2011). To further complicate matters, the desired mix of ecosystem services will typically evolve over time with changing societal values and preferences (Biggs *et al.* 2012b; Ernstson 2013). The inevitable trade-offs between disparate, changing societal goals requires resolution of collective-action dilemmas and intergroup conflict, a process that comes replete with power inequalities, asymmetric resource bases, and unequal outcomes (Robards *et al.* 2011). Decisions around which ecosystem services are the focus for resilience-building initiatives, and ensuring that these choices do not lead to undesirable lock-in effects that compromise the possibility for future adaptation and change, are far from trivial. The need to carefully consider these issues before applying any of the principles discussed in this book, particularly the potential for resilience-building initiatives to create, entrench or exacerbate social inequalities, is further discussed in Chapter 2. In the remainder of the book, we assume that some desired set of ecosystem services has been legitimately agreed upon and focus on how the resilience of these selected ecosystem services may be enhanced – both to unexpected shocks and slower, ongoing changes that may lead to changes in the preferred mix of ecosystem services over time.

1.4 IDENTIFYING PRINCIPLES FOR BUILDING RESILIENCE

The past two decades has seen rapid growth in research on social–ecological resilience (Gunderson *et al.* 1995; Berkes and Folke 1998; Gunderson and Holling 2002; Gunderson and Pritchard 2002; Berkes *et al.* 2003; Walker and Salt 2006, 2012; Armitage *et al.* 2007; Norberg and Cumming 2008; Chapin *et al.* 2009; Bodin and Prell 2011; Boyd and Folke 2011; Cumming 2011; Galaz 2014; Rockström *et al.* 2014). This literature has produced a number of insights on factors that promote resilience in SES, with an increasing focus in recent years on ecosystem services. While several studies have proposed general 'rules of thumb' for enhancing resilience across different types of SES (Anderies *et al.* 2006; Walker and Salt 2006; Walker *et al.* 2006), there does not yet exist a definitive set of resilience-enhancing principles backed up by extensive empirical results or a synthetic understanding of where and when these principles apply. Much of the work remains theoretical with empirical results focused on individual or small subsets of cases rather than more broadly generalizable studies (Biggs *et al.* 2012b). Furthermore, given the diversity of potential factors involved, the insights that have been published are substantially fragmented and dispersed across a range of different literatures, including ecology, social sciences and economics.

We set out to synthesize and make sense of this literature. Part of this process entailed an innovative 'mock court' in which a number of proposed principles for enhancing the resilience of ecosystem services were put 'on trial'. The first step in this process was for the project participants, all of whom have a PhD in resilience-related subjects and were associated with the Resilience Alliance Young Scholars (RAYS) network, to conduct an extensive literature review to identify an initial set of principles and debate the proposals. This process generated a list of ten principles. Each proposed principle, and the scientific knowledge in support of it, was described and assessed by a team of two to four RAYS authors in a background paper. Each author team was tasked with critically assessing the empirical evidence in support of a particular principle, examining the conditions under which each principle enhances or does not enhance the resilience of ecosystem services, and identifying critical research gaps. These background papers were circulated to all authors and participants in advance of the mock-court workshop held in October 2009 on Gabriola Island in Canada, in conjunction with a science meeting of the Resilience Alliance (RA).[1]

The intention of the two-day mock-court workshop was to critically examine the information in the background papers, and refine the list of proposed principles. Each principle was put on trial as follows. First, the key points from the background paper were presented to the court by the section authors – the 'defence attorneys'. A senior member of the RA then 'cross-examined' the evidence presented by the defence, looking for weaknesses. The cross-examiners were pre-selected for their expert knowledge of a particular principle (see acknowledgements for participants). This was followed by 20 minutes of general discussion, with questions from the audience

[1] http://www.resalliance.org.

who comprised various members of the RAYS and RA. In addition, two or three pre-selected participants acted as 'devil's advocates', posing questions from the stance of a critical outsider sceptical of resilience concepts. This structure was designed to help create a 'safe space' for more critical reflection and discussion of the work published by the RA community and others. Through this process we were able to clarify the definitions of the different principles and gain critical feedback on the evidence and research gaps identified by the section authors.

The mock-court workshop suggested the need for revising and refining the initial set of ten principles. In some cases, the cross-examiners made concrete suggestions of principles that should be combined (e.g. diversity and redundancy; slow variables and regulating ecosystem services) and broadened to include aspects of SES beyond the ecological. In other cases, the critique of the background paper and the discussion during the mock-court trial highlighted conceptual conflation, for instance between adaptive capacity and resilience. The outcome of this particular discussion was to conclude that rather than being a principle for enhancing resilience, adaptive capacity is itself an aspect of resilience particularly relevant in the context of social systems (and hence in some ways equivalent to resilience). This is supported by Folke *et al* (2010), and the adaptive capacity principle was therefore dropped.

Following the mock court and building on the feedback we received there, we interviewed resilience experts using a modified Delphi method (Landeta 2006) to elicit the expertise of the attendees of the 2009 RA science meeting, held directly after the mock-court workshop. The Delphi method has a long history of application in planning, decision-making and policy research, where the goal is to collect and synthesize expert judgements (Landeta 2006). A Delphi technique typically uses multiple rounds (two to three) with anonymous reviewers to generate feedback on a given issue or set of questions and move a group towards consensus. To implement this method we asked attendees of the 2009 RA science meeting:

'According to resilience theory, how can the resilience of SES be enhanced?' Each respondent (only senior RA members) generated an independent list of principles with notes as to their reasoning. Through an iterative process, project members categorized and structured the responses emerging from the expert interviews. This modified Delphi process provided an independent list of principles for enhancing resilience derived from leading experts in the field.

Comparison of the principles that emerged from the Delphi process with our original literature review and the principles discussed at the mock-court workshop showed a high correspondence. Based on the combination of these processes, we identified seven generic principles for enhancing the resilience of ecosystem services, first published in Biggs *et al.* (2012b): (P1) maintain diversity and redundancy, (P2) manage connectivity, (P3) manage slow variables and feedbacks, (P4) foster CAS thinking, (P5) encourage learning and experimentation, (P6) broaden participation and (P7) promote polycentric governance systems. A brief definition of each principle and other key concepts relevant to this book is given in Box 1.1. The high correspondence between the outcomes of these processes emphasizes the consensus on the importance of the principles presented in this book within the resilience community.

BOX 1.1 **Definitions of key concepts**

Complex adaptive systems (CAS): systems of interconnected components characterized by the potential for emergent and non-linear behaviour; the capacity for self-organization and adaptation based on past experience; and inherent uncertainties regarding system behaviour.

Connectivity (P2): the way and degree to which resources, species or social actors disperse, migrate or interact across ecological and social landscapes.

Diversity (P1): the range of different elements comprising three interrelated aspects: variety (how many different elements), balance (how many of each element) and disparity (how different the elements are from one another).

BOX 1.1 **Continued**

Ecosystem services: the benefits people obtain from their interaction with nature, including provisioning services (e.g. water, timber), regulating services (e.g. climate regulation) and cultural services (e.g. nature-based recreational and cultural activities).

Feedback (P3): a mechanism, process or signal that loops back to influence the SES component emitting the signal or initiating the mechanism or process. Monitoring is a specific form of feedback, in which the information about responses of the SES feeds back to actors so that they can change the way they utilize, affect or manage an SES.

Learning (P5): the process of modifying existing or acquiring new knowledge, behaviours, skills, values or preferences at individual, group or societal levels.

Mental models (P4): people's cognitive representations of external reality.

Modularity (P2): the extent to which a network or system consists of distinct compartments that are unconnected or only loosely connected to one another.

Participation (P6): active engagement of relevant stakeholders in SES management and governance.

Polycentricity (P7): a governance system with multiple, nested governing authorities at different scales.

Redundancy (P1): situations where several species or SES components perform the same function.

Regime shifts (P3): large, persistent and often abrupt changes in the structure and dynamics of SES that occur when there is a reorganization of the dominant feedbacks in a system.

Resilience approach: a perspective for the analysis of SES which assumes that SES behave as CAS and focuses on the capacity to deal with both unexpected shocks and ongoing change in such systems.

Resilience of SES: the capacity of an SES to sustain human well-being in the face of disturbance and change, both by buffering shocks and by adapting or transforming in response to change.

Resilience of ecosystem services: the capacity of an SES to reliably sustain a desired set of ecosystem services, in the face of disturbance and ongoing evolution and change.

> BOX 1.1 **Continued**
>
> **Response diversity (P1)**: the diversity of ways in which different species or SES elements respond to a disturbance.
>
> **Slow variable (P3)**: a variable whose rate of change is slow with respect to the timescales of ecosystem-service provision and management, and are for practical purposes often considered constant.
>
> **Social–ecological systems (SES)**: integrated systems of humans and nature that constitute a complex adaptive system with ecological and social components that interact dynamically through various feedbacks.
>
> **Sustainability**: achieving human well-being in the present without compromising the social, economic or environmental foundations that underpin the potential for future well-being.
>
> **Worldview (P4)**: a collection of ideas that allow individual people to construct a composite image of the world and understand their experiences and how they should act.

1.5 OBJECTIVES AND ORGANIZATION OF THE BOOK

This book aims to provide a practical synthesis of the contribution that a resilience approach can make to address the challenges of the Anthropocene. We do so by identifying a handful of underlying principles that can inform the practical governance and management of SES at local, regional and global scales. We focus specifically on enhancing the capacity of SES to sustain the production of desired sets of ecosystem services in the face of unexpected shocks and ongoing change.

The first two chapters set the stage for the book. In this first chapter we have introduced the resilience approach and the sustainability challenges that motivate it. We have also introduced the social–ecological perspective on ecosystem services that is adopted in this book, along with the process by which we identified the seven principles that form the core of the book. Before getting into a discussion of the actual principles, Chapter 2 delves more deeply into the political dimensions and social consequences that need to be considered before implementing any of the principles. In particular, given the inherent trade-offs that exist between different ecosystem services, Chapter 2 emphasizes that the winners and losers of any particular choice of ecosystem service to sustain in an SES need to be carefully considered before undertaking resilience-building initiatives, as these choices can create, entrench or exacerbate social inequalities and power disparities.

The core of the book focuses on the seven principles we have identified, expanding substantially on the analysis presented in Biggs et al. (2012b). Each principle comprises one chapter. For each we give a definition, review the state of knowledge about the underlying mechanism by which the principle enhances resilience of ecosystem services and the conditions under which resilience of ecosystem services may be compromised. We then present an initial set of guidelines on how each of the principles can be practically operationalized and applied, and conclude with a summary of major research and application gaps. Throughout, we have provided detailed examples to illustrate the text, and each chapter contains a box with an in-depth case study.

The ordering of the principles does not prioritize their importance. Rather, we grouped those principles that focus on generic SES properties and processes that enhance resilience (P1–P3), and those that focus on the way in which SES are governed (P4–P7) (Fig. 1.4). This follows the distinction made by Jentoft et al. (2007) between the 'system-to-be-governed' and the 'governance system'. We also distinguish between SES governance and SES management, where governance is taken to be the social and political process of defining goals for SES management and resolving trade-offs, while SES management is defined as the actions taken to achieve these goals, and includes monitoring and implementation (Pahl-Wostl 2009).

Interestingly, P1–P3 relate first to the nature of the SES components (P1 – Diversity), then to the structure of the connections amongst these components (P2 – Connectivity) and finally to the emergent system processes (P3 – Slow variables and feedbacks) of the

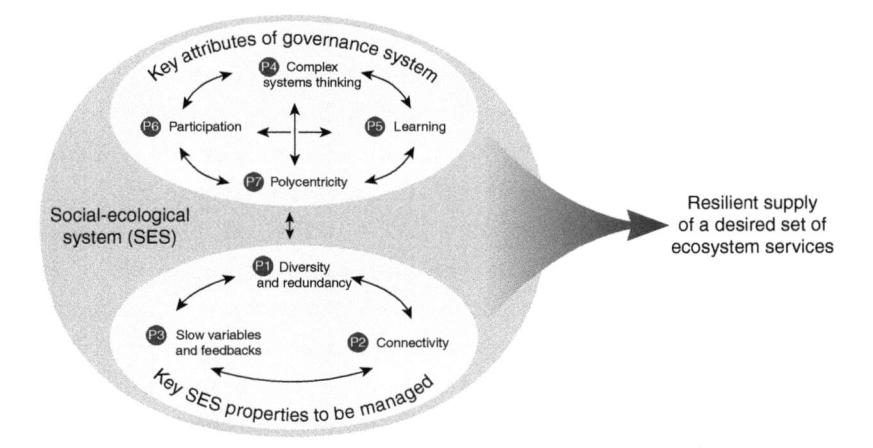

FIG. 1.4 The seven principles discussed in this book, grouped into those that relate to generic SES properties to be managed (P1–P3), and those that relate to key properties of the SES governance system (P4–P6). Modified from Biggs *et al.* (2012b).

SES. In contrast, the four governance system attributes relate to the underlying worldview adopted in governance and management (P4 – CAS thinking), the capacity for innovating and understanding change in the SES being governed (P5 – Learning), the importance of building trust and shared understanding in order to make decisions (P6 – Participation) and finally the governance structures that can help facilitate the various principles (P7 – Polycentricity). P4 in particular appears to be fundamental to being able to truly operationalize and apply the different principles.

While most of the principles are also important for the actual production of ecosystem services, we focus exclusively on how they affect the resilience of ecosystem services – i.e. not the quantity of ecosystem services produced, but the ability to sustain production of ecosystem services in the face of unexpected shocks and disturbance as well as slower ongoing change in SES. While we have attempted to separate individual principles for the sake of analysis and presentation, they are in practice of course highly interconnected and interdependent. We discuss these connections and synergies in the concluding Chapter 10, as well as reflecting on the obstacles that the CAS nature of SES pose for the study and analysis of these systems.

The principles we identify and discuss in this book are not intended to be definitive. Rather, our aim is to build on and synthesize seminal work in the field, and begin to distil essential elements that are important for building resilience in a way that can usefully inform sustainability policy and help focus further research efforts. We believe that the resilience field is reaching a level of maturity where we can start identifying general underlying principles that go beyond more tentative 'propositions'. For that reason we have broken with earlier language in this literature, and in this book take the bold step of positing a first-cut synthesis of underlying 'principles' for enhancing the resilience of SES and the ecosystem services they produce. We hope that this proposed set of principles will be interrogated, modified and refined over time as knowledge grows, and improve our capacity to more wisely manage the Earth and ensure the well-being of all citizens.

REFERENCES

Adger, W. N., Eakin, H., Winkels, A. (2009). Nested and teleconnected vulnerabilities to environmental change. *Frontiers in Ecology and the Environment*, 7, 150–157.

Anderies, J. M., Walker, B. H., Kinzig, A. P. (2006). Fifteen weddings and a funeral: case studies and resilience-based management. *Ecology and Society*, 11, 21.

Armitage, D., Berkes, F., Doubleday, N., eds. (2007). *Adaptive Co-Management: Collaboration, Learning, and Multi-Level Governance*. Vancouver: UBC Press.

Barnosky, A. D., Hadly, E. A., Bascompte, J. et al. (2012). Approaching a state shift in Earth's biosphere. *Nature*, 486, 52–58.

Beilin, R., Lindborg, R., Stenseke, M. et al. (2014). Analysing how drivers of agricultural land abandonment affect biodiversity and cultural landscapes using case studies from Scandinavia, Iberia and Oceania. *Land Use Policy*, 36, 60–72.

Berkes, F. and Folke, C., eds. (1998). *Linking Social and Ecological Systems*. Cambridge: Cambridge University Press.

Berkes, F., Colding, J., Folke, C., eds. (2003). *Navigating Social–Ecological Systems: Building Resilience for Complexity and Change*. Cambridge: Cambridge University Press.

Berkes, F., Hughes, T. P., Steneck, R. S. *et al.* (2006). Globalization, roving bandits, and marine resources. *Science*, 311, 1557–1558.

Biggs, D., Biggs, R., Dakos, V., Scholes, R. J., Schoon, M. L. (2011). Are we entering an era of concatenated global crises? *Ecology and Society*, 14, 32.

Biggs, R., Blenckner, T., Folke, C. *et al.* (2012a). Regime shifts. In *Encyclopedia of Theoretical Ecology*. Hastings, A. and Gross, L., eds. Berkeley, CA: University of California Press.

Biggs, R., Schlüter, M., Biggs, D. *et al.* (2012b). Towards principles for enhancing the resilience of ecosystem services. *Annual Review of Environment and Resources*, 37, 421–448.

Bodin, Ö. and Prell, C., eds. (2011). *Social Networks and Natural Resource Management: Uncovering the Social Fabric of Environmental Governance.* Cambridge: Cambridge University Press.

Bolund, P. and Hunhammar, S. (1999). Ecosystem services in urban areas. *Ecological Economics*, 29, 293–301.

Bond, M. T., Seiler, V. L., Seiler, M. J. (2002). Residential real estate prices: a room with a view. *Journal of Real Estate Research*, 23, 129–138.

Boyd, E. and Folke, C., eds. (2011). *Adapting Institutions: Governance, Complexity and Social–Ecological Resilience*. Cambridge: Cambridge University Press.

Carpenter, S. R., Walker, B. H., Anderies, J. M., Abel, N. (2001). From metaphor to measurement: resilience of what to what? *Ecosystems*, 4, 765–781.

Carpenter, S. R. (2003). *Regime Shifts in Lake Ecosystems: Pattern and Variation.* Oldendorf/Luhe: International Ecology Institute.

Chapin, F. S., Kofinas, G. P., Folke, C., eds. (2009). *Principles of Ecosystem Stewardship: Resilience-Based Natural Resource Management in a Changing World.* New York, NY: Springer.

CIA (2013). *The World Factbook 2013–14.* Washington, DC: Central Intelligence Agency.

Clark, W. C. and Dickson, N. M. 2003. Sustainability science: the emerging research program. *Proceedings of the National Academy of Sciences USA*, 100, 8059–8061.

Crutzen, P. J. and Stoermer, E. F. (2000). The 'Anthropocene'. *Global Change NewsLetter*, 41, 17–18.

Cumming, G. S. (2011). *Spatial Resilience in Social–Ecological Systems.* Heidelberg: Springer.

de Groot, R. S., Ramakrishnan, P. S., van de Berg, A. *et al.* (2005). Cultural and amenity services. In *Ecosystems and Human Well-Being: Current State and Trends*. Hassan, R., Scholes, R. J., Ash, N., eds. Washington, DC: Island Press.

Diamond, J. (2004). *Collapse: How Societies Choose to Fail or Succeed*. New York, NY: Viking.

Enfors, E. (2013). Social–ecological traps and transformations in dryland agro-ecosystems: using water system innovations to change the trajectory of development. *Global Environmental Change*, 23, 51–60.

Ernstson, H. (2013). The social production of ecosystem services: a framework for studying environmental justice and ecological complexity in urbanized landscapes. *Landscape and Urban Planning*, 109, 7–17.

Farman, J. C., Gardiner, B. G., Shanklin, J. D. (1985). Large losses of total ozone in Antarctica reveal seasonal ClO_x/NO_x interaction. *Nature*, 315, 207–210.

Finlayson, C. M., D'Cruz, R., Aladin, N. *et al.* (2005). Inland water systems. In *Ecosystems and Human Well-Being: Current State and Trends*. Hassan, R., Scholes, R. J., Ash, N., eds. Washington, DC: Island Press.

Foley, J. A., DeFries, R., Asner, G. P. *et al.* (2005). Global consequences of land use. *Science*, 309, 570–574.

Folke, C. (2006). Resilience: the emergence of a perspective for social–ecological systems analyses. *Global Environmental Change*, 16, 253–267.

Folke, C., Carpenter, S. R., Walker, B. H. *et al.* (2010). Resilience thinking: integrating resilience, adaptability and transformability. *Ecology and Society*, 15, 20.

Folke, C., Jansson, Å., Rockström, J. *et al.* (2011). Reconnecting to the biosphere. *AMBIO*, 40, 719–738.

Fraser, E. D. G. and Rimas, A. (2010). *Empires of Food: Feast, Famine, and the Rise and Fall of Civilizations*. New York, NY: Free Press.

Funtowicz, S. O., Martinez-Alier, J., Munda, G., Ravetz, J. R. (1999). *Information Tools for Environmental Policy Under Conditions of Complexity*. Luxembourg: European Environmental Agency.

Galaz, V., Crona, B., Österblom, H., Olsson, P., Folke, C. (2012). Polycentric systems and interacting planetary boundaries – emerging governance of climate change – ocean acidification–marine biodiversity. *Ecological Economics*, 81, 21–32.

Galaz, V. (2014). *Global Environmental Governance, Technology and Politics: The Anthropocene Gap*. Cheltenham: Edgar Elgar.

Gibbons, M., Limoges, C., Nowotny, H. *et al.* (1994). *The New Production of Knowledge: The Dynamics of Science and Research in Contemporary Societies*. London: Sage Publications.

Gros, C. (2008). *Complex and Adaptive Dynamical Systems: A Primer*. Berlin: Springer-Verlag.

Gunderson, L. H., Holling, C. S., Light, S. S. (1995). *Barriers and Bridges to the Renewal of Ecosystems and Institutions*. New York, NY: Columbia University Press.

Gunderson, L. H. and Holling, C. S., eds. (2002). *Panarchy: Understanding Transformations in Human and Natural Systems*. Washington, DC: Island Press.

Gunderson, L. H. and Pritchard, L., eds. (2002). *Resilience and the Behavior of Large-Scale Systems*. Washington, DC: Island Press.

Holling, C. S. (1973). Resilience and stability of ecological systems. *Annual Review of Ecology and Systematics*, 4, 1–23.

Holling, C. S. (2001). Understanding the complexity of economic, ecological, and social systems. *Ecosystems*, 4, 390–405.

Huntsinger, L. and Oviedo, J. L. (2014). Ecosystem services are social–ecological services in a traditional pastoral system: the case of California's Mediterranean rangelands. *Ecology and Society*, 19, 8.

IPCC (2014). *Climate Change 2014: Impacts, Adaptation, and Vulnerability*. Cambridge: Cambridge University Press.

James, P., Tzoulas, K., Adams, M. D. et al. (2009). Towards an integrated understanding of green space in the European built environment. *Urban Forestry and Urban Greening*, 8, 65–75.

Jentoft, S., van Son, T. C., Bjørkan, M. (2007). Marine protected areas: a governance system analysis. *Human Ecology*, 35, 611–622.

Kates, R. W., Clark, W. C., Corell, R. et al. (2001). Sustainability science. *Science*, 292, 641–642.

Kareiva, P., Tallis, H., Ricketts, T. H., Daily, G. C., Polasky, S., eds. (2011). *Natural Capital: Theory and Practice of Mapping Ecosystem Services*. Oxford: Oxford University Press.

Lambin, E. F., Geist, H. J., Lepers, E. (2003). Dynamics of land-use and land-cover change in tropical regions. *Annual Review of Environment and Resources*, 28, 205–241.

Lancaster, H. O. (1990). *Expectations of Life: A study in the Demography, Statistics, and History of World Mortality*. New York, NY: Springer-Verlag.

Landeta, J. (2006). Current validity of the Delphi method in social sciences. *Technological Forecasting and Social Change*, 73, 467–482.

Levin, S. A. (1999). *Fragile Dominion: Complexity and the Commons*. New York, NY: Perseus Books.

Levin, S., Xepapadeas, T., Crépin, A. S. et al. (2013). Social–ecological systems as complex adaptive systems: modeling and policy implications. *Environment and Development Economics*, 18, 111–132.

MA (2003). *Ecosystems and Human Well-Being: A Framework for Assessment.* Washington, DC: Island Press.

MA (2005a). *Ecosystems and Human Well-Being: Synthesis.* Washington, DC: Island Press.

MA (2005b). *Ecosystems and Human Well-Being: Current State And Trends.* Washington, DC: Island Press.

Martin, J. (2007). *The Meaning of the 21st Century: A Vital Blueprint For Ensuring Our Future.* New York, NY: Riverhead Books.

Norberg, J. and Cumming, G. S., eds. (2008). *Complexity Theory for a Sustainable Future.* New York, NY: Columbia University Press.

Österblom, H., Sissenwine, M., Symes, D. et al. (2011). Incentives, social–ecological feedbacks and European fisheries. *Marine Policy*, 35, 568–574.

Ostrom, E. (2009). A general framework for analyzing sustainability of social–ecological systems. *Science*, 325, 419–422.

Pahl-Wostl, C. (2009). A conceptual framework for analysing adaptive capacity and multi-level learning processes in resource governance regimes. *Global Environmental Change*, 19, 354–365.

Peters, D. P., Groffman, P. M., Nadelhoffer, K. J. et al. (2008). Living in an increasingly connected world: a framework for continental-scale environmental science. *Frontiers in Ecology and the Environment*, 6, 229–237.

Raudsepp-Hearne, C., Peterson, G. D., Bennett, E. M. (2010). Ecosystem service bundles for analyzing tradeoffs in diverse landscapes. *Proceedings of the National Academy of Sciences USA*, 107, 5242–5247.

Reyers, B., Biggs, R., Cumming, G. S. et al. (2013). Getting the measure of ecosystem services: a social–ecological approach. *Frontiers in Ecology and the Environment*, 11, 268–273.

Robards, M. D., Schoon, M. L., Meek, C. L., Engle, N. L. (2011). The importance of social drivers in the resilient provision of ecosystem services. *Global Environmental Change*, 21, 522–529.

Rockström, J., Steffen, W. L., Noone, K. et al. (2009). A safe operating space for humanity. *Nature*, 461, 472–475.

Rockström, J., Falkenmark, M., Folke, C. et al. (2014). *Water Resilience for Human Prosperity.* Cambridge: Cambridge University Press.

Rodríguez, J. P., Beard, T. D., Bennett, E. M. et al. (2006). Trade-offs across space, time, and ecosystem services. *Ecology and Society*, 11, 28.

Scheffer, M., Carpenter, S. R., Foley, J. A., Folke, C., Walker, B. H. (2001). Catastrophic shifts in ecosystems. *Nature*, 413, 591–596.

Scheffer, M. (2009). *Critical Transitions in Nature and Society.* Princeton, NJ: Princeton University Press.

Spangenberg, J. H., Görg, C., Truong, D. T. et al. (2014). Provision of ecosystem services is determined by human agency, not ecosystem functions. Four case studies. *International Journal of Biodiversity Science, Ecosystem Services & Management*, 10, 40–53.

Steffen, W. L., Sanderson, A., Tyson, P. D. et al. (2004). *Global Change and the Earth System: A Planet Under Pressure*. Berlin: Springer-Verlag.

Steffen, W. L., Crutzen, P. J., McNeill, J. R. (2007). The Anthropocene: are humans now overwhelming the great forces of Nature? *AMBIO*, 36, 614–621.

Steffen, W., Persson, Å., Deutsch, L. et al. (2011). The Anthropocene: from global change to planetary stewardship. *AMBIO*, 40, 739–761.

TEEB (2010). *The Economics of Ecosystems and Biodiversity (TEEB): Ecological and Economic Foundations*. London: Earthscan.

UN (2004). *World Population to 2300*. New York, NY: United Nations, Department of Economic and Social Affairs, Population Division.

UN (2013). *World Population Prospects: The 2012 Revision*. New York, NY: United Nations, Department of Economic and Social Affairs, Population Division.

Walker, B. H., Holling, C. S., Carpenter, S. R., Kinzig, A. (2004). Resilience, adaptability and tranformability in social–ecological systems. *Ecology and Society*, 9, 3.

Walker, B. H. and Salt, D. (2006). *Resilience Thinking: Sustaining Ecosystems and People in a Changing World*. Washington, DC: Island Press.

Walker, B. H. and Salt, D. (2012). *Resilience Practice: Building Capacity to Absorb Disturbance and Maintain Function*. Washington, DC: Island Press.

Walker, B. H., Gunderson, L. H., Kinzig, A. et al. (2006). A handful of heuristics and some propositions for understanding resilience in social–ecological systems. *Ecology and Society*, 11, 13.

Walker, B. H, Barrett, S., Polasky, S. et al. (2009). Looming global-scale failures and missing institutions. *Science*, 325, 1345–1346.

Willox, A. C., Harper, S. L., Ford, J. D. et al. (2013). Climate change and mental health: an exploratory case study from Rigolet, Nunatsiavut, Canada. *Climatic Change*, 121, 255–270.

World Bank (2014). *World Development Indicators 2014*. Washington, DC: World Bank.

Worster, D. (2004). *Dust Bowl – The Southern Plains in the 1930s*. Oxford: Oxford University Press.

2 Politics and the resilience of ecosystem services

Michael L. Schoon, Martin D. Robards, Katrina Brown, Nathan Engle[1], Chanda L. Meek and Reinette Biggs

SUMMARY

Different sectors of society typically value, need and demand different bundles of ecosystem services. At the same time, important trade-offs exist between the production of different services, and it is not possible to increase the resilience of all ecosystem services simultaneously. Decisions about which services to sustain in a particular social–ecological system therefore require trade-offs that are inherently political. Politics can be described as 'the authoritative allocation of values for a society' (Easton 1965). To further complicate matters, the desired mix of services will evolve with changing societal values and preferences, and the resilience of ecosystem services is only one among many desired outcomes (e.g. equality, human rights, democracy) of social–ecological systems. Resolving these trade-offs requires resolution of collective-action dilemmas and intergroup conflicts, a process that comes replete with power inequalities, asymmetric resource bases and unequal outcomes. This chapter discusses some of the asymmetries and power dynamics that underlie decisions of which ecosystem services should form the focus for resilience-building initiatives; the remainder of the book assumes these choices

---

[1] The findings, interpretations and conclusions expressed in this publication are those of the author(s) and should not be attributed in any manner to the World Bank, its Board of Executive Directors, or the governments they represent.

Principles for Building Resilience: Sustaining Ecosystem Services in Social–Ecological Systems, eds R. Biggs, M. Schlüter and M. L. Schoon. Published by Cambridge University Press. © Cambridge University Press 2015.

have been made and focuses on how the resilience of some agreed-on mix of ecosystem services may be enhanced. Here, we focus specifically on the social consequences of trade-offs between ecosystem services; asymmetries in the distribution of ecosystem services; and we briefly discuss the broad literature of how these may be addressed through wider deliberative processes. We find that issues associated with the allocation of ecosystem services are poorly integrated into the resilience literature, and suggest that an improved understanding of allocation trade-offs could result from more applied research on use of ecosystem services that integrates perspectives from the social sciences about how and why people make and respond to decisions concerning ecosystem services.

2.1 INTRODUCTION

Prompted by escalating rates of environmental change, resilience thinking is one emerging applied field that explicitly seeks to inform managers and policy-makers in the governance of social–ecological systems (SES) and the ecosystem services they produce (Berkes *et al.* 2000; Walker and Salt 2006). Much of this research has moved beyond the dichotomous separation of social and ecological systems, towards studying coupled or linked SES. It also moves away from traditional top-down management approaches, premised on static or linear notions of ecosystems and social organization. The research incorporates greater attention to the existence of multiple possible ecosystem and social states or regimes, the possibility of rapid non-linear change, linkages across and among scales, and the idea that different SES states and their associated ecosystem services benefit different groups of people (Holling and Meffe 1996; MA 2005) (Chapter I).

This chapter analyses some of the important political and power dimensions inherent in the governance of SES and the implicit or explicit societal choices about which sets of ecosystem services to build resilience of, and try to sustain, in the face of disturbance and change. Any particular set of ecosystem services for which we build resilience will involve trade-offs – both between actor groups and between different bundles of ecosystem services – with decisions influenced (to a greater or lesser extent) by issues of power and inequality. Uncritically applying the principles put forward in this book may accomplish some groups' goals, but may also intensify ecosystem-service trade-offs and power differentials. While these issues are ubiquitous to the process of political decision-making, this chapter seeks to highlight the political and power dimensions that can influence the selection of specific sets of ecosystem services to build resilience of, and to emphasize the need to reflect on these issues before applying the principles put forward in this remainder of this book.

In particular, we emphasize the inherent danger in ecosystem governance approaches that do not incorporate and consider the social mechanisms by which governance and institutions accomplish their goals (Brown and Westaway 2011; Hatt 2012). Any set of ecosystem services 'chosen' as the focus for resilience-building initiatives is an emergent outcome resulting from both explicitly and implicitly political processes. Too often, initiatives aimed at building resilience do not consider the existing socio-political and economic inequalities in the system, and the extent to which strategies aimed at building resilience may reinforce and aggravate these disparities and inequalities. This does not mean that perfect equality is achievable, but rather that increasing levels of inequality may reach dangerous levels. Scientists themselves may contribute to the problem if an overly technocratic approach is adopted and societal goals are not more widely deliberated. While scientific analyses may provide valuable information about the different magnitude and mix of ecosystem services that might be provided by different SES states, this information does not necessarily make clear what SES states and ecosystem services are most desirable, nor is the aim of scientific analysis to do so. Choosing to build resilience of a particular set of ecosystem services reflects an implicit valuation of a specific set of services by specific groups of people at particular times and places, and either explicitly (or not) includes the inherent trade-offs that accompany those choices. Consequently,

Carpenter *et al.* (2001) caution that resilience of such a chosen set of services is a 'normative concept' and Armitage and Johnson (2006, p. 14) urge that consideration of resilience under such circumstances should be 'situated in the context of contested and evolving human interests and the uncertainties of human interaction'. Ultimately, all initiatives aimed at building resilience of ecosystem services have distributional implications, and are a matter of justice within and between generations (Norgaard 2010).

Throughout the rest of the book, we focus on general principles that might be employed to build resilience of different sets of ecosystem services, and assume that some process has been followed to arrive at the selected one. We do not define this 'desired' set of ecosystem services, as it will vary between places and groups, and change over time as societal preferences change. Here, we emphasize the critical necessity of reflecting on the implicit or explicit choice about which ecosystem services to build resilience of before attempting to apply any of the principles. In this way we ensure that initiatives aimed at building such resilience of ecosystem services do not simply advance and entrench the position of more powerful groups in society. To do so, this chapter first discusses some of the trade-offs between ecosystem services implicit in building resilience for a given set of ecosystem services. We then explore the challenges and repercussions of distribution that result from these trade-offs. Finally, we highlight some asymmetries and how these may be reduced to increase legitimacy in the selection of ecosystem services that can, in turn, provide greater support for maintaining specific sets of ecosystem services.

2.2 THE TRADE-OFFS OF SELECTING BETWEEN BUNDLES OF ECOSYSTEM SERVICES

Different bundles of ecosystem services often trade off against one another, and the selection of one bundle may eliminate the possibility for the production of other bundles of ecosystem services, as highlighted in Box 2.1 (MA 2005; Bennett *et al.* 2009) (Chapter 1). For instance, the preservation of global biodiversity as a public good

BOX 2.1 **Ecosystem services and community-based conservation in the Richtersveld National Park, Southern Africa**

Community-based conservation (CBC), promoting local participation and sustainable use of resources, arose in the 1990s as a response to failures of top-down command and control approaches to conservation. Paralleling the discourse in this chapter, past conservation efforts often reinforced deep power asymmetries of groups favouring different bundles of ecosystem services. In the case of protected areas, the global conservation movement led by international environmental NGOs and their supporters pushed for greater protection of biodiversity at a global scale and, in support of financial sustainability of parks, advocated for ecotourism within the parks. However, this collection of ecosystem services often came at the expense of local resource users. While CBC should not be viewed as a panacea, and local communities as a romanticized, homogeneous group in sustainable balance with nature, we do see instances where broader participation assuages some of the trade-offs of ecosystem services identified in the chapter.

In |Ai-|Ais/Richtersveld Transfrontier Park, straddling the border of Namibia and South Africa (Fig. 2.1), initial management followed top-down conservation methods. Although Richtersveld National Park in South Africa, created in 1991, arose out of the settlement of land claims between the local community and the national government and the creation of a contractual park, restrictions to local users often meant closing access to grazing of sheep and goats as well as the collection of other resources. In the words of the park manager, 'tourists won't pay to see goats' (personal communication, 2008). Once again, biodiversity conservation goals and tourist expectations trumped local ecosystem-service decisions. Yet this approach to conservation comes with well-known drawbacks. Resource restrictions may compound poverty and worsen subsistence viability. For these reasons as well as basic concepts of equality, it often lacks legitimacy in the surrounding communities. In turn, monitoring and enforcement of regulations and restrictions becomes difficult, expensive and often ineffective. Through the contractual park, in which the local community owned the land and collaboratively managed the park with the

FIG. 2.1 (a) The Succulent Karoo ecosystem of |Ai-|Ais/Richtersveld Transfrontier Park looks harsh but is home to high biodiversity richness and a suite of ecosystem services. (b) The Orange or Gariep River forms the international boundary between Namibia and South Africa and forms a political divide in the ecosystem, separating |Ai-|Ais Hot Springs from Richtersveld National Park. Photo credits: Christo Fabricius.

BOX 2.1 **Continued**

South African National Parks Board, the local Nama people and park officials began a deliberative process regarding access, use and management of natural resources. As a result of this deliberation, grazing was again allowed back in the park.

As community members became more involved in a conservation initiative of their own development, they became emboldened and created Richtersveld Cultural and Botanical Landscape, a community conservancy. In 2007, the conservancy was granted UNESCO World Heritage status. World Heritage status was granted with 'the traditional land-use system of the Nama ... seen as part of the protection system' (whc.unesco.org). Specifically, the sustainable resource use of the transhumance grazing practices and the traditional use of grass for portable thatched roof housing were seen as integral elements to the cultural landscape. In effect, deliberation with the park service and self-determination put in place a series of events at the time of this writing and a dramatic shift in resource rules from strict restriction to increased access to a celebration of sustainable resource use.

advocated by predominantly Western environmental advocacy groups through increasing the area of national parks and minimizing resource extraction reduces the land available for subsistence use as arable land or as a source of food, lodging or medicinal products (Robards *et al.* 2011). Similarly, the creation of palm-oil plantations to cater to the global demand for oil products decreases the carbon sequestration possibilities of old-growth tropical forests (Butler *et al.* 2009). In such cases one set of ecosystem services reduces or obviates the possibility of other sets, and a dilemma emerges in that different groups of people benefit from one selection as opposed to another. These trade-offs can perpetuate the dispossession of lands and resources initiated during the era of European colonialism, and further the logic of enclosure in which resources formerly held in common become privatized commodities (Heynen and Robbins 2005).

The desired allocation or prioritization of ecosystem services at one level or scale often has direct trade-offs and may be radically opposed at another scale. For instance, the provision of wild meats in tropical forests at a local level may be essential for communities, but may be counter to global biodiversity goals; swidden (shifting cultivation) agriculture may sustain local economic or nutritional needs, but minimize global climate mitigation actions; and laissez-faire planning and urban sprawl may benefit local governments, but work against global goals for the reduction of fossil-fuel consumption. Such trade-offs may be accentuated by differing worldviews or cultures.

Because it is usually not possible to meet all societal needs and expectations, we must acknowledge that any particular set of ecosystem services involves trade-offs with other options. Usually these trade-offs are biased in favour of particular groups, or can only be mitigated through acknowledging the special interests of specific groups in society. Examples include the mitigation of global greenhouse-gas emissions by more powerful countries through capture of forest resources in tropical low- and middle-income countries, which may perpetuate poverty traps in which systemic influences reinforce the root causes of poverty through the control of resource access and use (Sachs 2005) or create them as a collateral repercussion of not wishing to bear the economic burden of emission reductions (Dow *et al.* 2006). In these ways, emission reduction efforts may lead to poverty traps similar to those arising from some past biodiversity conservation efforts (Adams *et al.* 2004), where access to resources by local communities may be restricted, leading to further impoverishment.

These examples demonstrate how trade-offs between ecosystem services can have significant social consequences. Selecting particular sets of ecosystem services can result in a number of ramifications that may reinforce the inequalities that led to those choices. In the following section, we draw further attention to such distributional questions that often arise from the trade-offs of ecosystem services.

2.3 THE CHALLENGES OF DISTRIBUTION

Distributional challenges emerge when certain groups of people have disproportionate and inequitable benefits from the selection of specific sets of ecosystem services. These benefits are often linked to the fact that those who benefit from the ecosystem services may institute rules, which give them access to these ecosystem services while other groups are precluded. For example, a Kenyan coastal SES's restrictions on fishing gear – specifically use of seine nets – aimed at conserving the fishery and building ecosystem resilience, potentially have important socially differentiated impacts. Specifically, women fish traders are disadvantaged as their access to small, cheap fish is undermined, thus eroding their livelihood opportunities and negotiating capabilities in setting access rules to the fishery (Daw et al. 2012).

Bundles of ecosystem services and related governing institutions are often directly affected by, if not products of, historical institutions relating to property rights, land-use decisions and the logic of appropriateness in resource use. Prior conditions and constraints may maintain a strong influence on contemporary ecosystem services. As an example, among other policies aimed at reducing pelagic sealing and more closely controlling the scale of early twentieth-century trade in fur seals, the United States restricted indigenous Unangan hunters from using modern technology in their hunt for fur seals. This type of restriction, while originally based on considerations of commerce as much as conservation eventually constituted a major restriction in the name of conservation under numerous international wildlife conventions including the North Pacific Fur Seal Convention of 1911 and the 1946 International Convention for the Regulation of Whaling (Meek 2011).

Human preferences often prioritize provisioning services over regulating services, and both of these are prioritized over cultural and supporting services (Rodriguez et al. 2006). These choices may exacerbate societal inequalities, and not only between different social groups; they also serve to privilege an immediate time horizon over a more sustainable long-term perspective, and current generations over future generations. For instance, lasting soil conservation and the minimization of *dongas* (dried, eroded waterways) through pasture rotation and limits on livestock often lacks support amongst local herders when they compare this to wealth maximization as measured by herd size in parts of southern Africa (Doran et al. 1979). While current generations may benefit from the increased cattle numbers, the loss of productive land can substantially reduce the potential of future generations to make a living.

Scientists may further complicate distributional trade-offs between societal groups by exerting power and influence through scientization of a political problem, often unknowingly or unintentionally using science to *mask* their own interests (Habermas 1970). Scientization suppresses the open discussion of value preferences and delegitimizes those without a scientific perspective to support their position. This often marginalizes those unable to speak the specialized language of science, which often includes the disenfranchised who bear the brunt of the negative trade-offs (Gismondi and Richardson 1991; Lemos 2003; Sarewitz 2004). In juxtaposition, politicization is when people – whether scientists, non-governmental organizations (NGOs), private industries or others – manipulate science to fit their desired political or legal interests (Joly et al. 2010). Politicians are not the only actors who can politicize science, as scientists can also use science to defend and pursue their own political interests (Pielke 2004). Politicization can inhibit corrective feedbacks that enable SES governance to respond to and incorporate different viewpoints or new scientific understanding.

Promotion of certain sets of ecosystem services by more powerful sectors of society results in a number of ramifications that may reinforce the inequalities that led to specific choices. These distributional disputes often result in strengthening the status quo. The conclusion of work focusing on ecosystem-service trade-offs is the need to find a balance among services to accomplish the 'greater good' (e.g. Nelson et al. 2009; Palumbi et al. 2009). However, this is no easy task. The following section discusses responses to emergent asymmetries and means for alleviating them, potentially providing a more legitimate and sustainable system.

2.4 RESPONDING TO EMERGENT ASYMMETRIES

At a landscape level, any initiatives to build resilience of ecosystem services entails implicit trade-offs, because it necessarily needs to privilege certain ecosystem services, and different groups of people will benefit to greater or lesser extents. As in many complex systems, there is no optimal set of ecosystem services or real-world Pareto frontier whereby no one can be made better off without someone else being worse off as a result (Levin 2002). Issues of equity and justice can be balanced to varying degrees, but not optimized due to their normative nature. The resultant discord between desired outcomes and the specific combination of ecosystem services that are captured by individuals, communities or society in general will produce asymmetric gaps as described by Lasswell and Kaplan (1950).

In prioritizing specific sets of ecosystem services, care must be given to ensuring that society builds resilience to a fair and equitable set of ecosystem services rather than entrenching the positions of a privileged few – or risk both moral (e.g. human rights (Hardin 1998) and practical (e.g. revolution (Scott 1998, 2009)) repercussions. Institutions that remove people's access to, or use of, a specific service need to more explicitly attend to what these people will do in response, and if they have the capacity and agency to adapt to or buffer that scarcity. History runs rife with examples of not attending to these questions. Although the very construct of ecosystem services implies a substitutable commodity rather than an outcome of contestation and historical paths, at the same time it may allow considerable transparency in evaluating trade-offs that might otherwise be taken for granted.

One means of building a more legitimate and broadly acceptable choice of ecosystem services is through broader deliberation. More fully deliberating the 'desirability' of ecosystem services in SES may not only balance competing conceptualizations of 'desirability', but can build further benefits towards sustainability or resilience of ecosystem services. It is here that long-standing philosophical debates (e.g. Hobbes, Foucault, Habermas) can be drawn upon in a process of social learning as well as the work of deliberative democracy scholars (Dewey 1927; Rawls 1993; Dryzek 2002), as we collectively seek to find legitimate sustainable relationships with each other and the world around us.

These ideas foreshadow our discussions on building resilience through the principles of learning (P5 – Learning), broader levels of participation (P6 – Participation) and innovative governance arrangements such as polycentricity (P7 – Polycentricity). The notion that participation leads to more resilient provision of ecosystem services stems in part from increasing legitimacy of the political process of selecting which ecosystem services to build resilience of. Increased participation also results in more respected monitoring and enforcement, as well as a means to change inequitable outcomes through collective choice bargaining (Schlager and Ostrom 1992). Similarly, polycentric governance arrangements may allow for learning and experimentation across geographic governance regions as well as a diversity of institutional options (Olsson *et al.* 2004).

2.5 THE BENEFITS OF WIDER DELIBERATION

Ecosystem-service governance outcomes are a result of balancing competing 'desires' of different groups; however, they are influenced by various asymmetries, leading some groups to get closer to their desired goals than others. As we have shown, agency of those in power to self-allocate the flow of ecosystem services may lead them to maintain their short-term benefits and the status quo in terms of inequalities and asymmetries. However, disenfranchisement of specific actors may lead to humanitarian issues or revolt of the disenfranchised. We have argued for the need to explicitly acknowledge trade-offs, distributional issues and the repercussions of not proactively incorporating the responses of, or repercussions to, the disenfranchised – in other words the need to consider appropriately the social ramifications of political decision-making when it comes to initiatives to build resilience of ecosystem services. Examples of processes to guide such thinking include companion modelling (Étienne 2011) or recent work on mental models (Biggs *et al.* 2011) (P4 – CAS thinking).

Openly deliberative processes may better incorporate feedbacks from the marginalized through providing for more inclusion, but will require the more powerful to incorporate pluralistic local needs and values into the dominant paradigms that they seek to maintain. Acting in this manner is no simple matter; however, self-restraint does emerge in governance. For example, constitutions favouring equal opportunity of all citizens may limit a government's ability to provide preferential allocation of resources to specific groups or communities. Establishing the degree to which global desires are being achieved at the cost of local repercussions will better illuminate priorities for action. Numerous authors have indicated that biodiversity goals in the tropics will not be met without addressing poverty first (e.g. Adams *et al.* 2004). Not only will change require better understanding of feedbacks associated with poverty traps and local agency, it will also need leaders and the elite (at multiple scales from local to global) to recognize these interrelationships, and to work towards more deliberative and open processes. For example, balancing mitigation of climate emissions through Reducing Emissions from Deforestation and Forest Degradation (REDD) in developing countries does not mask the need for comprehensive reductions in carbon emissions by the largest emitters, and may exacerbate poverty, which is inextricably linked to resource access in many regions (Angelson *et al.* 2009). Ignoring that linkage ignores the full cost of our carbon emissions.

More fully deliberating which ecosystem services should be the focus of resilience-building initiatives in SES can not only help balance competing conceptualizations of which ecosystem services society desires to sustain, but can build further benefits towards sustainability. Indeed, as Levin (2010, p. 13) concludes, 'one of the great challenges in achieving sustainability will be in understanding the basis for cooperation'. Without such an approach, society will struggle to develop a long-term strategy whereby we collectively live within the limits of the globe's ecosystems.

2.6 CONCLUSION

This chapter has highlighted some of the deep political issues and social implications underlying initiatives to build resilience of ecosystem services. Before applying the principles discussed in this book to foster the resilience of ecosystem services, critical attention should be directed towards understanding the context, contests, politics and history in which ecosystem services in a particular place are embedded. In particular, the current set of ecosystem services provided by a landscape may reflect deep asymmetries in which sectors or groups in society are supported or favoured, and strengthening the resilience of those ecosystem services may further entrench these inequalities. In some cases, repercussions from the disenfranchised may destabilize a system, while in other cases efforts to reduce inequity may be well meaning; however, changes to the existing ecosystem-service landscape may generate new conflicts and trade-offs. Reflecting on these issues can help illuminate who will be favoured or disadvantaged by choices to build resilience of certain sets of ecosystem services, and how this may itself influence the long-term resilience of these ecosystem services. Norgaard (2010, p. 1226) notes that 'while economists have been unusually successful at averting the ethical questions, and in the process supporting those who currently benefit from the governance structure, this avoidance has become central to the problems we now have in reaching a global accord'. The processes we summarize here and elsewhere (Robards *et al.* 2011) provide examples of what is being avoided and why. Where the flow of ecosystem services cannot fulfil all social and ecosystem needs, the feedbacks we discuss will need to be integrated into governance institutions to ensure that the resilience of ecosystem services is not incrementally eroded, with long-term repercussions for human or ecosystem health.

Given the diversity of potential ecosystem services and governance arrangements in most SES, the selection of bundles of ecosystem services is a traditional 'wicked' problem in which there can be no overall deliberative panel or institution to decide which ecosystem services should be the focus of resilience-building initiatives (Rittl and Webber 1973). Rather, the 'chosen' set of ecosystem services produced by a social–ecological landscape is an emergent, messy phenomenon that is the outcome of competition and negotiation between many different users and sectors of society at different scales, and the biophysical, economic and institutional constraints of the underlying SES. Social factors and processes shape and are shaped by the set of ecosystem services, in what can sometimes be a reinforcing process. This results in rigidity traps in which systems become highly connected, self-reinforcing and inflexible due to power differentials, sticky institutional arrangements and other mechanisms constraining governance changes, including externalization of trade-offs (Carpenter and Brock 2008). Such traps limit the ability of actors within the system to reorganize interactions, even if such a reorganization would benefit the provision of ecosystem services to society overall (Gunderson and Holling 2002). We have highlighted how trade-offs associated with ecosystem services can result in such traps, and are sometimes exacerbated through the scientization of the political discussion and politicization of scientific knowledge.

In providing these caveats to the resilience-building enterprise, we do not suggest that any decision-makers must have fully contextualized understanding and engage in all of the transaction costs implied in deliberative democratic practice. What is required is a measure of awareness and transparency regarding the political dimensions of potential ecosystem-service choices as well as potential futures for which we can build resilience.

REFERENCES

Adams, W. M., Aveling, R., Brockington, D. *et al.* (2004). Biodiversity conservation and the eradication of poverty. *Science*, 306, 1146–1149.

Angelsen, A., Brockhaus, M., Kanninen, M., eds. et al. (2009). *Realising REDD+: National Strategy and Policy Options*. Bogor: Center for International Forestry Research.

Armitage, D. R. and Johnson, D. (2006). Can resilience be reconciled with globalization and the increasingly complex conditions of resource degradation in Asian coastal regions? *Ecology and Society*, 11, 2.

Bennett, E. M., Peterson, G. D., Gordon, L. J. (2009). Understanding relationships among multiple ecosystem services. *Ecology Letters*, 12, 1–11.

Berkes, F., Folke, C., Colding, J., eds. (2000). *Linking Social and Ecological Systems: Management Practices and Social Mechanisms for Building Resilience*. Cambridge: Cambridge University Press.

Biggs, D., Abel, N., Knight, A. T. et al. (2011). The implementation crisis in conservation planning: could 'mental models' help? *Conservation Letters*, 4, 169–183.

Brown, K. and Westaway, E. (2011). Agency, capacity, and resilience to environmental change: lessons from human development, well-being, and disasters. *Annual Review of Environment and Resources*, 36, 321–342.

Butler, R. A., Lian P. K., Jaboury, G. (2009). REDD in the red: palm oil could undermine carbon payment schemes. *Conservation letters*, 2, 67–73.

Carpenter, S. R., Walker, B., Anderies, J. M., Abel, N. (2001). From metaphor to measurement: resilience of what to what? *Ecosystems*, 4, 765–781.

Carpenter, S. R. and Brock, W. A. (2008). Adaptive capacity and traps. *Ecology and Society*, 13, 40.

Daw, T., Brown, K., Rosendo, S., Pomeroy, R. (2012). Applying the ecosystem services concept to poverty alleviation: the need to disaggregate human well-being. *Environmental Conservation*, 38, 370–379.

Dewey, J. (1927). *The Public and its Problems: An Essay in Political Inquiry*. New York, NY: Henry Holt Press.

Doran, M. H., Low, A. R. C., Kemp, R. L. (1979). Cattle as a store of wealth in Swaziland: implications for livestock development and overgrazing in eastern and southern Africa. *American Journal of Agricultural Economics*, 61, 41–47.

Dow, K., Kasperson, R. E., Bohn, M. (2006). Exploring the social justice implications of adaptation and vulnerability. In *Fairness in Adaptation to Climate Change*. Cambridge, MA: MIT Press, pp. 77–96.

Dryzek, J. (2002). *Deliberative Democracy and Beyond: Liberals, Critics, Contestations*. Oxford: Oxford University Press.

Easton, D. (1965). *A Framework for Political Analysis*. Englewood Cliffs, NJ: Prentice-Hall.

Étienne, M., ed. (2011). *Companion Modelling. A Participatory Approach to Support Sustainable Development*. Dordrecht: Springer.

Gismondi, M. and Richardson, M. (1991). Discourse and power in environmental politics: public hearings on a bleached Kraft pulp mill in Alberta, Canada. *Capitalism Nature Socialism*, 2, 43–66.

Gunderson, L. H. and Holling, C. S., eds. (2002). *Panarchy: Understanding Transformations in Human and Natural Systems*. Washington, DC: Island Press.

Habermas, J. (1970). *Toward a Rational Society*. Boston, MA: Beacon.

Hardin, R. (1988). *Morality within the Limits of Reason*. Chicago, IL: University of Chicago Press.

Hatt, K. (2012). Social attractors: a proposal to enhance 'resilience thinking' about the social. *Society and Natural Resources*, 26, 30–43.

Heynen, N. and Robbins, P. (2005). The neoliberalization of nature: governance, privatization, enclosure and valuation. *Capitalism, Nature, Socialism*, 16, 5–8.

Holling, C. S. and Meffe, G. K. (1996). Command and control and the pathology of natural resource management. *Conservation Biology*, 10, 328–337.

Joly, J., Reynolds, J., Robards, M. D. (2010). Recognizing when the 'best scientific data available' isn't. *Stanford Environmental Law Journal*, 29, 247–282.

Lasswell, H. D. and Kaplan, A. (1950). *Power and Society: A Framework for Political Inquiry*. New Haven, CT: Yale University Press.

Lemos, M. C. (2003). A tale of two policies: the politics of climate forecasting and drought relief in Ceará, Brazil. *Policy Sciences*, 36, 101–123.

Levin, S. A. (2002). Complex adaptive systems: exploring the known, the unknown, and the unknowable. *Bulletin of the American Mathematical Society*, 40, 3–19.

Levin, S. A. (2010). Crossing scales, crossing disciplines: collective motion and collective action in the global commons. *Philosophical Transactions of the Royal Society, Series B*, 365, 13–18.

MA (2005). *Millennium Ecosystem Assessment: Ecosystems and Human Well-Being: A Framework for Assessment*. Washington, DC: Island Press.

Meek, C. L. (2011). Conservation of marine mammals in Alaska: the value of policy histories for understanding contemporary change. In *North by 2020 Synthesis*. Fairbanks, AK: University of Alaska Press, pp. 359–375.

Nelson, E., Mendoza, G., Regetz, J. et al. (2009). Modeling multiple ecosystem services, biodiversity conservation, commodity production, and trade-offs at landscape scales. *Frontiers in Ecology and the Environment*, 7, 4–11.

Norgaard, R. B. (2010). Ecosystem services: from eye-opening metaphor to complexity blinder. *Ecological Economics*, 69, 1219–1227.

Olsson, P., Folke, C., Berkes, F. (2004). Adaptive comanagement for building resilience in social–ecological systems. *Environmental Management*, 34, 75–90.

Palumbi, S. R., Sandifer, P. A., Allan, J. D. et al. (2009). Managing for ocean biodiversity to sustain marine ecosystem services. *Frontiers in Ecology and the Environment*, 7, 204–211.

Pielke Jr, R. A. (2004). When scientists politicize science: making sense of controversy over The Skeptical Environmentalist. *Environmental Science and Policy*, 7, 405–417.

Rawls, J. (1993). *Political Liberalism*, 4th edn. New York, NY: Columbia University Press.

Rittel, H. W. J. and Webber, M. M. (1973). Dilemmas in a general theory of planning. *Policy Sciences*, 4, 155–169.

Robards, M. D., Schoon, M. L., Meek, C. L., Engle, N. L. (2011). The importance of social drivers in the resilient provision of ecosystem services. *Global Environmental Change*, 21, 522–529.

Rodriguez, J. P., Beard, Jr, T. D., Bennett, E. M. et al. (2006). Trade-offs across space, time, and ecosystem services. *Ecology and Society*, 11, 28.

Sachs, J. (2005). *The End of Poverty: How We Can Make It Happen in Our Lifetime*. London: Penguin UK.

Schlager, E. and Ostrom, E. (1992). Property-rights regimes and natural resources: a conceptual analysis. *Land Economics*, 68, 249–262.

Scott, J. C. (1998). *Seeing Like a State: How Certain Schemes to Improve the Human Condition have Failed*. Yale, CT: Yale University Press.

Scott, J. C. (2009). *The Art of Not Being Governed: An Anarchist History of Upland Southeast Asia*. Yale, CT: Yale University Press.

Sarewitz, D. (2004). How science makes environmental controversies worse. *Environmental Science and Policy*, 7, 385–403.

Walker, B. and Salt, D. (2006). *Resilience Thinking: Sustaining Ecosystems and People in a Changing World*. Washington, DC: Island Press.

3 Principle 1 – Maintain diversity and redundancy

Karen Kotschy, Reinette Biggs, Tim Daw, Carl Folke and Paul West

SUMMARY

Diversity and redundancy in social–ecological system components such as species, landscape types, knowledge systems, actors, cultural groups or institutions provide options for responding to change and disturbance and for dealing with uncertainty and surprise. These options can increase both the reliability of ecosystem services and the potential for learning and innovation. Theoretical and empirical research suggests that it is specifically response diversity, in combination with functional redundancy, which is important for maintaining ecosystem services in the face of disturbance and ongoing change. However, both diversity and redundancy may be costly in terms of increasing system complexity and inefficiency, especially with regard to the social dimension, and this may negatively affect the resilience of certain ecosystem services. Enhancing the resilience of ecosystem services by investing in diversity and redundancy involves considering social–ecological interactions across different temporal

Principles for Building Resilience: Sustaining Ecosystem Services in Social–Ecological Systems, eds R. Biggs, M. Schlüter and M. L. Schoon. Published by Cambridge University Press. © Cambridge University Press 2015.

and spatial scales, and finding an appropriate balance between the costs and benefits of too much or too little diversity and redundancy.

3.1 INTRODUCTION

Diversity is widely held to be important for resilience because it provides options for responding to change and disturbance (Folke *et al.* 2003; Walker and Salt 2006; Norberg and Cumming 2008). Evidence from several fields of study suggests that systems with many different components are generally more resilient than systems with few components or less heterogeneous components, whether the components are molecules, species, habitat patches, livelihoods, actors, knowledge systems or institutions (Ellis 2000; Nyström and Folke 2001; Ostrom 2005; Di Falco and Chavas 2006; Cardinale *et al.* 2012). However, despite this general acceptance of the importance of diversity, attempts to develop a more detailed understanding of how diversity affects the functioning and resilience of social–ecological systems (SES) have typically produced a great deal of debate. In ecology, for example, the relationship between biodiversity and ecosystem functioning, and between biodiversity and ecosystem stability have both been the subject of lengthy debates (Holling *et al.* 1995; Levin 1998; McCann 2000; Naeem and Wright 2003). It has become increasingly clear that diversity, functioning and resilience are all multifaceted, scale-dependent concepts, making the relationships between them in SES far from simple (McCann 2000; Carpenter and Brock 2004; Ostrom 2005; Nelson *et al.* 2011; Barnes-Mauthe *et al.* 2013).

In this chapter we seek to evaluate the relationships between diversity, the related property of redundancy, and the resilience of ecosystem services, with the aim of developing a better understanding of how, when and where diversity and redundancy may enhance the resilience of ecosystem services, and how, when and where they may not.

3.2 WHAT DO WE MEAN BY DIVERSITY AND REDUNDANCY?

The concept of diversity is used in many different fields of study and has been defined in a large number of different ways. Stirling (2007) provided a useful framework for understanding diversity by identifying three interrelated but distinct aspects common to diversity concepts across many different fields, namely variety (how many different elements), balance (how many representatives of each element) and disparity (how different the elements are from one another) (Fig. 3.1). These three aspects together help to fully capture the property of diversity (Stirling 2007). Variety is the most well-studied aspect of diversity, and diversity is often taken to mean simply the number of different elements present, for example the number of species, landscape patches, cultural groups or institutions. Balance is often included to account for the fact that many systems show highly skewed 'distributions of wealth', with a few very abundant elements and a large number of rare ones (Nekola and Brown 2007), so that not all elements are equally represented. Disparity, or the nature of the similarities and differences between system elements, is not usually included in diversity concepts in ecology (Kotschy 2013), but is often more central to studies of diversity in social systems (Page 2007).

Depending on the elements being considered, many different types of diversity may be described within a particular SES. For example, we may describe functional diversity among plant or animal species in terms of the number of species present (variety), their relative abundances (balance) and the extent to which the species differ from each other functionally (disparity) (Kotschy 2013). Likewise, we may describe livelihood diversity as a function of the number of livelihood options available (variety), the extent to which each option is currently practiced (balance) and the degree of difference between the options (disparity), or cultural diversity as the number of cultural groups present (variety), the relative size or power of these groups (balance) and the differences between them (disparity). Since resilience is about coping

PRINCIPLE 1 – MAINTAIN DIVERSITY AND REDUNDANCY

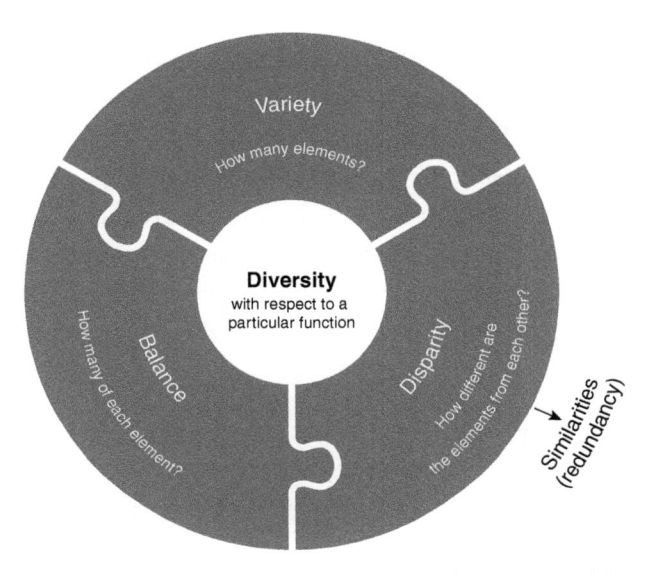

FIG. 3.1 Conceptual diagram showing the three aspects of diversity that affect the resilience of ecosystem services. Variety, balance and disparity all play a role in determining the capacity of a system to maintain a particular ecosystem service. Redundancy is related to disparity, being determined by the similarities rather than the differences among elements.

with change and disturbance, the ways in which SES elements differ from one another in their responses to disturbance ('response diversity') are thought to be particularly important for resilience (Elmqvist *et al.* 2003; Leslie and McCabe 2013; Mori *et al.* 2013).

Redundancy describes the replication of elements or pathways in a system (Walker 1992; Lawton and Brown 1993). Redundancy is determined by the number of elements that perform a particular function similarly (Walker 1992, 1995) (Fig. 3.1). Redundancy potentially provides 'insurance' for system functioning, by allowing some system elements to compensate for the loss or failure of others (Low *et al.* 2003; Nyström 2006; Vavouri *et al.* 2008). For example, impoverished small-scale farmers often plant several different food crops so that failure of any one crop will not have catastrophic impacts on food provision, ensuring a more continuous food supply than monoculture farming (Altieri 2009). Redundancy in this case is provided by the fact that several crops contribute to the provision of food and can be substituted for each other. Response diversity is provided by the fact that different crop types or species often respond differently to disturbances such as drought or disease and are therefore unlikely to all fail simultaneously. In general, elements that perform a particular function similarly provide redundancy for that function, while elements that respond differently to disturbances provide response diversity.

3.3 HOW DOES MAINTAINING DIVERSITY AND REDUNDANCY ENHANCE THE RESILIENCE OF ECOSYSTEM SERVICES?

We view ecosystem services as co-produced by the ecological and social components of an SES (Reyers *et al.* 2013) (Chapter 1). For example, the fish we eat (a provisioning ecosystem service) are produced by a combination of ecological processes and the human knowledge and skills to catch or farm the fish, store it and transport it to the place where it is consumed. The resilience of an ecosystem service may be influenced by redundancy and diversity pertaining to some or all of the various system elements involved in producing the ecosystem service.

The presence of multiple elements with similar functional roles (e.g. different species of edible fish) provides redundancy and allows for the possibility of substitution among elements, thus providing 'backup' or 'insurance' through a process known as functional compensation (Lawton and Brown 1993). Kenyan reef fisheries, for example, have to date not collapsed under heavy exploitation because of the large number of species available for harvest. Loss of larger species has been compensated for by an increase in smaller-bodied, more productive species (McClanahan *et al.* 2008). By decreasing reliance on the presence of particular elements (e.g. particular species of fish), redundancy increases the capacity of the system to maintain ecosystem-service provision over time despite changes in the identities of the elements.

Redundancy is even more valuable if the elements providing the redundancy also differ from each other in their responses to disturbance (response diversity). Such differences increase the chance that at least some elements will persist and continue delivering particular ecosystem services in the face of disturbance and change (Elmqvist *et al.* 2003) (Box 3.1). Differences in size, spatial scale or lifespan often translate into different ways of responding to disturbance, providing a cross-scale dimension to resilience (Peterson *et al.* 1998). For example, seed dispersal in Ugandan forests is performed by a range of different-sized mammals, from mice to chimpanzees. While the small mammals are negatively affected by localized disturbances, the larger, more mobile species are not, and can therefore maintain the seed dispersal function. This response diversity allows tree populations to persist through different-sized disturbances (Peterson *et al.* 1998). Similarly, differences in the responses of plant species to rainfall events allows grass production for grazing by livestock to be maintained during periods of variable rainfall. Species that increase their growth rate after rains can produce green biomass quickly but tend to dry out rapidly between showers. During dry periods, grazing is maintained by species which respond less rapidly to rainfall, but which dry out more slowly (McNaughton 1977).

Within the governance system a variety of organizational forms (e.g. government department, non-governmental organization (NGO), community organization) with overlapping domains of authority can provide both redundancy and response diversity (P7 – Polycentricity). If different organizations all play a similar role, for example regulating the use of a particular ecosystem service, redundancy is present because the regulatory function can still be performed even if one or more of the organizations become dysfunctional. Differences between organizational forms provide response diversity because organizations with different sizes, cultures, funding mechanisms and internal structures are likely to respond differently to various economic and political changes (Williamson 1985). Similarly, a diversity of institutional structures allows for a bigger range of responses to the myriad complex governance challenges faced by actors daily (Ostrom 2005).

Diverse groups of actors with different roles (often discussed in terms of heterogeneity) are critical in the resilience of SES, with overlapping functions and different strengths in performance during different phases of development (Folke *et al.* 2005; Page 2007; Westley *et al.* 2013). Roles include: knowledge carriers and retainers; interpreters and sense-makers; networkers and facilitators; stewards and leaders; visionaries and inspirers; innovators and experimenters; and followers and reinforcers. Creative teams and actor groups may emerge into a large connected community of practitioners with overlapping functions and redundancy that provide adaptive capacity and resilience for maintaining ecosystem services and dealing with disturbance and change (Folke *et al.* 2003). Baland and Platteau (1996) empirically demonstrated that heterogeneity of endowments in social groups is more likely to lead to sustainable outcomes in natural-resource management. This supports theoretical claims that privileged groups can enhance the possibilities for collective action (Olson 1965). However, the effects of social heterogeneity on collective action and the creation of long-enduring institutional arrangements remain disputed, as noted in the following section.

The above examples show how a function lost by the decline of certain elements (e.g. species, organizations) can be compensated for by other elements that are less severely affected by a particular disturbance. The differences in size or scale of operation between the elements involved in producing an ecosystem service confer upon them different strengths and weaknesses, so that a particular disturbance is unlikely to present the same risk to all elements at once, and enable the continued production of the ecosystem service. The same reasoning lies behind portfolio theory in economics, ensemble approaches in machine learning and the use of diverse problem solvers in decision-making (Page 2007; Whitacre and Bender 2010).

At the landscape level, spatial heterogeneity resulting from natural processes and/or human activities may also promote the resilience of ecosystem services. Landscape patches with different characteristics provide a form of response diversity, because different patches may be affected differently by a particular disturbance. For example, areas with lower fuel loads, such as rocky areas and watercourses, may be less susceptible to fire (Turner and Romme 1994), and urban and rural areas are affected differently by natural disasters such as floods or hurricanes (Wisner 2004). Spatial heterogeneity helps ensure that some landscape patches remain undisturbed and provide refuges for the maintenance of associated ecosystem services. Similarly, protected landscape patches such as conservation areas, sacred pools or forests, and reserve grazing areas often function as remnant sources of critical ecosystem services, such as water and fodder, during severe droughts or after wildfires (Berkes and Folke 2002; Bohensky et al. 2004). Remnant landscape patches may also become important sources of propagules for recolonization of bare areas after disturbances such as volcanic eruptions, hurricanes or extreme floods, provided there is sufficient connectivity to disturbed patches (Turner et al. 1998; Nyström and Folke 2001; Parsons et al. 2005) (P2 – Connectivity).

Spatial heterogeneity and habitat complexity also generally enhance species diversity (Kerr and Packer 1997; Tews et al. 2004), which is particularly important for the resilience of ecosystem services that are dependent on the combined functioning and interactions of many species, such as pollution control, climate regulation and nutrient cycling (Zhang et al. 2007; Cardinale et al. 2012) (Box 3.1). As the number of elements (variety) involved in producing an ecosystem service increases, both redundancy and response diversity tend to increase, because there is a greater chance that elements will overlap in certain aspects of their functioning, providing redundancy, while at the same time will also differ in other aspects of their functioning, providing response diversity (Bellwood et al. 2004; Kotschy 2013). As species richness (variety) increases in biological communities, species typically partition their use of resources over space, time and/or type. This differentiation in functioning provides complementarity in both function and time, which helps to maintain stability in the face of disturbance and change (de Mazancourt et al. 2013; Loreau and de Mazancourt 2013).

Diversity of values and perspectives in society can affect the resilience of ecosystem services by helping guard against fads and soaring demand for particular ecosystem services (Abrahamson 1991). Diversity amongst ecosystem services users and managers can also help improve understanding of the SES dynamics that underlie ecosystem services production, and broaden the set of potential management approaches (Norgaard and Baer 2005; Biggs et al. 2009) (P5 – Learning). For example, within fishing communities people of different ages, genders and financial means may favour different fishing methods and types of gear (Smith et al. 2005). This diversity among resource users contributes to resilience by enhancing the ability of the community as a whole to detect and understand ecological changes, because each user has a perspective on different parts of the system (Crona 2006). These different perspectives may also suggest a number of alternative management approaches (McClanahan and Cinner 2008) (P5 – Learning). However, diversity may also lead to conflicts over resource management, as described in Chapter 2 and in the following section.

The diversity of knowledge and experience embodied in institutions is a form of social–ecological memory which can be drawn upon when responding to future events (Gunderson and Holling 2002; Barthel et al. 2010). The greater the diversity of knowledge and experience present, the greater the range of possible responses, and the greater the chance of finding creative solutions to changes or disturbances that threaten ecosystem services. In this regard, there is growing interest in the potential of deliberately increasing the diversity of knowledge available by combining diverse types of knowledge, such as local ecological knowledge and scientific knowledge (Bohensky and Maru 2011) in various spheres, ranging from adaptation to climate change to management of natural resources such as fisheries, freshwater and biodiversity (e.g. Riedlinger and Berkes 2001; Aswani and Hamilton 2004; Lansing 2007).

Diversity and redundancy are also important for enabling adaptation to ongoing change in SES. Investment in diverse ecosystem services-based activities (e.g. fishing, ecotourism) can enhance the resilience of associated livelihoods as it enables people to adjust their livelihood portfolios in response to more long-lasting changes in market or environmental conditions (Ellis 2000). For example, a substantial number of farmers in the drier parts of South Africa and Namibia have shifted from cattle ranching to wildlife-based ecotourism in response to changing markets and growing preferences for cultural over provisioning ecosystem services (Scholes and Biggs 2004). Diverse livelihoods can also support options for responding to ecological change. In the western Indian Ocean region, for example, fishers from households with more diverse livelihood portfolios that included non-fishing activities were more able to consider leaving a fishery that was in decline (Daw *et al.* 2012). Not only does such livelihood flexibility increase the resilience of individual households, it also reduces the pressure on the parts of the system producing a particular ecosystem service, thereby enhancing the resilience of that ecosystem service.

3.4 UNDER WHAT CONDITIONS MAY RESILIENCE OF ECOSYSTEM SERVICES BE COMPROMISED?

There is substantial evidence that low levels of either diversity or redundancy can compromise resilience. If a key SES function or ecosystem service is produced by only one or a few system elements (i.e. has low redundancy), these elements are referred to as 'keystone species' or 'key actors' (Mills *et al.* 1993; Folke *et al.* 2005).

Loss of key species or actors typically leads to the loss of many other entities because the remaining species or actors are unable to compensate effectively (Mills *et al.* 1993; Solé and Montoya 2001). For example, the North American beaver (*Castor canadensis*) functions as an ecosystem engineer, altering the hydrology and biogeochemistry by cutting trees and building dams, creating a complex floodplain landscape that supplies a variety of ecosystem services (Naiman et al. 2005). Extensive trapping of beaver between 1500 and 1800 led to a widespread reduction in wetland habitat and associated ecosystem services (Butler and Malanson 2005). Similarly, work on key actors has shown that the loss of a key actor involved in managing ecosystem services, such as an institutional or policy entrepreneur who serves as a glue in social networks, can seriously hamper the resilience of ecosystem services (Scheffer et al. 2003; Westley et al. 2013).

There are several other well-documented examples of dramatic changes resulting from the loss of elements playing keystone roles. On Caribbean coral reefs, herbivory is crucial for maintaining a balance between coral and algae. Redundancy between herbivorous fish and urchins allowed grazing to continue despite overfishing. However, once the herbivorous fish were removed, redundancy and response diversity were lost as the grazing function depended on a single species of urchin. The loss of resilience was dramatically illustrated when a disease removed the dominant urchin species and the corals became overgrown by algae (Hughes 1994). Similarly, network analyses have shown that the targeted removal of highly connected nodes dramatically increases the risk of network collapse compared to random removal of nodes (Solé and Montoya 2001) (P2 – Connectivity).

Studies of keystone species and key actors have highlighted an important feature of SES, namely that the resilience of particular ecosystem services can be compromised by the presence of keystone entities with low redundancy, even when the overall diversity and/or redundancy levels in the system are high (Kotschy 2013). Diversity and redundancy levels therefore need to be assessed for each ecosystem service separately, because diversity and redundancy pertaining to one ecosystem service do not necessarily enhance the resilience of other ecosystem services produced by the same system.

In other cases, high redundancy may occur in combination with low response diversity. In such cases, many elements contribute to a particular ecosystem service, but all elements are very similar either by design (if they are human institutions or activities) or due to environmental or historical constraints. As long as disturbances remain within the natural range of variation experienced by the system, provision of ecosystem services is expected to be resilient. However, the system is likely to be vulnerable to new types of disturbances because of the limited options available for responding to the new conditions (Janssen et al. 2007).

There is some evidence that very high levels of diversity and/or redundancy can have negative impacts on ecosystem service resilience, by increasing the possibility for stagnation within some aspects of SES (Fig. 3.2). For example, the diversity of interests, preferences, expected climate-change impacts and response capacity among nations has been identified as an important contributing factor in the stalemate surrounding climate negotiations (Harris 2007).

At more local levels, diversity of ethnicity can significantly influence social network structure, affecting the extent of linkage to outside industry leaders, officials and members of the scientific community, and creating challenges for stakeholder collaboration across groups (Barnes-Mauthe et al. 2013). As noted in the previous section, the empirical evidence for the effects of social heterogeneity – economic, cultural, religious and political – on the functioning of groups is ambiguous (Agrawal 2002). Shared values or cultural *homogeneity* often facilitates cooperation in the governance of resources (Bardhan and Dayton-Johnson 2002). The relationship between social heterogeneity and the resilient provision of ecosystem services is further complicated by conflation of the multiple aspects of social heterogeneity that often vary by context. Diversity of ideas and individuals, diversity in the level of experience, diversity in worldviews and diversity in the perception of the most

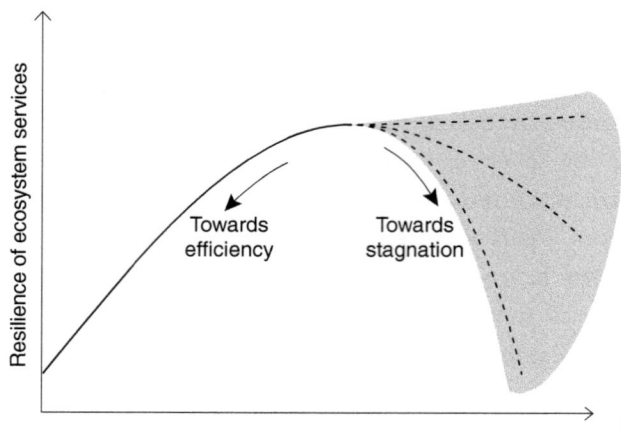

FIG. 3.2 There is substantial evidence that low levels of diversity or redundancy are associated with lower levels of ecosystem service resilience. There is also some evidence that very high levels of diversity in some SES elements, especially in the social dimension, may reduce the resilience of ecosystem services. However, it is unclear whether resilience always declines at high levels of diversity/redundancy, and there is substantial uncertainty over the exact form of the curve, as reflected by the dotted lines in the figure. The shape of the curve may vary depending on the spatial and temporal scales and the SES elements considered. Modified from Lietaer et al. (2010).

important problem facing an SES can all lead to disagreement and conflict and to poorer outcomes in collaborative resource management (Meinzen-Dick and Zwarteveen 1998; Page 2007; Bell et al. 2011).

Similarly, high redundancy in management organizations may hinder ecosystem-service governance, because it tends to increase administrative costs, coordination and other types of transaction costs, and also the potential for power struggles and contradictory regulations, which can compromise the ability of governance systems to respond effectively to change (Jentoft et al. 2009). There is less evidence of negative effects of high diversity or redundancy in the ecological domain. However, antagonistic interactions between species have been shown to be detrimental to aspects of system functioning at high diversity in bacterial communities (Becker et al. 2012). Greater diversity and redundancy may therefore not always increase ecosystem-service resilience.

More generally, it has been proposed that there is a trade-off between efficiency and increasing diversity and redundancy in SES (Ulanowicz et al. 2009) (Fig. 3.2). Low levels of diversity and/or redundancy can create greater efficiencies, such as more efficient food production (Reidsma and Ewert 2008) or more efficient global trade (Lietaer et al. 2010), but provide fewer options to draw on in adapting to change. In contrast, as highlighted above, high levels of diversity and/or redundancy can be extremely complex to manage, reducing the nimbleness of the system to respond to disturbances or adapt to ongoing change. High diversity and redundancy tend to be associated with a large number of system elements (Cardinale et al. 2012; Kotschy 2013). As the number of elements in a system increases, the possible interactions between them tend to rise exponentially, as does the possibility of complex, non-linear system dynamics (Ives and Carpenter 2007). This increased complexity may hinder the establishment of efficient, directional pathways for the processing of matter, energy or information, and lead to 'stagnation', or a reduced ability of the SES to maintain key processes and retain its essential character (Ulanowicz et al. 2009; Lietaer et al. 2010). Much work is still required in understanding the relationship between diversity/redundancy and resilience of ecosystem services in different contexts.

3.5 HOW CAN THE PRINCIPLE OF MAINTAINING DIVERSITY AND REDUNDANCY BE OPERATIONALIZED AND APPLIED?

To put this principle into practice, the value of both diversity and redundancy must be recognized and incorporated into SES management. In this section we suggest some ways in which this may be achieved.

- **Monitor diversity and redundancy in relation to key ecosystem services.** Measuring and monitoring diversity and redundancy is challenging, but essential for operationalizing this principle. Monitoring and assessment should be linked to particular ecosystem services as far as possible, rather than relying on 'general' measures. For example, biodiversity conservation programmes often focus on the number of species present as a general measure of diversity. However, species richness alone is not always a good measure of the resilience associated with particular ecosystem services, as described in Section 3.3. What is needed is an understanding of the species, actors, institutions, organizations and critical processes involved in producing each ecosystem service, and the ways in which diversity and redundancy in these different parts of the SES affect resilience. Identifying and managing vulnerable points in the system, such as those controlled by keystone entities, may be a practical way to maintain the resilience of ecosystem services because it allows for targeted monitoring and action (Box 3.1).
- **Conserve and value redundancy.** Redundancy is seldom explicitly conserved or managed (Kotschy 2013), but is just as important as diversity in providing resilience. Particular attention should be paid to important functions or ecosystem services with low redundancy, such as those controlled by keystone species or key actors. In some cases it may be possible to increase the amount of redundancy associated with these ecosystem services (Box 3.1). Alternatively, key system elements may need to be specifically conserved or protected (e.g. Bellwood et al. 2004), or the ability of the system to adapt to the loss of particular ecosystem services must be developed (see the last point below). However, care must be taken with the complex interplay between redundancy and efficiency for institutional infrastructure.
- **Maintain ecological diversity.** Several authors have published guidelines for managing ecosystems and production landscapes for resilience, which include strategies to maintain or enhance diversity (e.g. Fischer et al. 2006). These strategies include maintaining or creating structural complexity in the landscape, creating buffers around sensitive areas, creating corridors to maintain connectivity (P3 – Connectivity), maintaining landscape heterogeneity, applying appropriate disturbance regimes and controlling overabundant invasive species. Other strategies focus on merging biodiversity conservation and production imperatives, for example through

agroforestry or organic farming methods (Altieri 1999; Bengtsson et al. 2005) (Box 3.1). Besides contributing to multiple ecosystem services such as pollination, pest control, nutrient cycling and waste assimilation, natural biodiversity improves the resilience of these ecosystem services by providing a reservoir of redundancy and response diversity (Tscharntke et al. 2005) and by reducing the dependence of the production system on external inputs of fodder, fertilizers and pesticides (Folke et al. 1998; Maeder et al. 2002). In a similar way, 'green infrastructure' in the form of vegetated open-space networks in cities can provide ecosystem services such as stormwater management in a more resilient way than traditional 'grey infrastructure' such as concrete pipes, because green infrastructure provides multiple benefits and its value tends to appreciate rather than depreciate over time (Benedict and McMahon 2006).

- **Build diversity and redundancy into SES governance systems.** Institutions and systems need to recognize the value of diverse sources of knowledge and the potential resilience conferred by redundancy, for example between government, NGO and local community organizations (this is evident in polycentric governance arrangements (P7 –Polycentricity)). This, however, needs to be balanced against costs in terms of resources, the risk of overly complex and inflexible structures and conflicting agendas. For instance, overlapping mandates between multiple government departments can provide sources of innovation or insurance against failure, but can also lead to conflict, inertia and problems 'falling between the cracks' (McGinnis 2011). The diversity of perspectives obtained by engaging diverse user groups can improve problem-solving and support learning and innovation under certain conditions (P5 – Learning; P6 – Participation). This can allow for quicker recovery and/or maintenance of ecosystem-service provision after disturbance. Likewise, diverse management approaches can support learning and understanding of the best ways to manage SES to ensure the sustained provision of ecosystem services and to facilitate adaptation to changes in ecosystem services over time (Walters and Holling 1990; Boyd and Folke 2012). However, being able to leverage the value of this diversity often requires a shared overall vision (Bouwen and Taillieu 2004).
- **Change the focus of management paradigms from maximum efficiency to maintaining resilience of ecosystem services over time, even if this is more costly in the short term.** In managing SES for production of ecosystem

services, the resilience value of diversity and redundancy should be explicitly recognized so that it can be weighed against the gains in efficiency derived from streamlining towards optimal exploitation types. For example, fisheries can be managed with an explicit aim to maintain a diverse portfolio of fishing methods, which (1) can provide livelihoods for a diverse range of stakeholders, (2) can be resilient to fluctuations in the availability or price of individual target species, (3) can spread the ecological impact of exploitation amongst a range of trophic levels and life histories to maintain natural community and size structures (Zhou et al. 2010). Although conventional economic development has promoted specialization to maximize efficiency, consideration of resilience suggests that policies should facilitate and provide incentives for livelihood diversity as a strategy for resilience against ecological, market or conflict shocks (Walker et al. 2009; Cifdaloz et al. 2010). Alternative livelihood development programmes can be guided by principles of disparity and response diversity (Ellis 2000; Leslie and McCabe 2013). For example, in farming communities, alternative livelihood options that are more disparate, such as a tourism-related activity rather than alternative types of farming, will provide greater response diversity, and thus resilience, to shocks such as market shocks. Specific incentives can be created to encourage such diversification at the individual farmer level.

3.6 KEY RESEARCH AND APPLICATION GAPS

Understanding the relationships between diversity, redundancy and resilience requires the development of practical methods for measuring diversity and redundancy. A substantial part of our understanding of the value of diversity and redundancy for resilience of ecosystem services is based on theoretical arguments. Empirical evidence for the role of diversity and redundancy, especially in the social system, is in short supply, partly because it is difficult to measure both redundancy and response diversity (Kotschy 2013; Leslie and McCabe 2013).

In particular, we need better methods for identifying critical processes or keystone entities that underlie the resilience of ecosystem services in different SES. Network approaches may be one way of achieving this. Analysis of social or ecological networks can inform our understanding of the roles of diversity and redundancy in particular systems, for example by identifying highly influential system elements that serve to connect a large number of diverse elements, or elements that interact in a similar way, providing redundancy (Tononi et al. 1999; Bodin et al. 2006).

The interplay between the different aspects of diversity (variety, balance and disparity) in intertwined SES remains a largely unexplored area of research. We know that diversity in terms of variety increases the probability that there is redundancy in the system such that multiple elements can fulfil the same function. We also know that the disparity aspect of diversity, which describes the similarities and differences among system elements (Fig. 3.1), is particularly important for the resilience of ecosystem services, as it underlies response diversity, ensuring that some elements are more robust to disturbances and change. The balance aspect of diversity implies a portfolio of elements that provide a function and reduce the quantitative impact of the loss of any individual element. However, the effects of balance on resilience have seldom been studied. The available evidence from plant communities suggests that redundancy for a given function is provided by groups of species with a wide range of different abundances (Walker et al. 1999; Kotschy 2013). The relative abundance or importance of the elements may influence whether functional compensation occurs rapidly (where elements providing redundancy have similar abundances and are immediately available to compensate for lost functioning) or more slowly (where less abundant elements must first increase in abundance before they can effectively compensate for the functioning lost by the decline of more abundant elements). Better understanding the SES elements for which it is important to maintain balance, and not just variety in order to ensure resilience of ecosystem services, is a critical research need. This also includes better understanding the importance of balance in respect of social dimensions of ecosystem-service production, especially balance in the form of power inequalities between social groups.

A final research need is to develop our ability to determine how much diversity and redundancy is 'sufficient'. This pertains to the hypothesized non-linear relationship in Fig. 3.2, which needs to be explored in different systems, for different system elements and at different scales, to improve our understanding of the roles of diversity and redundancy in managing social–ecological systems for resilience. The importance of managing diversity and redundancy for maintaining ecosystem services is increasing as we move into novel social–ecological terrain in the Anthropocene (Crutzen 2002). With changes in the frequency, duration and magnitude of disturbances expected, the required levels of diversity and redundancy will need to be related not only to historical observations, but also to the likelihood of novel shocks and surprises. Managing diversity and redundancy for dealing with uncertainty and the unknown, and for turning crisis into opportunity, becomes central in this context.

> BOX 3.1 **Managing diversity and redundancy to enhance the resilience of crop pollination services**
>
> Many important crop species require insect pollinators to produce marketable fruit, including canola, sunflower, tomato, watermelon and many types of nuts and berries. The critical ecosystem service of crop pollination can be performed by a variety of insect species. However, the agricultural sector worldwide has come to rely heavily on the honeybee, *Apis mellifera*, with managed beehives being transported onto farms during the crop flowering season (Fig. 3.3). While the large colony sizes and social habits of honeybees make them ideal providers of such managed pollination services, these factors also make honeybees susceptible to parasites and diseases. The dangers of relying too heavily on a single species to provide this important ecosystem service have been brought into sharp focus recently in the United States, where honeybee populations have undergone sharp declines due to a number of interacting factors (Martin 2001; Chen

FIG. 3.3. Managed honeybee colonies (a) are important for pollination of crops such as watermelon (b) and almond (c) in California, but heavy dependence on a single pollinator species creates a point of vulnerability. Maintaining habitat and floral resources for native pollinators in farming landscapes (d) increases the resilience of pollination services by increasing the number of insect species able to effectively pollinate these crops. Photo credits: (a, b): morgueFile.com; (c): wanderbored (flickr.com, licensed under a Creative Commons Attribution 2.0 Generic Licence); (d): Akos Kokai (flickr.com, licensed under a Creative Commons Attribution 2.0 Generic licence).

BOX 3.1 **Continued**

(c)

(d)

FIG. 3.3. (Cont.)

et al. 2006). The decline in honeybees has led to declines in crop production, affecting food security and the livelihoods of farmers (Allen-Wardell *et al.* 1998).

Scientists in California have sought to increase the resilience of pollination services by enhancing both the redundancy and diversity associated with pollination (Kremen 2005 Balvanera *et al.* 2005). Research has shown that native bees can contribute substantially to the pollination of many crops, even meeting 100% of the pollination needs of highly insect-dependent crops such as watermelon. Native bees are in some cases more efficient pollinators than honeybees. However, native pollinators often have limited effectiveness because of the limited availability of natural vegetation on conventional farms, as well as 'bee-unfriendly' practices like excessive tillage and use of pesticides (Kremen *et al.* 2002). Encouraging pollination of crops by native bees, and increasing the abundances of these species on farms, adds redundancy to the ecosystem service of crop pollination by increasing the number of species that contribute to this service. This helps to buffer the pollination ecosystem service against fluctuations in the population sizes of any particular pollinator species. Increasing the number of pollinator species contributing to crop pollination also increases the response diversity associated with this ecosystem service, because bee species differ in many aspects of their biology, including foraging ranges and behaviour, morphology, nesting requirements, susceptibility to diseases, and responses to disturbances and land-use changes at various scales (Greenleaf and Kremen 2006; Winfree and Kremen 2009).

Farmers, landowners and scientists in California are working together to enhance access of wild pollinators to crops, by manipulating spatial diversity (designing and maintaining a network of patches of natural vegetation both on and off farms) and managing the temporal diversity of food sources available (Kremen *et al.* 2004). This is done by, for example, planting a diversity of native plants in hedgerows and along roadsides, allowing weeds to grow alongside the crop and providing suitable nesting sites for bees. A spatially explicit ecosystem-service planning model has been developed, similar to those used by conservation planners (Kremen 2005). In a regional sense, encouraging a diversity of land uses and crop types also enhances the diversity of pollinators contributing to the pollination ecosystem service.

REFERENCES

Abrahamson E. (1991). Managerial fads and fashions: the diffusion and rejection of innovations. *Academy of Management Review*, 16, 586–612.

Agrawal, A. (2002). Common resources and institutional sustainability. In *The Drama of the Commons*. Washington, DC: National Academy Press, pp. 41–85.

Allen-Wardell, G., Bernhardt, P., Bitner, R. et al. (1998). The potential consequences of pollinator declines on the conservation of biodiversity and stability of food crop yield. *Conservation Biology*, 12, 8–17.

Altieri, M. A. (1999). The ecological role of biodiversity in agroecosystems. *Agriculture, Ecosystems and Environment*, 74, 19–31.

Altieri, M. A. (2009). Agroecology, small farms, and food sovereignty. *Monthly Review*, 61, 102–113.

Aswani S. and Hamilton R. (2004). Integrating indigenous ecological knowledge and customary sea tenure with marine and social science for conservation of bumphead parrotfish (*Bolbometopon muricatum*) in the Roviana Lagoon, Solomon Islands. *Environmental Conservation*, 31, 69–83.

Baland, J-M. and Platteau, J-P. (1996). *Halting Degradation of Natural Resources: Is There a Role for Rural Communities?* Rome: Food and Agriculture Organization of the United Nations.

Balvanera, P., Kremen, C., Martinez-Ramos, M. (2005). Applying community structure analysis to ecosystem function: examples from pollination and carbon storage. *Ecological Applications*, 15, 360–375.

Bardhan, P. and Dayton-Johnson, J. (2002). Unequal irrigators: heterogeneity and commons management in large-scale multivariate research. In *The Drama of the Commons*. Washington, DC: National Academy Press, pp. 87–112.

Barnes-Mauthe, M., Arita, S., Allen, S. D., Gray, S. A., Leung, P. S. (2013). The influence of ethnic diversity on social network structure in a common-pool resource system: implications for collaborative management. *Ecology and Society*, 18, 23.

Barthel, S., Folke, C., Colding, J. (2010). Social–ecological memory in urban gardens: retaining the capacity for management of ecosystem services. *Global Environmental Change*, 20, 255–265.

Becker, J., Eisenhauer, N., Scheu, S., Jousset, A. (2012). Increasing antagonistic interactions cause bacterial communities to collapse at high diversity. *Ecology Letters*, 15, 468–474.

Bell, A. R., Engle, N. L., Lemos, M. C. (2011). How does diversity matter? The case of Brazilian river basin councils. *Ecology and Society*, 16, 42.

Bellwood, D. R., Hughes, T. P., Folke, C., Nystrom, M. (2004). Confronting the coral reef crisis. *Nature*, 429, 827–833.

Benedict, M. and McMahon, E. T. (2006). *Green Infrastructure: Linking Landscapes and Communities*. Washington, DC: Island Press.

Bengtsson, J., Ahnström, J., Weibull, A-C. (2005). The effects of organic agriculture on biodiversity and abundance: a meta-analysis. *Journal of Applied Ecology*, 42, 261–269.

Berkes, F. and Folke, C. (2002). Back to the future: ecosystem dynamics and local knowledge. In *Panarchy: Understanding Transformations in Human and Natural Systems*. Washington, DC: Island Press, pp. 121–146.

Biggs, R, Carpenter, S. R., Brock, W. A. (2009). Spurious certainty: how ignoring measurement error and environmental heterogeneity may contribute to environmental controversies. *BioScience*, 59, 65–76.

Bodin, Ö., Crona, B., Ernstson, H. (2006). Social networks in natural resource management: what is there to learn from a structural perspective? *Ecology and Society*, 11, 2.

Bohensky, E., Reyers, B., van Jaarsveld, A. S., Fabricius C. (2004). *Ecosystem Services in the Gariep Basin*. Stellenbosch: Sun Press.

Bohensky, E. L. and Maru, Y. (2011). Indigenous knowledge, science, and resilience: what have we learned from a decade of international literature on 'integration'? *Ecology and Society*, 16, 6.

Bouwen, R. and Taillieu, T. (2004). Multi-party collaboration as social learning for interdependence: developing relational knowing for sustainable natural resource management. *Journal of Community and Applied Social Psychology*, 14, 137–153.

Boyd, E. and Folke, C., eds. (2012). *Adapting Institutions: Governance, Complexity and Social–Ecological Resilience*. Cambridge: Cambridge University Press.

Butler, D. R. and Malanson, G. P. (2005). The geomorphic influences of beaver dams and failures of beaver dams. *Geomorphology*, 71, 48–60.

Cardinale, B. J., Duffy, J. E., Gonzalez, A. *et al.* (2012). Biodiversity loss and its impact on humanity. *Nature*, 486, 59–67.

Carpenter, S. R. and Brock, W. A. (2004). Spatial complexity, resilience and policy diversity: fishing on lake-rich landscapes. *Ecology and Society*, 9, 8.

Cifdaloz, O., Regmi, A., Anderies, J. M., Rodriguez, A. A. (2010). Robustness, vulnerability, and adaptive capacity in small-scale social–ecological systems: the Pumpa irrigation system in Nepal. *Ecology and Society*, 15, 39.

Chen, Y., Evans, J., Feldlaufer, M. (2006). Horizontal and vertical transmission of viruses in the honeybee, *Apis mellifera*. *Journal of Invertebrate Pathology*, 92, 152–159.

Crona, B. I. (2006). Supporting and enhancing development of heterogeneous ecological knowledge among resource users in a Kenyan seascape. *Ecology and Society*, 11, 32.

Crutzen, P. J. (2002). Geology of mankind: the anthropocene. *Nature*, 415, 23.

Daw, T. M., Cinner, J. E., McClanahan, T. R. et al. (2012). To fish or not to fish: factors at multiple scales affecting artisanal fishers' readiness to exit a declining fishery. *PLoS ONE*, 7, e31460.

de Mazancourt, C., Isbell, F., Larocque, A. et al. (2013). Predicting ecosystem stability from comunity composition and biodiversity. *Ecology Letters*, 16, 617–625.

Di Falco, S. and Chavas, J-P. (2006). Crop genetic diversity, farm productivity and the management of environmental risk in rainfed agriculture. *European Review of Agricultural Economics*, 33, 289–314.

Ellis, F. (2000). The determinants of rural livelihood diversification in developing countries. *Journal of Agricultural Economics*, 51, 289–302.

Elmqvist, T., Folke, C., Nyström, M. et al. (2003). Response diversity, ecosystem change, and resilience. *Frontiers in Ecology and the Environment*, 1, 488–494.

Fischer, J., Lindenmayer, D. B., Manning, A. D. (2006). Biodiversity, ecosystem function, and resilience: ten guiding principles for commodity production landscapes. *Frontiers in Ecology and the Environment*, 4, 80–86.

Folke, C., Kautsky, N., Berg, H., Jansson, C. and Troell, M. (1998). The Ecological Footprint concept for sustainable seafood production: a review. *Ecological Applications (Supplement)*, 8, 63–71.

Folke, C., Colding, J., Berkes, F. (2003). Synthesis: building resilience and adaptive capacity in social–ecological systems. In *Navigating Social–Ecological Systems: Building Resilience for Complexity and Change*. Cambridge: Cambridge University Press, pp. 352–387.

Folke, C., Hahn, T., Olsson, P., Norberg, J. (2005). Adaptive governance of social–ecological systems. *Annual Review of Environment and Resources*, 30, 441–473.

Greenleaf, S. S. and Kremen, C. (2006). Wild bee species increase tomato production but respond differently to surrounding land use in Northern California. *Biological Conservation*, 133, 81–87.

Gunderson, L. H. and Holling, C. S., eds. (2002). *Panarchy: Understanding Transformations in Human and Natural Systems*. Washington, DC: Island Press.

Harris, P. G. (2007). Collective action on climate change: the logic of regime failure. *Natural Resources Journal*, 47, 195–224.

Holling, C. S., Schindler, D. W., Walker, B. H., Roughgarden, J. (1995). Biodiversity in the functioning of ecosystems: an ecological synthesis. In *Biodiversity Loss: Economic and Ecological Issues*. Cambridge: Cambridge University Press, pp. 44–83.

Hughes, T. P. (1994). Catastrophes, phase shifts, and large-scale degradation of a Caribbean coral reef. *Science*, 265, 1547–1551.

Ives, A. R. and Carpenter, S. R. (2007). Stability and diversity of ecosystems. *Science*, 317, 58–62.

Janssen, M. A., Anderies, J. M., Ostrom, E. (2007). Robustness of social–ecological systems to spatial and temporal variability. *Society and Natural Resources*, 20, 307–322.

Jentoft, S., Bavinck, M., Johnson, D. S., Thomson, K. T. (2009). Fisheries co-management and legal pluralism: how an analytical problem becomes an institutional one. *Human Organization*, 68, 27–38.

Kerr, J. T. and Packer, L. (1997). Habitat heterogeneity as a determinant of mammal species richness in high-energy regions. *Nature*, 385, 252–254.

Kotschy, K. A. (2013). Biodiversity, redundancy and resilience of riparian vegetation under different land management regimes. PhD Thesis, Johannesburg: University of the Witwatersrand.

Kremen, C., Williams, N. M., Thorp, R. W. (2002). Crop pollination from native bees at risk from agricultural intensification. *Proceedings of the National Academy of Sciences USA*, 99, 16812–16816.

Kremen, C., Williams, N. M., Bugg, R. L., Fay, J. P., Thorp, R. W. (2004). The area requirements of an ecosystem service: crop pollination by native bee communities in California. *Ecology Letters*, 7, 1109–1119.

Kremen, C. (2005). Managing ecosystem services: what do we need to know about their ecology? *Ecology Letters*, 8, 468–479.

Lansing, J. S. (2007). *Priests and Programmers: Technologies of Power in the Engineered Landscape of Bali*. Princeton, NJ: Princeton University Press.

Lawton, J. H. and Brown, V. K. (1993). Redundancy in ecosystems. In *Biodiversity and Ecosystem Function*. Berlin: Springer, pp. 255–270.

Leslie, P. and McCabe, J. T. (2013). Response diversity and resilience in social–ecological systems. *Current Anthropology*, 54, 114–143.

Levin, S. A. (1998). Ecosystems and the biosphere as complex adaptive systems. *Ecosystems*, 1, 431–436.

Lietaer, B., Ulanowicz, R. E., Goerner, S. J., McLaren, N. (2010). Is our monetary structure a systemic cause for financial instability? Evidence and remedies from nature. *Journal of Futures Studies*, 14, 89–108.

Loreau, M. and de Mazancourt, C. (2013). Biodiversity and ecosystem stability: a synthesis of underlying mechanisms. *Ecology Letters*, 16, 106–115.

Low, B., Ostrom, E., Simon, C., Wilson, J. (2003). Redundancy and diversity: do they influence optimal management? In *Navigating Social–Ecological Systems: Building Resilience for Complexity and Change*. Cambridge: Cambridge University Press, pp. 83–114.

Maeder, P., Fliessbach, A., Dubois, D. et al. (2002). Soil fertility and biodiversity in organic farming. *Science*, 296, 1694–1697.

Martin, S. J. (2001). The role of Varroa and viral pathogens in the collapse of honeybee colonies: a modelling approach. *Journal of Applied Ecology*, 38, 1082–1093.

McCann, K. S. (2000). The diversity–stability debate. *Nature*, 405, 228–233.

McClanahan, T. R. and Cinner, J. E. (2008). A framework for adaptive gear and ecosystem-based management in the artisanal coral reef fishery of Papua New Guinea. *Aquatic Conservation: Marine and Freshwater Ecosystems*, 18, 493–507.

McClanahan, T. R., Hicks, C. C., Darling, E. S. (2008). Malthusian overfishing and efforts to overcome it on Kenyan coral reefs. *Ecological Applications*, 18, 1516–1529.

McGinnis, M. D. (2011). Costs and challenges of polycentric governance: an equilibrium concept and examples from US health care. Conference on Self-Governance, Polycentricity and Development, Renmin University of China, Beijing, 8 May.

McNaughton, S. J. (1977). Diversity and stability of ecological communities: a comment on the role of empiricism in ecology. *American Naturalist*, 111, 515–525.

Meinzen-Dick, R. and Zwarteveen, M. (1998). Gendered participation in water management: issues and illustrations from water users' associations in South Asia. *Agriculture and Human Values*, 15, 337–345.

Mills, L. S., Soulé, M. E., Doak, D. F. (1993). The keystone-species concept in ecology and conservation. *BioScience*, 43, 219–224.

Mori, A., Furukawa, T., Sasaki, T. (2013). Response diversity determines the resilience to environmental change. *Biological Reviews*, 88, 349–364.

Naeem, S. and Wright, J. P. (2003). Disentangling biodiversity effects on ecosystem functioning: deriving solutions to a seemingly insurmountable problem. *Ecology Letters*, 6, 567–579.

Naiman, R. J., Décamps, H., McClain, M. E. (2005). *Riparia: Ecology, Conservation, and Management of Streamside Communities*. Amsterdam: Elsevier Academic Press.

Nekola, J. C. and Brown, J. H. (2007). The wealth of species: ecological communities, complex systems and the legacy of Frank Preston. *Ecology Letters*, 10, 188–196.

Nelson, M. C., Hegmon, M., Kulow, S. R. et al. (2011). Resisting diversity: a long-term archaeological study. *Ecology and Society*, 16, 25.

Norberg, J. and Cumming, G. S., eds. (2008). *Complexity Theory for a Sustainable Future*. New York, NY: Columbia University Press.

Norgaard, R. B. and Baer, P. (2005). Collectively seeing complex systems: the nature of the problem. *BioScience*, 55, 953–960.

Nyström, M. (2006). Redundancy and response diversity of functional groups: implications for the resilience of coral reefs. *AMBIO*, 35, 30–35.

Nyström, M. and Folke, C. (2001). Spatial resilience of coral reefs. *Ecosystems*, 4, 406–417.

Olson, M. (1965). *The Logic of Collective Action: Public Goods and the Theory of Groups*, Harvard Economic Studies 124. Cambridge, MA: Harvard University Press.

Ostrom, E. (2005). *Understanding Institutional Diversity*. Princeton, NJ: Princeton University Press.

Page, S. E. (2007). *The Difference: How the Power of Diversity Creates Better Groups, Firms, Schools, and Societies*. Princeton, NJ: Princeton University Press.

Parsons, M., McLoughlin, C. A., Kotschy, K. A., Rogers, K. H., Rountree, M. W. (2005). The effects of extreme floods on the biophysical heterogeneity of river landscapes. *Frontiers in Ecology and the Environment*, 3, 487–494.

Peterson, G., Allen, C. R., Holling, C. S. (1998). Ecological resilience, biodiversity, and scale. *Ecosystems*, 1, 6–18.

Reidsma, P. and Ewert, F. (2008). Regional farm diversity can reduce vulnerability of food production to climate change. *Ecology and Society*, 13, 38.

Reyers, B., Biggs, R., Cumming, G. S. et al. (2013). Getting the measure of ecosystem services: a social–ecological approach. *Frontiers in Ecology and the Environment*, 11, 268–273.

Riedlinger, D. and Berkes. F. (2001). Contributions of traditional knowledge to understanding climate change in the Canadian Arctic. *Polar Record*, 37, 315–328.

Scheffer, M., Westley, F., Brock, W. (2003). Slow responses of societies to new problems: causes and costs. *Ecosystems*, 6, 493–502.

Scholes, R. J. and Biggs, R. eds. (2004). *Ecosystem Services in Southern Africa: A Regional Assessment*. Pretoria: CSIR.

Smith, L. E. D., Khoa, S. N., Lorenzen, K. (2005). Livelihood functions of inland fisheries: policy implications in developing countries. *Water Policy*, 7, 359–383.

Solé, R. V. and Montoya, M. (2001). Complexity and fragility in ecological networks. *Proceedings of the Royal Society of London B*, 268, 2039–2045.

Stirling, A. (2007). A general framework for analysing diversity in science, technology and society. *Journal of the Royal Society Interface*, 4, 707–719.

Tews, J., Brose, U., Grimm, V. et al. (2004). Animal species diversity driven by habitat heterogeneity/diversity: the importance of keystone structures. *Journal of Biogeography*, 31, 79–92.

Tononi, G., Sporns, O., Edelman, G. M. (1999). Measures of degeneracy and redundancy in biological networks. *Proceedings of the National Academy of Sciences USA*, 96, 3257–3262.

Tscharntke, T., Klein, A. M., Kruess, A., Steffan-Dewenter, I., Thiess, C. (2005). Landscape perspectives on agricultural intensification and biodiversity–ecosystem service management. *Ecology Letters*, 8, 857–874.

Turner, M. G. and Romme, W. H. (1994). Landscape dynamics in crown fire ecosystems. *Landscape Ecology*, 9, 59–77.

Turner, M. G., Baker, W. L., Peterson, C. J., Peet, R. K. (1998). Factors influencing succession: lessons from large, infrequent natural disturbances. *Ecosystems*, 1, 511–523.

Ulanowicz, R. E., Goerner, S. J., Lietaer, B., Gomez, R. (2009). Quantifying sustainability: resilience, efficiency and the return of information theory. *Ecological Complexity*, 6, 27–36.

Vavouri, T., Semple, J. I., Lehner, B. (2008). Widespread conservation of genetic redundancy during a billion years of eukaryotic evolution. *Trends in Genetics*, 24, 485–488.

Walker, B. H. (1992). Biodiversity and ecological redundancy. *Conservation Biology*, 6, 18–23.

Walker, B. H. (1995). Conserving biological diversity through ecosystem resilience. *Conservation Biology*, 9, 747–752.

Walker, B. H and Salt, D. (2006). *Resilience Thinking: Sustaining Ecosystems and People in a Changing World*. Washington, DC: Island Press.

Walker, B. H., Kinzig, A., Langridge, J. (1999). Plant attribute diversity, resilience, and ecosystem function: the nature and significance of dominant and minor species. *Ecosystems*, 2, 95–113.

Walker, B. H., Abel, N., Anderies, J. M., Ryan, P. (2009). Resilience, adaptability, and transformability in the Goulburn–Broken Catchment, Australia. *Ecology and Society*, 14, 12.

Walters, C. J. and Holling, C. S. (1990). Large-scale management experiments and learning by doing. *Ecology*, 71, 2060–2068.

Westley, F., Tjörnbo, O., Schultz, L. *et al.* (2013). A theory of transformative agency in linked social–ecological systems. *Ecology and Society*, 18, 27.

Whitacre, J. M. and Bender, A. (2010). Networked buffering: a basic mechanism for distributed robustness in complex adaptive systems. *Theoretical Biology and Medical Modelling*, 7, 20.

Williamson, O. E. (1985). *The Economic Institutions of Capitalism*. New York, NY: Free Press.

Winfree, R. and Kremen, C. (2009). Are ecosystem services stabilized by differences among species? A test using crop pollination. *Proceedings of the Royal Society of London B*, 276, 229–237.

Wisner, B., ed. (2004). *At Risk: Natural Hazards, People's Vulnerability and Disasters*. London: Routledge.

Zhang, W., Ricketts, T. H., Kremen, C., Carney, K., Swinton, S. M. (2007). Ecosystem services and dis-services to agriculture. *Ecological Economics*, 64, 253–260.

Zhou, S., Smith, A. D. M., Punt, A. E. *et al.* (2010). Ecosystem-based fisheries management requires a change to the selective fishing philosophy. *Proceedings of the National Academy of Sciences USA*, 107, 9485–9489.

4 Principle 2 – Manage connectivity

Vasilis Dakos, Allyson Quinlan, Jacopo A. Baggio, Elena Bennett, Örjan Bodin and Shauna BurnSilver

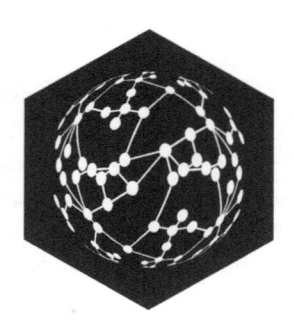

SUMMARY

Connectivity refers to the *structure* and s*trength* with which resources, species or social actors disperse, migrate or interact across patches, habitats or social domains. Here we discuss how connectivity may confer resilience to the supply of ecosystem services. High levels of connectivity can facilitate recovery after a disturbance. At the same time, highly connected systems increase the potential for disturbances to spread. Additionally, the structure characterizing how system components are connected appears to play a role. Thus, the effect of connectivity on the provision of ecosystem services is highly context dependent. Despite increasing theoretical work that evaluates how connectivity affects the resilience of social–ecological systems, we still largely lack empirical studies that quantify these effects. We discuss this disparity and suggest new areas for further research.

Principles for Building Resilience: Sustaining Ecosystem Services in Social–Ecological Systems, eds R. Biggs, M. Schlüter and M. L. Schoon. Published by Cambridge University Press. © Cambridge University Press 2015.

4.1 INTRODUCTION

Ecosystem services are integrated within systems in which social and ecological components interact across multiple spatial and temporal scales. For this reason, connectivity between these components can be influential in conferring resilience to the production and/or supply of specific sets of ecosystem services in response to disturbances. For instance, isolated forest patches in a fragmented landscape may escape fire (Peterson 2002), whereas highly connected agricultural landscapes may suffer the spread of pests or diseases (Davis *et al.* 2008). Densely connected social networks may facilitate governance of ecological resources (Bodin and Prell 2011), although at the risk of reducing diversity in management strategies that may potentially undermine the resilience of the managed resources (Bodin and Norberg 2005; McAllister *et al.* 2006). The implications of connectivity for the resilience of ecosystem services are further complicated by the fact that the above processes operate simultaneously at different scales. The recent financial meltdown across the world economy and droughts in major bread baskets, coupled with spikes in food prices, are clear examples of how increasing global connectivity and novel interconnections at different scales have implications for the resilience of such complex systems (Biggs *et al.* 2011). In the following, we draw from the growing body of theoretical work, and the few empirical studies that explicitly test the relationship between connectivity and resilience of ecosystem services, to explore how connectivity may affect the resilience of the provision of ecosystem services to disturbances in social–ecological systems (SES).

4.2 WHAT DO WE MEAN BY CONNECTIVITY?

Connectivity refers to the way in which parts of an SES (i.e. entities that have similar features such as species, landscape patches, individuals, organizations and so forth) interact with each other (i.e. exchange information, transfer material, transform energy, etc.). For example, consider the case of forest patches and their connections in a landscape. The forested landscape is the *system*, the forest patches are the *parts* of the system and their *interactions* dictate how easy it is for an organism to move from one patch to another. Here, however, we do not only consider connectivity in the context of a spatially explicit landscape. In every system that can be conceptualized as a sum of individual components, connectivity refers to the nature and the strength of the interactions between these components. In that sense, in any ecological or social 'landscape', connectivity is the way by which (*structure*) and the extent to which (*strength*) resources, species or social actors disperse, migrate or interact across patches, habitats or social domains (Bodin and Prell 2011). While these interactions are primarily mapped statically, they also change through time (Raudsepp-Hearne *et al.* 2010). However, in this chapter, we do not consider the consequences of temporal changes in connectivity, but only focus on how the structure and strength of connectivity influences the resilience of ecosystem services in coupled SES.

Alternatively, we can also think of connectivity from a network perspective. In a network all individual components of a system are *nodes* embedded in a web of connections that constitute the *links* (Fig. 4.1). Examples of links are species interactions (like feeding interactions in a food web), vegetation corridors across habitats or communication channels between human communities (Table 4.1). The way the links are distributed within an SES determines the structure of the SES. For instance, links may be present or absent between components; they may be one-way interactions or mutual (reciprocal) interactions. At the same time, some components/nodes may be highly connected (i.e. have many links), while others may have few connections (like an isolated patch of trees at the edge of a forest). Links are also characterized by their strength, which refers to the intensity with which nodes are connected or interact. Strength can be determined by various factors, such as corridor quality among habitats, preferences of a predator for specific prey, the visitation rate of a pollinator insect to a plant or the frequency of interactions between social actors.

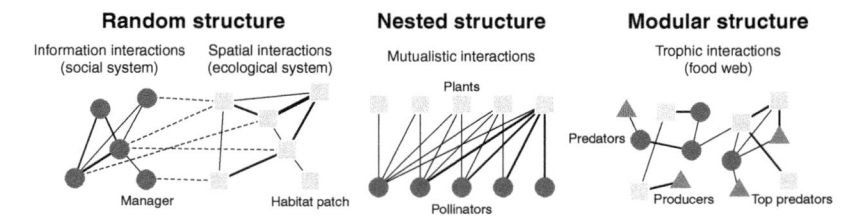

FIG. 4.1 Toy representations of the architecture of connectivity in SES. SES can be organized in random, nested or modular ways. In a random network each node has on average the same number of links to other nodes and no particular characteristic. Nested networks are usually bipartite (meaning that they are made of nodes that belong to a distinct group). In nested networks, nodes interact with only a subset of nodes in a hierarchical way. In a modular (or compartmentalized) network, the nodes are organized in distinct compartments that are connected to one another with very few links. Lines indicate interactions (edges/links) between components (nodes), which can be of various sorts. For example, in food webs, links between producers define competition interactions, while links between predators and producers define trophic links. Dashed lines indicate interactions across SES. The thickness of the lines indicates the strength of interaction (connectivity strength). Different shades and shapes correspond to different types of system components (e.g. parts/actors/patches/species).

4.3 HOW DOES CONNECTIVITY ENHANCE THE RESILIENCE OF ECOSYSTEM SERVICES?

Connectivity in SES generally facilitates the flow of energy, material or information necessary for the resilience of ecosystem services. In particular, the strength and structure of connectivity may safeguard ecosystem services against a disturbance either by facilitating recovery or by constraining locally the spread of a disturbance (Nyström et al. 2001).

The importance of connectivity for the recovery of disturbed SES and thus for the maintenance of resilience of their ecosystem services can be demonstrated in the recolonization of coral reefs. The extent of reef recolonization is related to the degree of connectivity between remnant coral patches, which is determined by the

Table 4.1 *Examples of nodes and links for ecological and social systems across different scales*

Scale		Ecological	Social
Local	Node	Patch, species	Individual, household
	Link	Migration, energy (kcal)	Information, trust, food, labour, money, equipment
Intermediate (Regional)	Node	Landscape patches, populations, trophic levels	Community, organization (e.g. NGOs), firm, geographical region
	Link	Migration, genetic material, energy (kcal)	Information, opinion, ideas, trust, money, expertise, food, equipment, labour
Global	Node	Ecosystems, biomes	Nation states, governance entities, stakeholder groups
	Link	Migration, genetic material, energy (kcal)	Rules, norms, decisions, information, trust, finances

prevailing currents that allow coral recruitment between neighbouring reefs (Treml *et al.* 2007; Mumby and Hastings 2008). Similarly, in disturbance experiments of macrobenthic communities, recovery was largely determined by the degree of connectivity across metacommunities (Thrush *et al.* 2008). Closely situated habitats with no physical barriers enhance the recolonization of nearby sites, safeguarding against loss of species and ensuring the maintenance of their functions. Thus, approaches of protecting, maintaining and restoring connectivity underlie many conservation initiatives that focus on enhancing the resilience of SES and the ecosystem services they produce, as in for instance the design of networks of marine protected areas in the Great Barrier Reef off the coast of Australia (McCook *et al.* 2010). The basic mechanism behind these cases is that maintaining connections to areas that serve as refuges can accelerate the restoration of disturbed areas and their associated ecosystem services, as these refuges provide a critical habitat that reduces larvae and juvenile mortality and enhances recruitment in other less-resilient habitats (Nyström *et al.* 2001).

Instead of facilitating recovery from a disturbance, connectivity may also enhance the resilience of ecosystem services by acting as a barrier to the spread of disturbances (like the spread of fire or of a disease vector). This capacity is usually maximized in moderately connected SES that are highly heterogeneous (P1 – Diversity). While local disturbances can cause local regime shifts with local losses of ecosystem services, limited connectivity reduces the possibility of large-scale global effects (e.g. Bodin and Norberg 2007). In other words, the potential loss of ecosystem services is locally contained due to the existence of bottlenecks in the landscape. Generally, the effect of connectivity on these two processes of recovery and constraint can be conceptualized by sink–source dynamics with compensating effects (Dias 1996). Sources are parts of the system that produce or maintain resources, whereas sinks are parts that do not. For example, some reefs act as nursing grounds for fish and produce larvae (sources), and other reefs are receiving larvae from the source reefs to populate their own fish community (sinks). In marine systems, resilient local systems may act as sources whereas non-resilient systems act as sinks. Depending on the type and size of disturbance, the overall resilience of systems that can maintain local fishing communities (McCook *et al.* 2010) will be dependent on the strength of the dispersal processes between local sink and source parts (Nyström *et al.* 2008).

Perhaps the most highlighted positive effect of connectivity on the resilience of SES is that it facilitates the maintenance of biodiversity in the landscape, which underlies the production of many ecosystem services. The reason is that among well-linked habitat patches local species extinctions may be compensated by the inflow of species from their surroundings. This rescue effect (Hanski 1991) has been demonstrated experimentally in moss microecosystems (Gonzalez *et al.* 1998) and supports the idea of a spatial insurance hypothesis (Loreau *et al.* 2003). According to this hypothesis spill-over effects have been shown to be overall beneficial for the maintenance of biodiversity (Brudvig *et al.* 2009) and for reducing the risk of extinction (Gilbert *et al.* 1998). Clearly, all these effects are a function of connectivity in the landscape. As connectivity affects diversity (both functional and genetic, P1 – Diversity), it will also indirectly have an effect on the resilience of ecosystem services provided by a high diversity. For instance, reduced connectivity caused by human-induced fragmentation, like roads and dams, has a negative effect on population viability (Fahrig and Rytwinski 2009) especially for large mammal populations (Beier and Noss 1998). The Yellowstone-to-Yukon project is an example of conservation planning that focuses on reconnecting large habitat patches by establishing corridors to minimize the effects of reduced genetic diversity in isolated large-carnivore populations (Raimer and Ford 2005). Managers even mimic connectivity in fragmented landscapes through additions of species or individuals to decrease the risk of extinction of local populations. The successful design of such schemes depends largely on conserving keystone patches in the landscape, creating new patches in the vicinity of vulnerable ones or managing highly connected patches that all can maximally contribute to the resilient provision of ecosystem services (Janssen *et al.* 2006). However, the relationship between connectivity and the maintenance of biodiversity is not straightforwardly linear. Theoretical work suggests that a certain level of connectivity is required in order to prevent extinctions, but an overly connected system may reduce the probability of population survival when all populations are experiencing the same strong exploitation practices (Baggio *et al.* 2011; Salau *et al.* 2012).

Although a growing body of literature highlights the effects of connectivity on resilience of SES, empirical evidence of the explicit relationship of connectivity and the resilience of ecosystem services remains limited (Mitchell *et al.* 2013). It has been shown that ecosystem functions that affect ecosystem productivity are influenced by the strength of dispersal across habitats in the landscape (Staddon *et al.* 2010), which infers a positive relationship of connectivity to the resilience of a bundle of ecosystem services like provisioning and regulating services. Another example is crop pollination by insects that is tied to other ecosystem services such as food production and habitat provision. It has been shown that connected patches in the landscape have an effect on plant–animal interaction by increasing pollination (Tewksbury *et al.* 2002) or changing patterns of butterfly movements (Haddad *et al.* 2001). As pollination is strongly influenced by the distance between plants that require pollination and suitable habitats for their pollinators (Kearns *et al.* 1998; Ricketts *et al.* 2008), it may be inferred that connectivity in such agroecosystems will be important for the provision of pollination, food and habitat services. Similarly, bundles of ecosystem services associated with water flowing in streams and rivers within a watershed (e.g. drinking-water provision, erosion control, water-quality regulation, recreation opportunities, etc.) can be simultaneously affected by changes in landscape connectivity of riparian buffering corridors. How intact native vegetation remains along the shoreline of urban streams affects their physical and biological condition, with less-connected buffer zones having reduced erosion control leading to poorer stream conditions (McBride and Booth 2005).

In human social networks, it has been argued that connectivity can facilitate the resilience of ecosystem services through enhanced governance opportunities. High levels of connectivity between different social groups increase information-sharing and help develop the trust and reciprocity necessary for collective action (P6 – Participation) (Brondizio et al. 2009). Certain actors can serve as connectors to other actors or landscapes, bringing outside perspectives and new ideas to local issues (P5 – Learning) (Bodin and Crona 2009). Empirical studies in social networks demonstrate that the strength of connectivity (e.g. frequency or duration of interactions) may have different effects on the resilience of ecosystem services depending on the aspirations and importance of the interacting social actors. For example, it appears that actors are most likely to have strong ties to actors with similar characteristics (Mcpherson et al. 2001). This homogeneity of characteristics can lead, for instance, to a high connectivity of resource users with similar perspectives and knowledge about the resources they exploit: the 'who you know is what you know' phenomenon (Ruef 2002; Crona and Bodin 2006; Bodin and Norberg 2007; Little and McDonald 2007). Increasing levels of network connectivity across different social groups gives individuals opportunities for new information, and development of trust and reciprocity necessary for collective action (Diani 2003). These findings suggest that social network connectivity can facilitate resilience of ecosystem services through enhanced governance (Bodin and Crona 2009), while high levels of connectivity among actors with similar types of knowledge or economic preferences can hinder collective action or aid in cases of resource overexploitation of resources (see Section 4.4).

Another relatively novel and largely unexplored feature of the way connectivity affects the resilience of SES is the actual structure of SES. Network theory suggests that non-random configurations (like modular and nested structures) of food webs, mutualistic communities (seed-dispersers–plants, plants–pollinators) or habitat patches have a positive effect on their stability (Ash and Newth 2007; Galstyan and Cohen 2007; Bastolla et al. 2009) (Fig. 4.1). Modularity (or compartmentalization) refers to the extent to which subsets of densely connected nodes are loosely connected to other subsets of nodes, creating in essence distinct compartments within a network (Fig. 4.1). Nestedness is the degree to which specialist nodes (nodes with few links) interact with subsets of generalist nodes (nodes with a lot of links) (Fig. 4.1). Although progress to identify the effect of network architecture on the resilience of SES is recent (Scheffer et al. 2012), it appears that modular ecosystems, like lakes, are functionally organized in independent modules. In that sense disturbances are difficult to spread globally across modules or to cascade (Carpenter 2003), whereas nested communities can sustain higher levels of disturbances but at the cost of collapsing synchronously once a threshold is crossed (Lever et al. 2014). These preliminary studies highlight that the architecture of SES masks trade-offs between the provision of ecosystem services and their resilience (Box 4.1).

4.4 UNDER WHAT CONDITIONS MAY RESILIENCE OF ECOSYSTEM SERVICES BE COMPROMISED?

While connectivity can facilitate recovery or constrain the spread of a disturbance, in some cases it can also compromise the resilience of ecosystem services. Depending on the type and size of disturbance, in strongly connected systems without compartmentalization (i.e. fragmented parts or local weakly connected parts) and with dense pathways between parts of the system, disturbances can propagate rapidly, leading to widespread impacts on SES and associated ecosystem services (Van Nes and Scheffer 2005; Ash and Newth 2007). Pest outbreaks, disease epidemics, invasion of alien species, or even financial crises, such as the global spread of the 2008 recession triggered by the collapse of the US housing market, confirm the high risk of propagation of disturbances in strongly connected systems (Adger et al. 2009; Biggs et al. 2011). In some ecosystems, such as the pine forests of western North America, pest outbreak mechanisms rely on highly connected patches (Raffa et al. 2008). An intricate set of factors and conditions, all linked to high connectivity, are necessary to set in motion a bark beetle infestation such as the pine beetle outbreak that has been occurring across large expanses of forests in western Canada and northwestern USA. Pheromone-triggered mass attacks on trees by thousands of closely located beetles is facilitated by dense

BOX 4.1 **Social–ecological connectivity and preservation of forests in southern Madagascar**

Taking both social and ecological connectivity into account when analysing resilience is challenging from many perspectives. First, it involves an explicit integration of disciplines that have different practices, epistemologies and methods. Second, there is the issue of defining *relevant* units of analysis (i.e. actors, ecological resources) and *appropriate* types of links. Finally, linking patterns of connectivity to resilience is not necessarily theoretically straightforward. All these clearly pose a challenging task in deciphering the role of connectivity in the resilience of ecosystem services. Here we illustrate how a combined social and ecological network analysis can help to empirically disentangle how patterns of social–ecological connectivity might influence resilience.

The study system is an agricultural landscape in southern Madagascar that is interspersed with scattered forest patches of high biodiversity value that have been remarkably well preserved in spite of strong pressures on land and forest resources (Fig. 4.2) (Tengö et al. 2007; Bodin and Tengö 2012). The forest patches are protected by taboos restricting access and use, and the patches generate essential ecosystem services, such as micro-climate regulation and crop pollination (Bodin et al. 2006). Furthermore, the forests provide cultural ecosystem services as they are important ancestral burial grounds, sites for ceremonies and a symbol of the link between people and land (Tengö et al. 2007).

The puzzle is whether an analysis of the patterns of social–ecological connectivity can help explain why these forest patches have been preserved in spite of an increasing demand for land. More specifically, this example focuses on the control and use of ecosystem services stemming from the forest patches. The forest patches are defined as the nodes of the ecological part of the SES. These patches are geographically located within a village with approximately 9000 inhabitants. In the social part of the SES, nodes are the social actors and are made up of the six main clans in the village, alongside two additional clans residing elsewhere but with a stake in the forests. The social links between the clans were assessed through interviews with clan

BOX 4.1 **Continued**

(a)

(b)

FIG. 4.2 The agricultural landscape (a) in Androy, southern Madagascar, is interspersed with scattered forest patches (b) of high biodiversity value that have been remarkably well preserved due to various taboos restricting access and use (Tengö and von Heland 2011). Photo credits: Maria Tengö.

BOX 4.1 **Continued**

authorities, and the ecological links between the forest patches were assessed based on the potential for seed dispersal between patches (Bodin and Tengö 2012). Finally, the social to ecological links were defined based on access and use rights of the forest patches. The complete social–ecological network describing the study system consisted of 14 ecological and 8 social nodes (Fig. 4.3a).

A network analysis of the complete social–ecological network would involve the estimation of the average number of links, the distribution of links among nodes or the relative compartmentalization for each part of the SES network. In this example, however, it was more sensible to use a micro-scale approach. This is because a simplified network might be easier to link, at least theoretically, to some governance challenges of interest that have implications for the resilience of ecosystem services. In particular, by analysing how often a set of three micro-scale social–ecological networks (also called 'motifs') occurred in the complete network, it was found that shared forest access generally implied social connectivity (Fig. 4.3b). In other words, if two clans were utilizing one and the same forest patch, they tended to also be socially connected. This means that resource sharing (i.e. competition) is often accompanied with social connectivity. According to common-pool resource theory (Ostrom 1990), this configuration of social–ecological connectivity may increase the potential for negotiating and regulating resource use in a sustainable way. Thus, the relatively high frequency of this presumably favourable motif in the larger network may provide a possible explanation of why the forest patches have been preserved in this otherwise heavily exploited agricultural landscape.

There is another overrepresented motif in the network (Fig. 4.3b). That is the motif where the clans share two forest patches that are also connected. Thus, highly interconnected clusters of clans and forest patches seem to occur relatively frequently. The third most common motif is the one of symmetric pair-wise coupling of social and ecological nodes (Fig. 4.3b). The occurrence of such motif patterns indicates that (1) socially connected clans tend to share sets of patches that are ecologically connected and (2) unconnected patches are divided between unconnected clans. Overall, this implies a positive alignment of social and ecological patterns of connectivity, or social–ecological

BOX 4.1 **Continued**

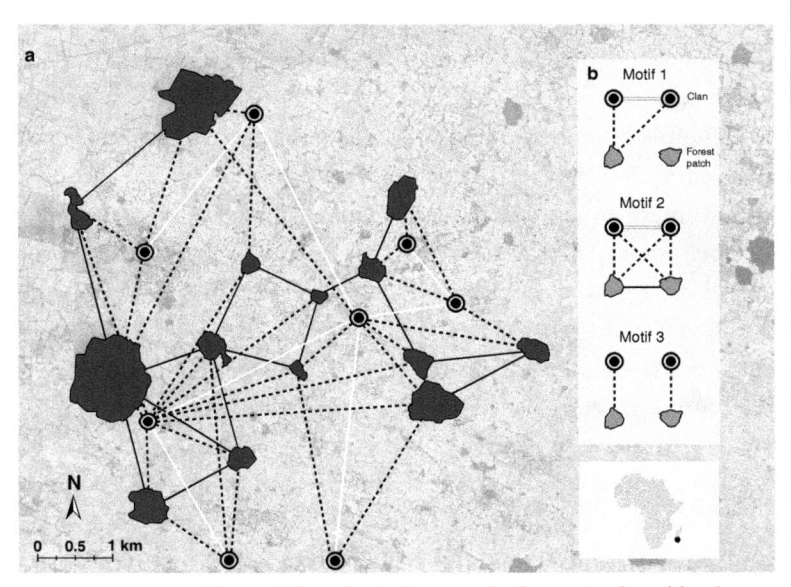

FIG. 4.3 The social–ecological network of an agricultural landscape in southern Madagascar. Dark grey areas represent the 14 forest patches (ecological nodes of the SES), and the circled black dots are the 8 clans that are maintaining the forest and constitute the social nodes of the SES. The white lines are the interrelationships between the clans, while the solid lines are the dispersal rates of seeds between the forest patches based on a measure of distance. The dasked lines depict the relationship (ownership, management) of each clan to each forest patch. (b) The micro-scale social–ecological networks (motifs). Motif 1 shows shared forest patch access combined with social connectivity between clans. In motif 2, complete connectivity between clans and forest patches exists, and in motif 3 there is a pair-wise coupling of the clans and the forest patches.

'fit' that generally suggests increased capacity to manage ecosystems in a sustainable way.

In summary, this example demonstrates how, by analysing connectivity patterns of SES, one may partly explain the successful governance of biodiversity-rich forest patches. Such analysis of specific patterns of connectivity of SES may highlight mechanisms to enhance the resilience of ecosystem services.

host-tree stands that have become structurally similar due to environmental factors such as drought or temperature (Raffa et al. 2008). In this case, the resilience of ecosystem services, such as wood resource production and pest regulation, is negatively impacted by high connectivity.

High levels of connectivity between social actors can also be detrimental to the resilience of ecosystem services through a different mechanism. In this case, strong links may lead to synchronized behaviour that translates into intense unsustainable resource extraction or strong norm barriers for giving up unsustainable practices (Bodin and Prell 2011). For example, Satake et al. (2007) found that in dense social networks with preferences for immediate gains over long-term resilience, information about a change in market price for timber can spread quickly and result in deforestation as multiple actors take advantage of market conditions to cut and sell their timber at the same time. Moreover, highly connected networks may limit social learning and reduce the capacity to find optimal solutions and reduce the ability for novel experimentation (P5 – Learning). For example, modelling studies show that when homogenization of norms occurs, explorative ability drops, leading to a lock-in situation in which actors believe themselves to be doing well while they are actually driving their managed ecosystems towards unsustainable pathways (Bodin and Norberg 2005). In the case of SES, these results suggest that overly connected networks can lead to homogenization of strategies when imitation and social influence are strong. Lack of diversity may lead to maladaptation: instead of people adapting to the changing environment, the effect is that the environment itself must adapt to human norms (Levinthal 1997), with negative consequences for the resilience of ecosystem services.

Another way that connectivity can jeopardize the resilience of ecosystem services is by weakening or disrupting links across different compartments. For instance destruction of breeding or refuge grounds of species with diverse life cycles disrupts their recruitment and can make SES less resilient. Mumby and Hastings (2008) have shown that shallow coral reefs become less resilient due to the destruction of mangroves that serve as breeding grounds for parrotfish larvae that play a crucial part in the functioning of the reef. In this case, one of the services provided by mangroves, i.e. provision of parrotfish breeding habitat, is disrupted. Such types of interdependencies are commonly found across ecological and social domains at multiple scales (Brondizio *et al.* 2009). It has been suggested that in recent years, due to the increased interlocking of systems like markets and global food distribution networks, local disruptions or scarcities had disproportional impacts on the resilience of SES on distance scales that have been unknown so far (Biggs *et al.* 2011).

In highly modular (compartmentalized) systems, resilience of ecosystem services may be jeopardized if some components become overly important compared to others, in the sense that the whole system relies heavily on some individual parts (Strogatz 2001). Removal of important components, such as keystone species or highly connected patches, may trigger cascading waves of extinctions (P1 – Diversity). For example, models of Madagascar's dry-forest dynamics suggest that rapid declines in pollination services could occur if small forest patches are removed from the landscape, owing to their impacts on the spatial configuration of the remaining forest area (Bodin *et al.* 2006). If subgroups that actively use certain ecosystem services are not engaged in the management of those ecosystem services, critical knowledge of systems' functioning and monitoring can be missed (P5 – Learning) (Gelcich *et al.* 2006), and there may be a reduced potential for collective action (P6 – Participation).

4.5 HOW CAN THE PRINCIPLE OF CONNECTIVITY BE OPERATIONALIZED AND APPLIED?

Operationalizing connectivity to enhance the resilient provision of ecosystem services is clearly an ambitious goal. As with all principles, operationalization is inevitably context-dependent. Different SES will have different potentials for intervention, while the resilience of individual ecosystem services will be variably affected. Thus, system-specific properties will determine how connectivity should be managed (e.g. by modulating strength, manipulating structure). Here we attempt to postulate some general principles for operationalizing and managing connectivity, although further research is needed to substantiate these principles. We discuss these gaps in the next section.

- **Map connectivity**. In order to understand the effect of connectivity on the resilience of ecosystem services, the first step is to clearly map the relevant parts of the SES, their scale, interactions and the currency of connectivity (see Table 4.1 and Box 4.1). Based on this information, visualization and network analysis tools can assist to map the structure (random, nested, modular), the units flowing across links (information, animals, energy, resources) and the strength (weak, moderate, strong) of connectivity in the SES. Such mapping can help determine the overall level of connectivity to develop hypotheses of the relative effect of connectivity on the resilience of ecosystem services.
- **Identify important elements/interactions**. To guide interventions and optimize the effect of connectivity on the resilience of ecosystem services, network tools can help to identify keystone, highly connected nodes or isolated patches in the SES. This helps to identify vulnerable and resilient parts in the SES, and highlight groups of actors that are overly connected. In parallel, it is important to characterize these elements in terms of their diversity (P1 – Diversity) as the combination of their structure and uniqueness can determine their relative importance. By doing so, one can rank nodes based on their potential effect on the resilience of ecosystem services and can explore the potential for managing structure and/or strength of connectivity in the SES through particular nodes or interactions.
- **Restore connectivity**. The restoration of connectivity involves the creation of nodes, or conservation of keystone nodes in the SES depending on the ecosystem service that needs to be enhanced and the type of disturbance against which one wants to protect. Alternatively, one can also maintain or strengthen connections to more resilience nodes that serve as refuge nodes. For example, habitat loss caused by the conversion of forest to crop or pasture land or the disruption of blue corridors that convey fish, nutrients and sediment when dams are built in rivers are a few examples that demonstrate how disrupting connectivity can jeopardize the provision and

resilience of ecosystem services these systems provide. Restoring connectivity in such cases can directly restore ecosystem functioning and the supply of ecosystem services. For example, the Yellowstone-to-Yukon (Y2Y) project in North America, mentioned above, focuses on reconnecting large patches of wildlife habitat by restoring corridors between patches. The approach of Y2Y primarily involves purchasing land or enacting land trusts in large, intact watersheds, connecting habitats to ensure species and genetic diversity (Baldwin *et al.* 2012). Similarly, the Montérégie Connection project in southern Quebec, Canada, is about connecting forests and people to make the landscape, and its provision of ecosystem services, more resilient to climate change and other global and regional changes (http://www.monteregieconnection.com). Here, the focus is on a much smaller scale; the science primarily addresses how the size and connectedness of forest patches is likely to influence the provision of ecosystem services across the region (Mitchell *et al.* 2013).

- **Optimize current connectivity patterns**. In other cases, it may be more useful to manage current connectivity patterns to minimize the effect of a disturbance on the resilience of ecosystem services and to contain the risk of a systemic failure. This can be achieved by disrupting the connections of extremely vulnerable components from the rest of the SES. Alternatively, the goal might be to increase modularity in the structure of the SES in order to create compartments that can act as bottlenecks for containing a disturbance. The loss of electricity across the eastern USA and Canada in 2003, affecting an estimated 50 million people, is an example of a network where local failures could not be contained and the system experienced a systemic collapse. In this case, the high degree of connectivity and lack of modularity of the power grid was largely responsible for the extensive blackout (Andersson *et al.* 2005). Thus, in some cases, connectivity may need to be reduced or otherwise changed structurally to increase the resilience of the system. Nonetheless, determining and achieving the appropriate structure and degree of strength remains a challenge. This especially applies when analyses take social and ecological connectivity into account simultaneously. Some attempts have recently been taken in this direction, although much work remains to be done for fully integrated social–ecological connectivity analyses (Box 4.1) (Bodin and Tengö 2012; Schoon *et al.* 2014).

4.6 KEY RESEARCH AND APPLICATION GAPS

Connectivity in an SES can facilitate recovery after a disturbance in an ecological landscape or the development of trust necessary for collective action in social systems. However, at the same time, highly connected systems increase the potential for disturbances to spread and enhance the risk of homogenization of knowledge, which can lead to suboptimal management. The relationship between connectivity and the resilience of SES or the ecosystem service they provide is far from simple. Despite the bulk of theoretical work that evaluates how connectivity affects the resilience of SES, we are largely lacking empirical studies. New work (e.g. Mitchell *et al.* 2013; Ziter *et al.* 2013) that summarize the effect of connectivity on the provision of ecosystem services are emerging, but still much remains to be understood regarding the impact of connectivity on the resilience of ecosystem services.

This gap in our knowledge stems mostly from the difficulty in identifying and measuring connectivity. The suggestions for operationalizing connectivity outlined in Section 4.5 are not easy to generalize. This is due to the large number of currencies employed for quantifying connectivity in SES (e.g. flow of energy, resources, information, interaction strengths, species movements) that make it challenging to quantify and compare the strength of connectivity across different SES. Moreover, difficulties arise in defining the boundaries and/or agents in network representations of SES (Bodin and Prell 2011). Most network theory has focused on well-defined subsets of ecological interactions, like feeding relationships in food webs or mutualistic interactions in plant–pollinator communities, but the integration of multiple interaction types is still largely unexplored (Fontaine *et al.* 2011; Mougi and Kondoh 2012). The consequences of integrating such a diversity of interactions for the resilience of ecological systems are unclear (Scheffer *et al.* 2012) and at the same time are difficult to grasp conceptually. Furthermore, when one adds social network dynamics, the task of disentangling the effects of connectivity on the resilience of ecosystem services becomes even more challenging. So far there is little understanding on the effect of integrating both types of interactions (social and ecological) on the resilience of SES. This challenge is aggravated by the fact that connectivity is not a constant property, as the strength and structure of links may vary over time.

Equally challenging is to know how to practically manage connectivity to enhance the resilience of ecosystem services. Despite some general statements about how to operationalize the level and type of connectivity to improve the resilience of ecosystem services, future research needs to focus on clear applications of connectivity management based on a theoretical understanding of the impacts of connectivity. As the tools and methods for estimating ecosystem services improve, initiatives that aim to quantify the impact of restoring landscape connectivity on ecosystem services will be better able to demonstrate how specific actions translate into increased resilience of ecosystem services.

Despite these challenges, recent advances in network tools for mapping and analysing complex relationships in SES, as well as rapid developments of quantifying ecosystem services, create new opportunities for testing how managing the connectivity of SES may increase the resilience of the ecosystem services they provide. At the same time, increasing access to information such as remote-sensing data, combined with (a) novel representations of social–ecological interactions (Box 4.1), (b) individual-based modelling for simulating SES and (c) theoretical advancements in understanding the effect of architecture on the dynamics of complex networks may all offer new insights into the relationship between connectivity and resilience of ecosystem services.

REFERENCES

Adger, W. N., Eakin, H., Winkels, A. (2009). Nested and teleconnected vulnerabilities to environmental change. *Frontiers in Ecology and the Environment*, 7, 150–157.

Andersson, G., Donalek, P., Farmer, R. et al. (2005). Causes of the 2003 major grid blackouts in North America and Europe, and recommended means to improve system dynamic performance. *IEEE Transactions on Power Systems*, 20, 1922–1928.

Ash, J. and Newth, D. (2007). Optimizing complex networks for resilience against cascading failure. *Physica A: Statistical Mechanics and its Applications*, 380, 673–683.

Baggio, J. A., Salau, K., Janssen, M. A., Schoon, M. L., Bodin, Ö. (2011). Landscape connectivity and predator–prey population dynamics. *Landscape Ecology*, 26, 33–45.

Baldwin, R.F., Reed, S.E., McRae, B.H., Theobald, D.M., Sutherland, R.W. (2012). Connectivity restoration in large landscapes: modeling landscape condition and ecological flows. *Ecological Restoration*, 30, 274–279.

Bastolla, U., Fortuna, M.A., Pascual-Garcia, A. et al. (2009). The architecture of mutualistic networks minimizes competition and increases biodiversity. *Nature*, **458**, 1018–1020.

Beier, P. and Noss, R. (1998). Do habitat corridors provide connectivity? *Conservation Biology*, 12, 1241–1254.

Biggs, D., Biggs, R., Dakos, V., Scholes, R. J., Schoon, M. L. (2011). Are we entering an era of concatenated global crises? *Ecology and Society*, 16, 27.

Bodin, Ö. and Crona, B. I. (2009). The role of social networks in natural resource governance: what relational patterns make a difference? *Global Environmental Change*, 19, 366–374.

Bodin, Ö. and Norberg, J. (2005). Information network topologies for enhanced local adaptive management. *Environmental Management*, 35, 175–193.

Bodin, Ö. and Norberg, J. (2007). A network approach for analyzing spatially structured populations in fragmented landscape. *Landscape Ecology*, 22, 31–44.

Bodin, Ö. and Prell, C., eds. (2011). *Social Networks and Natural Resource Management: Uncovering the Social Fabric of Environmental Governance*. Cambridge: Cambridge University Press.

Bodin, Ö. and Tengö, M. (2012). Disentangling intangible social–ecological systems. *Global Environmental Change*, 22, 430–439.

Bodin, Ö., Tengö, M., Norman, A., Lundberg, J., Elmqvist, T. (2006). The value of small size: loss of forest patches and ecological thresholds in southern Madagascar. *Ecological Applications*, 16, 440–451.

Brondizio, E. S., Ostrom, E., Young, O. R. (2009). Connectivity and the governance of multilevel social–ecological systems: the role of social capital. *Annual Review of Environment and Resources*, 34, 253–278.

Brudvig, L. A., Damschen, E. I., Tewksbury, J. J., Haddad, N. M., Levey, D. J. (2009). Landscape connectivity promotes plant biodiversity spillover into non-target habitats. *Proceedings of the National Academy of Sciences USA*, 106, 9328–9332.

Carpenter, S. R. (2003). *Regime Shifts in Lake Ecosystems: Pattern and Variation*. Oldendorf/Luhe, Germany: International Ecology Institute.

Crona, B. and Bodin, Ö. (2006). What you know is who you know? Communication patterns among resource users as a prerequisite for co-management. *Ecology and Society*, 11, 7.

Davis, S., Trapman, P., Leirs, H., Begon, M., Heesterbeek, J. A. (2008). The abundance threshold for plague as a critical percolation phenomenon. *Nature*, 454, 634–637.

Diani, M. (2003). Introduction: social movements, contentious actions, and social networks: from metaphor to substance. In *Social Movements and Networks: Users Without a Subscription are Not Able to See the Full Content. Social Movements and Networks: Relational Approaches to Collective Action*. Oxford: Oxford University Press, pp. 1–20.

Dias, P. C. (1996). Sources and sinks in population biology. *Trends in Ecology and Evolution*, 11, 326–330.

Fahrig, L. and Rytwinski, T. (2009). Effects of roads on animal abundance: an empirical review and synthesis. *Ecology and Society*, 14, 21.

Fontaine, C., Guimarães, P. R Jr, Kéfi, S. et al. (2011). The ecological and evolutionary implications of merging different types of networks. *Ecology Letters*, 14, 1170–1181.

Galstyan, A. and Cohen, P. (2007). Cascading dynamics in modular networks. *Physical Review E*, 75, 36109.

Gelcich, S., Edwards-Jones, G., Kaiser, M.J., Castilla, J. C. (2006). Co-management policy can reduce resilience in traditionally managed marine ecosystems. *Ecosystems*, 9, 951–966.

Gilbert, F., Gonzalez, A., Evans-Freke, I. (1998). Corridors maintain species richness in the fragmented landscapes of a microecosystem. *Proceedings of the Royal Society of London B*, 265, 577–582.

Gonzalez, A., Lawton, J. H., Gilbert, F. S., Blackburn, T. M., Evans-Freke, I. (1998). Metapopulation dynamics, abundance, and distribution in a microecosystem. *Science*, 281, 2045–2047.

Haddad, N. M., Tilman, D., Haarstad, J., Ritchie, M., Knops, J. M. (2001). Contrasting effects of plant richness and composition on insect communities: a field experiment. *American Naturalist*, 158, 17–35.

Hanski, I. (1991). Single-species metapopulation dynamics: concepts, models and observations. *Biological Journal of the Linnean Society*, 42, 17–38.

Janssen, M. A., Bodin, Ö., Anderies, J. M. et al. (2006). Toward a network perspective of the study of resilience in social–ecological systems. *Ecology and Society*, 11, 15.

Kearns, C. A., Inouye, D. W., Waser, N. M. (1998). Endangered mutualisms: the conservation of plant–pollinator interactions. *Annual Review of Ecology and Systematics*, 29, 83–112.

Lever, J. J., van Nes, E. H., Scheffer, M., Bascompte, J. (2014). The sudden collapse of pollinator communities. *Ecology Letters*, 17, 350–359.

Levinthal, D. A. (1997). Adaptation on rugged landscapes. *Management Science*, 43, 934–950.

Little, L. R. and McDonald, A. D. (2007). Simulations of agents in social networks harvesting a resource. *Ecological Modelling*, 204, 379–386.

Loreau, M., Mouquet, N., Gonzalez, A. (2003). Biodiversity as spatial insurance in heterogeneous landscapes. *Proceedings of the National Academy of Sciences USA*, 100, 12765–12770.

McAllister, R. R., Gordon, I. J., Janssen, M. A., Abel, N. (2006). Pastoralists' responses to variation of rangeland resources in time and space. *Ecological Applications*, 16, 572–583.

McBride, M. and Booth, D. B. (2005). Urban impacts on physical stream condition: effects of spatial scale, connectivity, and longitudinal trends. *Journal of the American Water Resources Association*, 98195, 565–580.

McCook, L. J., Ayling, T., Cappo, M. et al. (2010). Adaptive management of the Great Barrier Reef: a globally significant demonstration of the benefits of networks of marine reserves. *Proceedings of the National Academy of Sciences USA*, 107, 18278–18285.

Mcpherson, M., Smith-lovin, L., Cook, J. M. (2001). Birds of a feather: homophily in social networks. *Annual Reviw of Sociology*, 27, 415–444.

Mitchell, M. G. E., Bennett, E. M., Gonzalez, A. (2013). Linking landscape connectivity and ecosystem service provision: current knowledge and research gaps. *Ecosystems*, 16, 894–908.

Mougi, A. and Kondoh, M. (2012). Diversity of interaction types and ecological community stability. *Science*, 337, 349–351.

Mumby, P. J. and Hastings, A. (2008). The impact of ecosystem connectivity on coral reef resilience. *Journal of Applied Ecology*, 45, 854–862.

Nyström, M. and Folke, C. (2001). Spatial resilience of coral reefs. *Ecosystems*, 4, 406–417.

Nyström, M., Graham, N. A. J., Lokrantz, J., Norström, A. V. (2008). Capturing the cornerstones of coral reef resilience: linking theory to practice. *Coral Reefs*, 27, 795–809.

Ostrom, E. (1990). *Governing the Commons: The Evolution of Institutions for Collective Action*. Cambridge: Cambridge University Press.

Peterson, G. D. (2002). Contagious disturbance, ecological memory, and the emergence of landscape pattern. *Ecosystems*, 5, 329–338.

Raffa, K.F., Aukema, B. H., Brentz, B. J. *et al.* (2008). Cross-scale drivers of natural disturbances prone to anthropogenic amplification: the dynamics of bark beetle eruptions. *BioScience*, 58, 501.

Raimer, F. and Ford, T. (2005). Yellowstone to Yukon (Y2Y) – one of the largest international wildlife corridors. *Ecological Perspectives for Science and Society*, 14, 182–185.

Raudsepp-Hearne, C., Peterson, G. D., Bennett, E. M. (2010). Ecosystem service bundles for analyzing tradeoffs in diverse landscapes. *Proceedings of the National Academy of Sciences USA*, 107, 5242–5247.

Ricketts, T. H., Regetz, J., Steffan-Dewenter, I. *et al.* (2008). Landscape effects on crop pollination services: are there general patterns? *Ecology Letters*, 11, 499–515.

Ruef, M. (2002). Strong ties, weak ties and islands: structural and cultural predictors of organizational innovation. *Industrial and Corporate Change*, 11, 427–449.

Salau, K., Schoon, M. L., Baggio, J. A., Janssen, M. A. (2012). Varying effects of connectivity and dispersal on interacting species dynamics. *Ecological Modelling*, 242, 81–91.

Satake, A., Leslie, H. M., Iwasa, Y., Levin, S. A. (2007). Coupled ecological–social dynamics in a forested landscape: spatial interactions and information flow. *Journal of Theoretical Biology*, 246, 695–707.

Scheffer, M., Carpenter, S. R., Lenton, T. M. *et al.* (2012). Anticipating critical transitions. *Science*, 338, 344–348.

Schoon, M.L., Baggio, J.A., Salau, K., Janssen, M. (2014). Insights for managers from modeling species interactions across multiple scales in an idealized landscapes. *Environmental Modelling and Software*, 55, 53–59.

Staddon, P., Lindo, Z., Crittenden, P. D., Gilbert, F., Gonzalez, A. (2010). Connectivity, non-random extinction and ecosystem function in experimental metacommunities. *Ecology Letters*, 13, 543–552.

Strogatz, S. H. (2001). Exploring complex networks. *Nature*, 410, 268–276.

Tengö, M. and von Heland, J. (2011). Adaptive capacity of local indigenous institutions – the case of the taboo forests in southern Madagascar. In *Adapting Institutions Governance, Complexity, and Social–Ecological Resilience*. Boyd, E. and Folke, C., ed. Cambridge: Cambridge University Press, pp. 37–74.

Tengö, M., Johansson, K., Rakotondrasoa, F. *et al.* (2007). Taboos and forest governance: informal protection of hot spot dry forest in southern Madagascar. *AMBIO*, 36, 683–691.

Tewksbury, J. J., Levey, D. J., Haddad, N. M. *et al.* (2002). Corridors affect plants, animals, and their interactions in fragmented landscapes. *Proceedings of the National Academy of Sciences USA*, 99, 12923–12936.

Thrush, S. F., Halliday, J., Hewitt, J. E., Lohrer, A. M. (2008). The effects of habitat loss, fragmentation, and community homogenization on resilience in estuaries. *Ecological Applications*, 18, 12–21.

Treml, E. A., Halpin, P. N., Urban, D. L., Pratson, L. F. (2007). Modeling population connectivity by ocean currents, a graph-theoretic approach for marine conservation. *Landscape Ecology*, 23, 19–36.

Van Nes, E. H. and Scheffer, M. (2005). Implications of spatial heterogeneity for regime shifts in ecosystems. *Ecology*, 86, 1797–1807.

Ziter, C., Bennett, E.M., Gonzalez, A. (2013). Functional diversity and management mediate aboveground carbon stocks in small forest fragments. *Ecosphere*, 4, 1–21.

5 Principle 3 – Manage slow variables and feedbacks

Reinette Biggs, Line Gordon, Ciara Raudsepp-Hearne, Maja Schlüter and Brian Walker

SUMMARY

Many social–ecological systems can exist in different self-organizing configurations or 'regimes'. Each of these configurations produces a different set of ecosystem services, with differing consequences for different users. Changes in controlling slow variables can cause a system to shift from one regime to another if certain thresholds are exceeded and there is a change in dominant feedback processes in the social–ecological system. Such shifts are often associated with large, rapid changes in ecosystem services, and can have substantial impacts on human societies. In other cases, feedbacks may trap a system in a regime that produces a very limited set of desired ecosystem services, and make it very difficult to shift the system to a different configuration. The importance of managing slow variables and feedbacks to maintain social–ecological regimes that produce desired bundles of ecosystem services, restore social–ecological systems to more desired configurations or transform systems to entirely new configurations is

Principles for Building Resilience: Sustaining Ecosystem Services in Social–Ecological Systems, eds R. Biggs, M. Schlüter and M. L. Schoon. Published by Cambridge University Press. © Cambridge University Press 2015.

widely acknowledged in the resilience literature. However, identifying and managing key slow variables and feedbacks to avoid system thresholds or facilitate systemic transformations is often difficult in practice. Maintaining regulating ecosystem services as a proxy for managing slow variables may be one practical way forward. Other strategies focus on better understanding slow variables and feedbacks that underlie different social–ecological configurations, monitoring changes in slow variables and feedbacks, managing the strength of feedbacks and addressing missing feedbacks between drivers and impacts on ecosystem services.

5.1 INTRODUCTION

This chapter examines how slow variables and feedbacks influence the 'configuration' of a social–ecological system (SES) – i.e. the self-organizing processes and structure of an SES. These processes and structures directly affect the set of ecosystem services that the SES generates (Chapter 1), which in turn impacts who in society benefits and loses (Chapter 2). For example, it has been shown that in substantial parts of the world rainfall and soil conditions are such that it is possible for ecosystems to be configured either as forests or as savannas (systems that consist of a mixture of trees and grasses) (Hirota et al. 2011). These different configurations provide different ecological systems: forests provide wood for cooking fires, heating and building, while savannas deliver valuable grazing services for cattle ranching. Different user groups or commercial companies therefore tend to benefit or lose in these different system configurations. In addition to the policy implications of different SES configurations, shifts between different SES configurations often occur unexpectedly and very rapidly. Such shifts typically have large and abrupt impacts on the set of ecosystem services produced by the SES, often in ways society does not want or finds difficult to cope with or adapt to (MA 2005).

Similarly, it has been suggested that changes in river management approaches, for instance the potential for shifting from command-and-control to 'live-with-the-river' approaches in the

Tisza River in Hungary, can be described as alternate SES configurations that would have marked impacts on ecosystem services such as flood regulation in the region (Sendzimir *et al.* 2007). Likewise, one may consider a country under autocratic rule as one configuration of that system within the context of today's geopolitical world, with democracy often representing a possible alternate configuration. As an example, the transition in South Africa from white minority rule under Apartheid to a full participatory democracy in 1994 can be seen as two alternate self-organizing socio-political configurations of the country that have had marked consequences for the governance and use of ecosystem services, human well-being and the country's trajectory of development (Bohensky 2008; Herrfahrdt-Pähle and Pahl-Wostl 2012).

In most SES, it appears that a limited set of key variables and internal feedback processes interact to control the configuration of the system (Holling 2001; Gunderson and Holling 2002; Walker and Salt 2006). In the forest–savanna example, a key controlling variable is mean annual precipitation, which influences internal feedback processes related to fire. Such controlling variables generally change relatively slowly compared to the states of the ecosystem service variables that are of concern to people, such as cattle production. In the case of the political shift in South Africa, a key slow variable was changing societal norms about the ethics of racial discrimination, both internationally as well as in South Africa, which weakened support for and tolerance of the government's oppressive policies (Clark and Worger 2011). This was imposed for instance through economic sanctions, which substantially weakened the national economy over time, and ultimately contributed to the political transition.

The self-organizing, complex adaptive systems (CAS) nature of SES (Chapter 1) means that SES often do not respond in linear ways to disturbance or gradual changes in key controlling (usually slow) variables. Instead, SES often show little change in response to disturbance or ongoing gradual change (e.g. drought, long-term changes in rainfall patterns), but once a critical threshold of change is exceeded, they may undergo large, sudden changes to a different system configuration that may be difficult or impossible to reverse (Scheffer et al. 2001; Scheffer 2009). For instance, as temperatures rise with global warming, it is predicted that the world's major ice sheets in Greenland and Antarctica will not melt gradually, but instead are likely to undergo sudden collapse once a critical temperature threshold is reached (Joughin et al. 2014). This will have major impacts on a variety of ecosystem services. Similarly, where actions are undertaken to actively transform an SES into a new configuration they often appear to have little or no impact for a substantial period of time, until at some point the system suddenly and very rapidly reorganizes. For instance, the African National Congress (ANC) campaigned for decades to end Apartheid with seemingly little effect, but once the door for negotiations opened and Nelson Mandela was released from prison in 1990, the shift happened in less than five years, far more rapidly than political leaders anticipated (Slabbert 2006).

A central aspect of maintaining the resilience of ecosystem services in the face of disturbance and change therefore involves identifying and managing the key controlling variables and feedbacks that underpin and control the configuration of an SES. If the current system configuration produces a desired set of ecosystem services (taking into account diverse stakeholder needs and power relations, Chapter 2), this typically involves maintaining the current system configuration (e.g. a diverse coral reef system enjoyed by ecotourists or used by local fishermen), by focusing on avoiding changes in feedbacks and controlling variables that could cause the system to cross a critical threshold into another configuration. On the other hand, if the system is locked into an undesirable configuration, it may be necessary to weaken the feedbacks that keep it there, in order to restore a previous regime (e.g. in the case of degradation or invasion by alien plants (Suding et al. 2004)), or transform the SES to an entirely new configuration that produces a more desired set of ecosystem services (Walker et al. 2004; Folke et al. 2010).

5.2 WHAT DO WE MEAN BY SLOW VARIABLES AND FEEDBACKS?

SES consist of and are affected by a multitude of variables that change and interact on a range of timescales (Chapter 1). Some of these variables are 'slow', in the sense that they change much more gradually than other 'fast' variables. Provisioning ecosystem services such as crop production and freshwater usually represent fast variables. They are affected by slow variables such as soil composition and phosphorus concentrations in lake sediments. In the social domain, variables such as legal systems, values, traditions and worldviews (P4 – CAS thinking) can be important slow variables that affect ecosystem services, through for instance gradual changes in ecosystem service preferences (Abel *et al.* 2006). For example, a complex mix of gradual economic changes and changes in societal preferences has led, in many parts of the world, to fairly rapid shifts from agriculture-dominated landscapes to mixed land-use systems that provide a variety of additional ecosystem services related to tourism and 'lifestyle farming' (Beilin *et al.* 2014).

It is important to note that slow and fast variables do not have fixed timescales, but are relative to one another in the context of a specific SES (Walker *et al.* 2012). It is therefore entirely possible that a variable that is considered fast in one context or system might be considered slow in another. For any given SES, slow variables typically determine the underlying structure of SES, while the dynamics of the system arise from interactions and feedbacks between fast variables that respond to the conditions created by the slow variables (Gunderson and Holling 2002; Norberg and Cumming 2008). The variables that control the configuration of an SES, and whether or not a critical threshold is exceeded in a system, are therefore typically slow variables (Walker *et al.* 2012). Slow ecological variables are in turn often linked to regulating ecosystem services, such as erosion control, flood regulation and nutrient retention (MA 2003).

Feedbacks occur when a change in a particular variable, process or signal in an SES leads to changes in the system that eventually loop back to affect the original variable, process or signal. Feedbacks can either be reinforcing (also called positive feedbacks) if the effect creates more change of the same type, or dampening (also called negative feedbacks) if they counteract further similar changes. As an example of a reinforcing feedback, introduced grasses in Hawaii promote fire, which encourages further growth of the invasive grasses and suppresses the native shrub species. More grass therefore creates conditions for even more fire and grass production in a self-reinforcing feedback that is very difficult to break (Mack and D'Antonio 1998). On the other hand, informal or formal social sanctioning when someone breaks a rule, such as harvesting threatened species, acts as a dampening feedback. If effective, punishment such as fines and social spurning of offenders acts as a dampening feedback by discouraging further misbehaviour by the individual, as well as discouraging others from misbehaving (Ostrom 1990).

5.3 HOW DO SLOW VARIABLES AND FEEDBACKS ENHANCE THE RESILIENCE OF ECOSYSTEM SERVICES?

All SES are continually exposed to shocks such as droughts and floods, as well as more gradual, ongoing changes, such as increasing global trade connectivity, which often affect slow, controlling variables. The feedbacks within an SES are critical in determining how the SES responds to such shocks and ongoing changes. In general, the configuration of a particular SES (e.g. village and surrounding landscape), and shifts between different SES configurations, arise from the interplay between the internal feedback processes of an SES and the levels of key controlling variables (e.g. rainfall, soil type, land tenure or political system).

In many situations, the configuration of an SES can be derived from the levels of the key controlling variables (e.g. at high rainfall levels we tend to find forest). Somewhat surprisingly, however, the interplay between underlying controlling variables and the complex adaptive internal SES feedbacks means that, for a given set of conditions, it is sometimes possible for an SES to be 'configured' in two or more substantively different ways. In other words, under for instance the same rainfall, soil and other conditions, a particular SES can be structured and can function very differently, and produce completely different sets of ecosystem services. For example, as alluded to in the introduction, in places with rainfall of around 1000–2500 mm per year, it has been shown that it is possible to have either open savannas or closed-canopy forests (Fig. 5.1). These vegetation differences cannot be explained by differences in soil type or other factors, and occur even in the absence of human modifications to the landscape (Sankaran et al. 2005; Hirota et al. 2011; Staver et al. 2011). In these situations, whether a particular place has savanna or forest at a particular point in time depends on the past configuration of the system (specifically, which feedback processes have been dominant). This runs counter to our standard conceptions of the world, as it means that for a particular set of controlling conditions (e.g. rainfall, soil type) two or more substantially different SES outcomes (or configurations) are possible, and these cannot be accounted for by adding additional explanatory variables.

What is more, in these situations, SES can abruptly shift from one configuration to another without any change in key controlling conditions. For instance, under rainfall conditions of 1000–2500 mm per year, it is possible for a forest to shift abruptly to a savanna configuration, due to, for instance, a drought or a large fire, without any change in key controlling variables such as average rainfall or land management practices (Sankaran et al. 2005; Hirota et al. 2011; Staver et al. 2011). Instead, the shift results from a 'flip' in internal feedback processes triggered by the disturbance. These 'surprising' features of SES have substantial implications for understanding, governing and managing SES and the ecosystem services they provide.

In general, controlling variables set certain bounds on the possible configurations of an SES, and to a significant extent determine its structure and processes. For example, under high rainfall conditions we typically find forests, while under low to medium rainfall conditions we tend to find savannas (Fig. 5.1) (Hirota et al. 2011). Similarly, SES landscapes around many cities, especially in the developed world, are

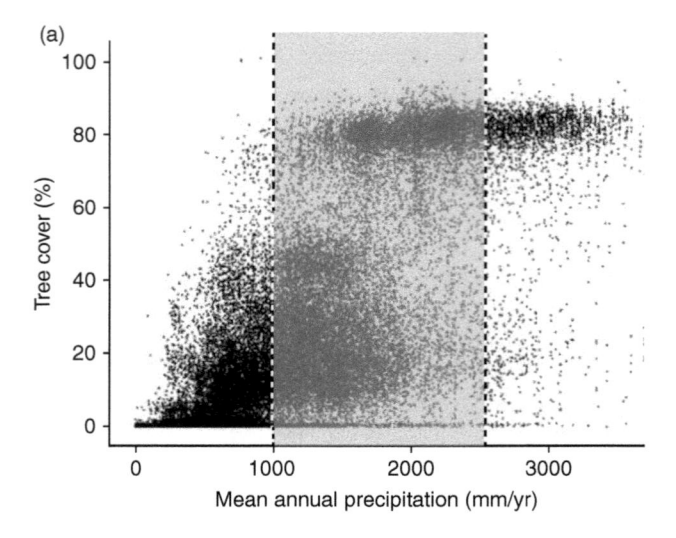

FIG. 5.1 (a) Data from around the world show that under intermediate rainfall conditions (around 1000–2500 mm per year, shaded area), landscapes can exist either as open savannas (20–40% tree cover) or as closed wooded landscapes (around 80% tree cover). At higher levels of rainfall only the closed woody state exists (b), while at lower rainfall amounts only open savanna (c), or at very low levels of rainfall, treeless savanna or deserts exist. (a) From Hirota *et al.* (2011). Photo credits: Hans Hillewaert, Creative Commons licence (b); Reinette Biggs (c).

substantially influenced by the demands of city inhabitants for various recreational and other cultural ecosystem services (Raudsepp-Hearne *et al.* 2010; Beilin *et al.* 2014). Controlling variables are often 'external' to the SES in the sense that they comprise factors over which the internal processes of the SES have little influence, or only a very gradual influence. Understanding the links between controlling variables and SES outcomes forms the focus for many scientific investigations.

SES do not, however, respond passively to disturbances or changes in controlling variables (which, as noted above, are usually slow variables). The self-organizing internal feedbacks of an SES typically buffer the impact of such changes. Dampening feedbacks in particular help counteract disturbance and change and keep the system functioning in the same kind of way, thereby maintaining the current system configuration. For example, the amount and type of crops an individual farmer decides to plant is partly influenced by expected selling prices. If there is a drought in one part of a country leading to lower maize production there, maize prices will tend to rise, and farmers in other parts of the country may be encouraged to plant more maize. The opposite will tend to happen when there is an oversupply of maize. Provided there are no other important factors regulating or distorting the market, this feedback process helps ensure a fairly constant supply of maize and provision of food to meet human needs, despite disturbances such as droughts and floods in different parts of a country (Common 1995).

However, there are limits to how large a shock or how much change an SES can be exposed to and still recover and keep functioning in the same way. If critical limits in controlling slow variables are exceeded, the feedbacks that keep the system in a particular configuration are unable to counteract the changes. For instance, in the forest–savanna example fire is a key reinforcing feedback that maintains the grassy savanna regime: more grass enables more hot fires to burn, which kills the small shrubs and trees and favours the growth of more grass. A critical slow variable that affects the strength of this feedback is the ratio of grass biomass to woody

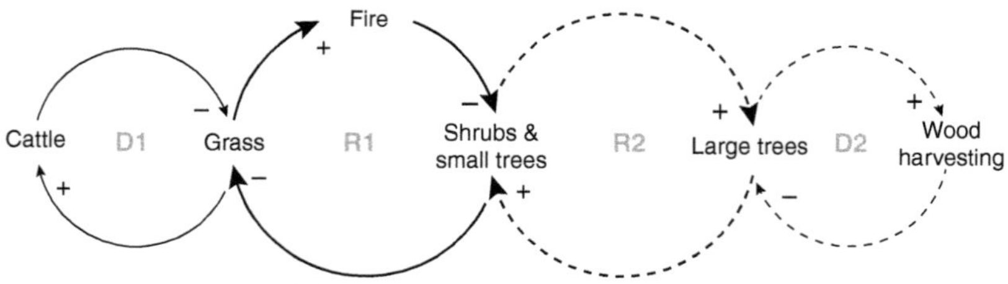

Fire → (diagram: Cattle —D1— Grass —R1— Shrubs & small trees —R2— Large trees —D2— Wood harvesting)

FIG. 5.2 Changes in the strength and balance between competing feedback loops can lead ecosystems to shift from open grassy savannas to closed wooded forest regimes. The open grassy regime is characterized by the dominance of reinforcing feedback R1 (solid lines), while the closed wooded regime is characterized by the dominance of reinforcing feedback R2 (dotted lines). D1 and D2 denote damping feedbacks related to the use of grazing and wood/timber ecosystem services. The critical threshold that causes a shift from the grassy to the wooded regime is the ratio of grass to woody vegetation, which affects whether the system can sustain sufficiently hot fires to kill small shrubs and trees, and prevent them growing into large trees. When feedback R1 is dominant the SES can support relatively large numbers of cattle, and provided cattle stocking rates and other disturbances do not cause the grass-to-woody-vegetation threshold to be exceeded, the system will remain in the grassy configuration. Conversely, when feedback R2 is dominant the system provides various forest-related ecosystem services, and provided wood harvesting rates and other disturbances do not cause a critical threshold to be exceeded, the system will remain in the wooded regime.

biomass, which decreases under heavy grazing pressure by cattle. When this ratio drops below a critical level there is too little grass to enable fires that are sufficiently hot to kill shrubs to burn. The SES will then shift into a closed-canopy forest configuration as the small shrubs grow into trees (Fig. 5.2) (Anderies et al. 2002).

Critical thresholds in controlling slow variables therefore typically correspond to points at which previously dominant feedbacks in an SES disappear, new feedbacks suddenly come into operation, or previously minor feedbacks become dominant (Bennett et al. 2005; Biggs et al. 2012). At these critical thresholds, changes in internal feedback processes cause the SES to reorganize, often abruptly, into a different configuration, where the system is structured and functions in a different way, and produces a different set of ecosystem services.

For example, lakes have been shown to shift from a clear-water to a algae-dominated configuration at the point where the level of nutrient inputs into a lake exceed the absorptive capacity of the rooted plants, which provides a strong dampening feedback (Carpenter 2003). At this critical threshold, the excess nutrients available in the water lead to the growth of algae which, when extensive, blocks sunlight and leads to the death of the rooted plants growing on the lake floor. The dampening feedback provided by the plants is then lost, and a new recycling feedback is introduced: as the plants die, the sediments on the lake floor that were stabilized by the plant roots become loose, and the nutrients that have been trapped there (sometimes for decades) also enter the water column, creating a reinforcing feedback that further fuels algal growth (Carpenter 2003).

Such large, persistent and often abrupt system reorganizations are known as regime shifts in the context of ecological systems, and have been documented in a wide range of ecosystems (Scheffer 2009; RSDB 2014). These shifts often occur unexpectedly, because the feedbacks that buffer change mean that there is often little observable change in the system (e.g. nutrient levels, algae) until the regime shift occurs. For the same reason, changes in controlling slow variables, and thus the gradual erosion of resilience in the system, usually go unnoticed. Sometimes gradual changes in the SES itself cause unexpected changes in the controlling variables. For example, it has been shown that increased cropping in the Horn of Africa and the Sahel region of West Africa can lead to changes in surface reflectivity and reduce the long-term average rainfall in the region (Taylor *et al.* 2002; Knorr and Schnitzler 2006; Otieno and Anyah 2012). The changed SES structures and processes associated with regime shifts often result in large and rapid changes in ecosystem services that society finds difficult to cope with. For example, the sudden collapse of Canada's Newfoundland cod fishery in the early 1990s directly affected the livelihoods of some 35 000 fishers and fish-plant workers, led to a decline of over $200 million dollars per annum in revenue from cod landings (DFO 2004) and had significant indirect impacts on the local economy and society (Finlayson and McCay 1998).

Different system configurations or regimes and the shifts between them are often visualized by the metaphor of the ball and cup (Fig. 5.3). The different cups represent the different potential configurations of the system under a particular set of key determinant conditions. As mentioned above, under some conditions or levels of a controlling slow variable, only one configuration of the system may be possible (represented by a single cup). However, under other conditions, two or more different configurations of the system may be possible, corresponding to different configurations of key variables and dominant feedback processes in the system (represented by two or more cups). When the system (ball) is in a given regime (cup), gradual changes in key controlling slow variables may erode the strength of the dominant feedbacks, and hence the resilience of a particular regime. This can be metaphorically thought of as reducing the size of the cup and/or making it shallower. These slow changes in the strength of the dominant feedbacks (size of the cup) make the system more vulnerable to undergoing a regime shift in the face of a disturbance such as a drought. Under these conditions, a disturbance that previously had no major impact on the system may now suddenly result in a regime shift. Of course, changes in controlling slow variables can also increase the strength of the dominant feedback processes, and increase resilience.

Where ongoing changes in internal or external controlling slow variables (e.g. global temperature increase, changes in land cover) occur, a critical threshold may be reached at which the feedbacks that create and maintain a particular regime become so weak that that the possibility of that configuration or regime (cup) disappears (Fig. 5.3). At this point, a different set of feedbacks will become dominant, and the system will reorganize into a new configuration – i.e. shift to a new cup. Once a system has

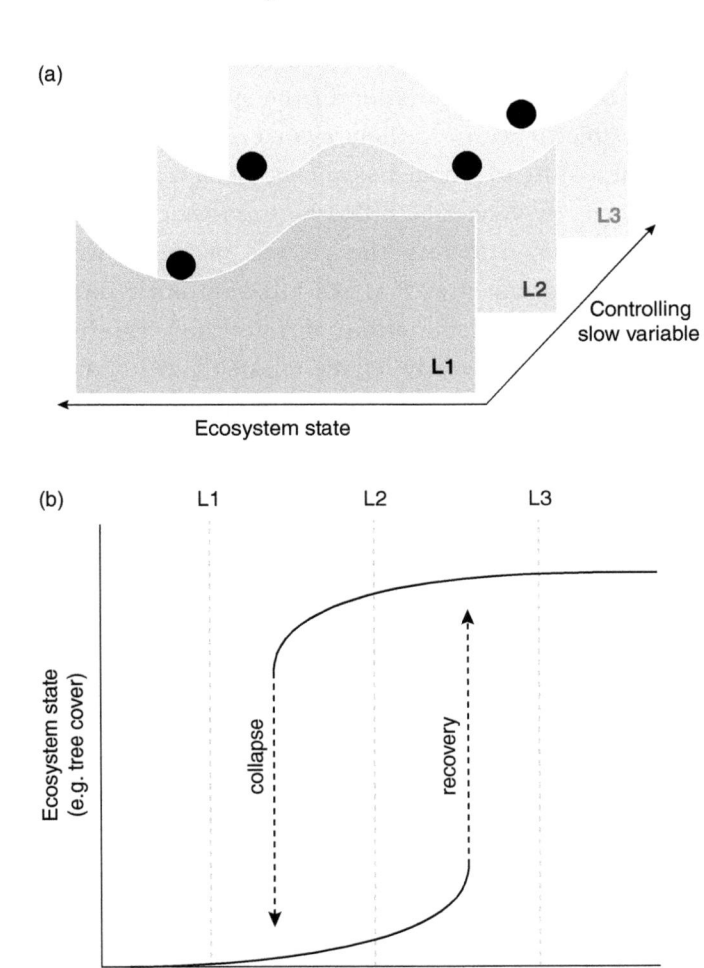

PRINCIPLE 3 – MANAGE SLOW VARIABLES AND FEEDBACKS

FIG. 5.3 (a) Regime shifts are often visualized with the metaphor of the ball and cup. Under conditions prevailing at levels L1 and L3 of the controlling slow variable there is only one cup, representing the fact that only one possible regime or SES configuration exists. Under the conditions at level L2 of the controlling slow variable there exist two possible alternate regimes. The resilience of each regime is depicted by the depth of the valley or bowl, and is determined by the strength of the dominant feedback processes. (b) Changes in the number of possible regimes and their resilience occur due to the interaction between changes in controlling slow variables and the strength of internal SES feedbacks. Based on Gordon et al. (2008).

shifted to a different regime, the new set of dominant feedbacks usually reinforce the new configuration of the system, making it difficult or impossible to return to the previous regime. For example, in the case of a shift to wooded savannas, once trees reach a certain size, they can no longer be killed by fire (Anderson et al. 2000). In addition, they suppress the growth of grass, which reduces the potential for hot fires that can kill new small shrubs, and therefore the further domination of trees and shrubs is favoured (Fig. 5.2). Once the woody regime is established it therefore becomes very difficult to reverse without mechanical removal of the trees to allow grasses to re-establish and fires to burn (Anderies et al. 2002). This 'stickiness' of the alternate regimes creates a phenomenon known as hysteresis, where the threshold and conditions required to shift the system in one direction are different from those required to reverse the shift (Carpenter 2003).

It has been proposed that exceeding critical thresholds in slow ecological variables can be avoided by better managing regulating ecosystem services, as these services are often linked to slow controlling variables (Gordon et al. 2008; Bennett et al. 2009). For instance, dryland salinization in Australia is related to the clearing of trees to make way for agricultural fields (Anderies et al. 2006). This has changed the hydrology of the landscape since the trees have a higher annual transpiration than agricultural crops, causing the water table to slowly rise. Australian soils are naturally salty and when the water table rises to less than 2 metres below the soil surface these salts are brought up to the soil surface through capillary action. The resulting salinization of the topsoil can dramatically affect crop yields, and is very difficult to reverse. Resilience to soil salinization can be enhanced by managing the hydrological regulation service of the landscape through intercropping trees and perennial crops among the annual crops to help keep water tables below the 2-metre threshold. Declines in regulating services such as erosion control and nutrient cycling, for example, also contributed to desertification-related regime shifts during the Dust Bowl years in the United States, and land degradation in many tropical drylands including the Sahel (MA 2005).

Although the two concepts have not often been linked, the notion of social–ecological 'transformation' (Olsson et al. 2004) appears to describe similar kinds of systemic reorganization as the idea of ecological regime shifts. The transformation literature has largely focused on changes in the social dimension of SES, and examples of changes from less desirable to more desirable SES configurations. Such transformations have also been understood in terms of substantive changes in feedback processes in an SES, leading to a reconfiguration of the system and a new trajectory of development (Olsson et al. 2006; Biggs et al. 2010). For instance, in the Kristianstad wetlands in southern Sweden, the emergence of a leader and the formation of a 'shadow network' of actors from both within and outside government were central to developing a vision of an alternate SES configuration for the region and influencing key actors in positions of authority to adopt this vision. These processes modified existing feedbacks in the system as well as introducing new feedbacks that ultimately led to a transformation in ecosystem management that substantially improved the diversity, flow and resilience of ecosystem services in the region (Olsson et al. 2004). Rather than focusing on critical thresholds, however, the transformations literature has stressed the importance of windows of opportunity for enabling transformation, actions to weaken key feedbacks in the 'old' regime to enable change, and, conversely, to strengthen key feedbacks once the system has shifted in order to build resilience of the new regime (Olsson et al. 2006). On the other hand, transformations have also been defined as conceptually distinct from regime shifts, and seen to entail the creation of an entirely new system rather than a reconfiguration of the system (Walker et al. 2004; Folke et al. 2010). Given these uncertainties, we have focused primarily on insights from the ecological regime shifts literature in this chapter, but note that there may be many parallels to transformations in the social dimension of SES, and that the connections between the two concepts are an active emerging area of research.

In summary, a critical aspect of enhancing the resilience of specific bundles of ecosystem services revolves around the management of slow variables and feedbacks to ensure that the SES remains in a configuration that produces those ecosystem services. For many systems, however, our understanding of which slow variables and feedbacks underlie desired SES configurations is limited, and this is an important area for future research. In addition, because we live in a rapidly changing world, these desired configurations will themselves be subject to change (Chapter 2). This is not only because the ecosystem services societies value may change over time, but also because of ongoing social and ecological changes that may cause some SES configurations to disappear and new possible configurations to arise. A better understanding of how the concept of social–ecological transformations connects to these types of changes, and of how to manage transformations to entirely new system configurations, is therefore critical.

5.4 UNDER WHAT CONDITIONS MAY RESILIENCE OF ECOSYSTEM SERVICES BE COMPROMISED?

While feedbacks can keep an SES in a configuration that produces a set of desired ecosystem services, they can also lock a system into an undesirable configuration or reduce its ability to adapt or transform in the face of external or internal change. For example, poverty in drylands is often associated with conditions where population growth has increased the demand for crop production and pressure on the land, for instance by reducing fallow time, or increasing biomass offtake so that little organic matter is left on the soil (Gordon and Enfors 2008). The resulting drop in soil fertility means that crop harvests are low and farmers have little or no surplus harvest to sell, and therefore no money to buy fertilizers to restore or increase soil fertility to increase their crop harvests. Consequently they remain trapped in a vicious cycle of poverty (Enfors 2013). In such cases, the resilience of a desired set of ecosystem services is compromised by reinforcing feedbacks that maintain SES configurations that do not produce these services.

As another example, in the Amudarya river basin in central Asia, reinforcing feedbacks in the agricultural system keep the system locked in an unsustainable water management regime that has led to the disappearance of the Aral Sea and an agricultural sector that is increasingly vulnerable to drought (Box 5.1) (Schlüter and Herrfahrdt-Pähle 2011). Key reinforcing feedbacks that trap this system are related to soil salinization (increasing soil salinization increases the need to leach fields with water, but due to poor drainage this leads to rising groundwater tables, and hence further increases soil salinization), vested interests of the elites and a patronage system where farmers often plant the water-intensive cash crop rice as demanded and facilitated by their patrons. In these situations, increasing the supply of desired ecosystem services requires weakening these key feedbacks that keep the SES trapped to enable the system to shift to an alternate configuration that supplies a more desired set of ecosystem services.

Management interventions that obscure, remove or ignore stabilizing feedbacks that underlie the provision of desired ecosystem services can also erode resilience of the SES configurations that produce these services. For example, the 2005 flood in New Orleans was partially caused by human-engineered modifications to the delta system that undermined the capacity of the natural sediment and flood dynamics to absorb changes in water flows (Constanza et al. 2006; Day et al. 2007). In other cases, policies or markets can send signals to resource users that change or overpower feedbacks. For example, spikes in global commodity prices can lead to overexploitation of local agricultural ecosystems if the incentive to make a lot of money quickly overpowers the incentive to maintain the long-term productive potential of the land (Allison and Hobbs 2004). In an example from Indonesia, a stabilizing feedback was removed when pesticide subsidies encouraged the use of so much pesticide that the

BOX 5.1 **Social–ecological traps in the Amudarya river basin**

The Amudarya river is the largest river of central Asia with an average annual runoff of 79 km^3. It originates in the Hindukush and Pamir mountains in Tajikistan and Afghanistan, where all river flow is generated, flows through the semi-arid Turan lowlands in Uzbekistan and Turkmenistan, and drains into the Aral Sea (Fig. 5.4). Water is a vital and strategic resource for all countries in the river basin because of their heavy reliance on irrigated agriculture. Today, more than 90% of the region's water resources are used in the agricultural sector of the downstream countries Uzbekistan and Turkmenistan. The ecological and social systems in the river basin are strongly linked by their water needs and multiple formal and informal institutions of land and water resources management. The delta of the river provides multiple ecosystem services for the local population and the national economy of Uzbekistan and Turkmenistan. These include agricultural crops such as cotton, rice and wheat, as well as fish, reeds, groundwater regulation and wind protection in the remaining wetlands (Schlüter and Herrfahrdt-Pähle 2011).

Changes in the slow variables of water use and rising groundwater tables in agricultural areas have caused regime shifts in the SES such as the disappearance of much of the southern Aral Sea, collapse of its fishery and loss of agricultural lands because of massive soil salinization (Fig. 5.5). Decreasing water flows to the delta and land-use changes such as the removal of the riverine Tugai forests have led to lowering of groundwater tables in the wetlands that have favoured encroachment of salt cedars. These have in turn further lowered groundwater tables creating a positive feedback that accelerates desertification. Climate change is also driving changes in other slow variables such as a shift in precipitation composition from snow to rain leading to temporal shifts in peak runoff with serious implications for agriculture. Together, these slowly changing variables and regime shifts have severely impacted ecosystem services in the basin, shifting the SES in the Uzbek part of the river basin into an undesirable regime that provides a much lower level of essential ecosystem services than it potentially could (Schlüter and Herrfahrdt-Pähle 2011).

BOX 5.1 **Continued**

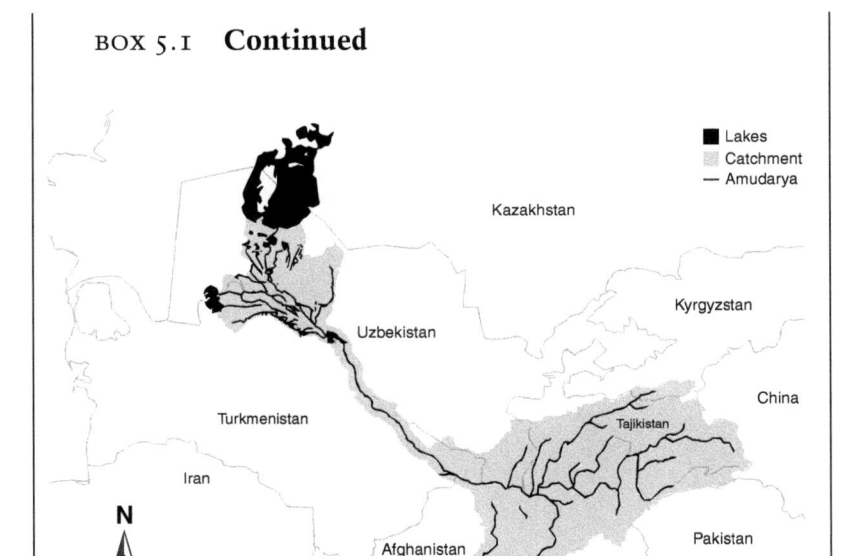

FIG. 5.4 The Amudarya river basin

Several strong social–ecological feedbacks keep the system trapped in a state where the resilience of ecosystem services is further degraded (Schlüter and Herrfahrdt-Pähle 2011). One well-known feedback is the massive use of water for irrigation, often following bad practices, that has led to high groundwater tables and soil salinization. Salinization of agricultural land increases water demand even further because of the need to leach fields to make them suitable for planting. Leaching of fields with bad drainage, however, increases groundwater levels even further. This reinforcing feedback could be weakened by managing the semi-natural vegetation in the delta. Natural vegetation such as poplars in Tugai forests can regulate groundwater tables. They have been planted in pilot areas alongside water-logged fields as a measure to remediate soils. In times of high uncertainty regarding water availability, farmers, however, prefer high water tables as an insurance against water scarcity despite their negative effects on soil quality. In order to effectively manage groundwater tables, institutional changes that provide more water security to farmers and change their

BOX 5.1 **Continued**

FIG. 5.5 (a) Dried out river bed during severe drought in 2000, (b) salinized agricultural fields (also showing massive deposits of gypsum), (c) the dried out Aral Sea and the Amudarya river delta (in the south), (d) selling of fish and fowl from the Amudarya delta at a local market. Photo credits: Maja Schlüter (a, b, d); CHELYS, Earth snapshot, http://www.eosnap.com (c).

perception of high water tables are therefore needed as much as are actions that reduce the water table levels themselves (Schlüter *et al.* 2010).

The low capacity of the current SES in the river basin to adapt to ongoing ecological and political changes (which became evident for example during the severe drought in 2000/2001) is also driven by a strong social feedback (Schlüter and Herrfahrdt-Pähle 2011). After the breakup of the Soviet Union, cotton production had to provide the financial means to fill the state budget hole that occurred after support from Moscow ceased. The Uzbek government thus retained its state order system for cotton which forces farmers to produce fixed cotton quotas and sell them to the state at state prices. The state in return

BOX 5.1 **Continued**

provides farmers with production inputs and serves as a guaranteed buyer. The latter is important because farmers lack access to markets. The farmers are thus dependent on the state order despite the fact that they would prefer to plant other more profitable crops. The state and its elites then export the cotton at world-market prices (Uzbekistan is the world's fourth largest cotton producer). The abuse of positions of authority for personal enrichment keeps the system in its current state and further decreases the resilience of ecosystem services with severe implications for human well-being, particularly in the delta region of the river. The mutual dependencies between farmers and elites in patronage relationships and strong social networks and informal institutions act to maintain the status quo and prevent any change in institutional or management arrangements. Even the large shock of the breakup of the Soviet Union and subsequent donor support that could have provided a window of opportunity to transform water use towards more sustainable practices did not result in any real changes in water use and governance in the region.

Many, often donor-driven, interventions neglect the social and social–ecological feedbacks and focus on technical measures to increase water use and drainage efficiency. In order to enhance the resilience of ecosystem services in the Amudarya river basin interventions need to address these persistent social and social–ecological feedbacks to allow for a transformation towards more sustainable land- and water-use practices, such as a multi-purpose water use that provides for diversification of livelihood practices (Schlüter et al. 2009) and a shift to less-water-intensive activities. The situation in the Amudarya river basin is an example of how social–ecological feedbacks have trapped the system in a configuration that produces a much lower level of essential ecosystem services such as crop production, fish, erosion control, micro-climate, etc. than the system could potentially provide. These feedbacks have also created a very rigid system that seems incapable of adapting or transforming in the face of massive external pressure arising from socio-political and climate change (Schlüter et al. 2010).

natural predator of the brown rice plant hopper was killed. This led to an explosion in the population of the hopper, resulting in US$1.5 billion loss in brown rice yields (De Moor and Calamai 1997). In such cases, more appropriate rules or incentives can maintain feedbacks that dampen the effect of disturbances and maintain the resilience of SES configurations to produce desired ecosystem services.

In many cases the resilience of desired SES configurations is eroded because there are no feedbacks from the system to the key factors driving change in that SES. For example, to build resilience in lakes at risk from eutrophication, management needs to occur beyond the boundaries of the lake at the catchment scale to reduce fertilizer runoff into the lake (Carpenter 2003). The agricultural practices of farmers have a direct impact on the lake, but farms are often distant from the lake and farmers use other water sources for their domestic and farming needs, so that there is no feedback or connection from impacts on the lake back to the farmer. In such cases, incentive-based feedbacks can be created to connect impacts on the lake to the farmers' practices, for example through the introduction of compensation or reward schemes for agricultural practices that enhance nutrient retention in the landscape. Managing the regulation of ecosystem services related to nutrient retention in lake catchments by keeping steep areas vegetated, leaving stubble on fields and maintaining riparian areas and wetlands can greatly reduce the risk of eutrophication and algae-dominated lakes since less nutrients end up in the lake (Carpenter 2003). Conceptually, the aim of such compensation and reward schemes is to widen the system boundaries to internalize key drivers that affect a particular SES so that there is a feedback from the system back to the key drivers of change.

Lack of knowledge about which key slow variables and feedbacks underlie particular SES configurations is a further important limitation that can lead to actions that unwittingly erode the resilience of those configurations. Detecting and understanding the feedbacks and dynamics underlying regime shifts is not a trivial task. For instance, it took several decades of observational and experimental research to clarify the mechanisms underlying freshwater eutrophication, one of the best-understood regime shifts today (Carpenter 2003). Even where slow variables and feedbacks are known, they may not be monitored, so that information about changes in these variables is not available to inform management. One of the key challenges in this regard is that monitoring systems often focus on fast variables. Consequently, the creeping changes taking place in controlling slow variables that potentially threaten the long-term production and resilience of valued ecosystem services often go unnoticed until a regime shift occurs (Walker and Salt 2006; Biggs *et al.* 2012), at which time it may be very difficult or impossible to reverse the changes.

Finally, even where knowledge and monitoring information exist, appropriate action may not occur for a variety of reasons. For instance, although several key controlling slow variables and feedbacks are known with respect to climate change, vested and competing interests, and lack of agreement on the appropriate responses, have hampered the implementation of a coordinated international response to avoid potential climate-driven regime shifts (Harris 2007). Another important problem is that governance institutions are often structured to operate on shorter timescales than the timescale over which important changes in controlling slow variables might occur (Crépin *et al.* 2012). Consequently, these variables are often treated as constant, and ignored. Developing governance institutions that can act on knowledge and information about key feedbacks and slow variables in SES is therefore critical (Walker *et al.* 2009).

5.5 HOW CAN THE PRINCIPLE OF MANAGING SLOW VARIABLES AND FEEDBACKS BE OPERATIONALIZED AND APPLIED?

Managing slow variables and feedbacks is a central aspect of managing resilience in SES and the ecosystem services they produce. A central aim in this regard is to foster SES configurations that produce desired sets of ecosystem services. Strategies for operationalizing this principle revolve around identifying and managing key stabilizing and destabilizing feedbacks and slow variables, removing barriers that obscure feedbacks in the system, introducing new feedbacks where they are missing, and developing effective monitoring systems and institutions that can respond to this information. Most often several of these strategies need to be implemented in tandem. Fundamental to all the strategies is systemic understanding of the system being managed, which often requires significant research investment.

- **Invest in a better understanding of key slow variables and feedbacks that underlie different SES configurations**. Our understanding of possible alternate SES configurations and the slow variables and feedbacks which underlie them is currently limited. This is partly because science has often focused on explaining SES outcomes as a one-to-one function of key internal and external determinant conditions. The possibility for multiple outcomes for the same set of determinant conditions (i.e. one-to-many relationships) has seldom been considered, and evidence for this has consequently seldom been sought. A better understanding of the possibility for alternate SES configurations, and the key controlling variables and feedbacks that underlie these configurations, is key to operationalizing this principle.
- **Strengthen feedbacks that maintain desired regimes**. Identifying and strengthening feedbacks that help maintain desired SES configurations can help build resilience of ecosystem services in the face of disturbances and external stresses such as climate change (Thrush et al. 2009). These include both balancing feedbacks as well as feedbacks that reinforce SES configurations that produce desired ecosystem services. For example, coral reefs can shift between regimes dominated by hard corals that provide ecosystem services such as fisheries and ecotourism, and regimes dominated by seaweed (Bellwood et al. 2004; Norström et al. 2009). The resilience of the hard coral regime can be enhanced by promoting the abundance of herbivores such as parrotfish that graze on seaweed, as it reduces the possibility for seaweed to become established in the face of shocks such as coral bleaching events (Nyström et al. 2012). Feedbacks in the governance system can also be created and strengthened to enhance the resilience of hard corals by, for instance, supporting the empowerment of reef users and providing incentives to prevent overfishing (Steneck et al. 2009).

- **Weaken or break feedbacks that trap SES in undesired regimes**. In other cases, it may be necessary to disrupt or weaken the feedbacks that keep an SES in a resilient but undesired regime. This can be particularly important in ecosystem restoration projects, or to facilitate the transformation of an SES into a different configuration that produces a more desirable set of ecosystem services (Suding et al. 2004; Young 2010). For instance, small-scale water-system innovations such as rainwater harvesting and conservation tillage can destabilize feedbacks that keep small-holder agricultural systems in Tanzania trapped in a low production state with high levels of poverty (Enfors 2013). This region is faced with recurrent droughts and dry spells, which cause dramatic crop losses for farmers and drain their financial and physical resources. Water-system innovations can help increase yields and allow for resource accumulation, thereby weakening some of the feedbacks that keep these systems poor (Enfors 2013).
- **Keep track of actions that obscure or disrupt stabilizing feedbacks**. Activities and subsidies that obscure or disrupt stabilizing feedbacks in SES can lead to economic and environmental costs that could be avoided. This often happens through the introduction of new feedbacks and connections at larger scales, such as those associated with processes of globalization (Adger et al. 2009). For example marine 'roving bandits' are fishing vessels that maintain high harvests by moving around the world and depleting multiple local fisheries (Berkes et al. 2006). In contrast, fishing enterprises that are tied to a specific location have an incentive to manage fish stocks sustainably to ensure continued harvests in the long term. Roving vessels break this local dependence feedback by simply moving to a new location once they have depleted a fishery. Identifying actions that break or conceal important feedbacks, and creating institutions that are able to address cross-scale dynamics that lead to the disruption or concealment of feedbacks, are crucial for managing resilience in today's highly connected world (Walker et al. 2009).
- **Address missing feedbacks, especially in relation to key drivers of SES change**. On the other hand, for many environmental problems, especially those involving cross-scale effects, there are missing feedbacks between the impacts on an SES and the key drivers of change in those systems. In economics, these are referred to as externalities. Various regulation-and incentive-based feedbacks can be created to internalize drivers and connect

them to SES changes. For example, the introduction of seafood labelling and certification for timber products aims to create a feedback between the production system and individual consumers (Ward and Phillips 2008). There are also a growing number of 'payments for ecosystem services' (PES) schemes, such as the Chinese 'Grain for Green' programme, which offers farmers grain in exchange for not clearing forested slopes, thereby reducing erosion and improving downstream water quality (Uchida et al. 2005). Better system definition and an understanding of cross-scale dynamics can often help identify missing feedbacks that need to be managed to enhance the resilience of desired SES configurations (Soranno et al. 2014).

- **Monitor slow variables that underlie key thresholds and feedback processes**. Monitoring known or suspected key slow variables and feedbacks is central to an adaptive SES management system. This ensures that important underlying changes in SES are detected and that timely adjustments in management can take place where needed (P5 – Learning). Slow variables are often ignored in monitoring and management, as attention tends to focus on fast variables that show more variability and response over short timescales and are often easier to observe (Biggs et al. 2012). Understanding the crucial role of slow variables and feedbacks can help managers recognize that investing in monitoring programmes and management strategies that focus on slow variables which underlie system resilience can be very cost-effective. It has been suggested that paying attention to regulating ecosystem services as a proxy for slow variables may be one effective approach to monitoring and managing resilience of ecosystem services (Bennett et al. 2009; Raudsepp-Hearne et al. 2010).

- **Establish governance structures that can respond to monitoring information in a timely manner**. Knowledge and monitoring information alone are insufficient to avoid loss of resilience. Establishing governance structures that can effectively respond to information about changes in slow variables are equally critical to preventing SES changes that undermine the provision of desired ecosystem services. One innovative example of an institution that links monitoring and management to avoid potential thresholds is the strategic adaptive management approach in the Kruger National Park, South Africa (Roux and Foxcroft 2011). This approach is based on large sets of carefully specified 'thresholds of potential concern' (TPCs) that, based on the best available current knowledge, define hypothesized thresholds for key environmental indicators (Biggs and Rogers 2003). The management process has been designed so that when monitoring indicates that a TPC has been reached or will soon be reached, it triggers a formal meeting where it is required that a decision is taken to implement a course of action to moderate the system change, or that the TPC be adjusted in the light of new knowledge. By embedding the monitoring process within a formal decision-making structure it helps ensure that the latest knowledge is incorporated in decision-making and there is a discreet point at which managers are required to act on monitoring information, something which seems obvious but often does not happen in practice (Rogers and Biggs 1999).

5.6 KEY RESEARCH AND APPLICATION GAPS

Several critical research and application gaps are evident in relation to improving our capacity to manage slow variables and feedbacks, and enhance the resilience of desired ecosystem services. First, we need to better understand what regime shifts are possible in different SES, under which conditions they occur and how they impact ecosystem services and human well-being. Several initiatives are making progress in this direction. Walker and Myer (2004) collated around one hundred examples of proposed and demonstrated examples of regime shifts in case studies around the world. The Regime Shifts Database (http://www.regimeshifts.org) builds on this initiative, focusing on expanding the set of case studies described in the literature; and, based on these, identifying different generic types of regime shifts (e.g. freshwater eutrophication, coral shifts, dryland degradation). For each regime shift, the database identifies the alternate regimes, the ecosystem services associated with each regime and which users benefit and lose from those ecosystem services, the key feedbacks that maintain each regime and the key drivers and slow variables that underlie regime shifts in these systems. The goal is to provide an accessible information resource for scientists, policy-makers and practitioners that advances our knowledge and understanding of what shifts are possible in different SES, under which conditions they occur, how much they matter in terms of impacts on ecosystem services and how resilience to undesired shifts might be enhanced.

Second, there is a particular need to better understand social–ecological regime shifts, i.e. shifts that arise entirely from feedbacks between social and ecological variables. Given the disciplinary divides in academia, most shifts that have been studied to date involve ecological regime shifts (i.e. shifts that arise from changes in ecological feedback processes), which are often caused by the impact of human activities, and which have consequences for human society. There are also examples of social regime shifts (i.e. shifts that arise from social feedback processes) that have consequences for ecosystems (Abrahamson 1991; Brock and Durlauf 1999; Scheffer et al. 2003). However, it is possible that some regime shifts may arise entirely from the interaction of social and ecological factors. For instance, Lade et al. (2013) demonstrated in a theoretical model that non-linear feedbacks between harvesters and the resource they are exploiting can trigger a regime shift that has significant consequences for human well-being and the sustainability of the ecosystem. In this model, increasing resource availability provides incentives for overharvesting, which triggers a reinforcing feedback that leads to the collapse of cooperation in the community and consequently resource overexploitation. This regime shift happens despite the fact that neither the resource nor social system exhibit regime shifts on their own.

Third, there is a need to explore and better integrate the concepts of transformation (Olsson et al. 2004) and regime shifts (Biggs et al. 2012), and to understand to what extent they describe similar phenomena, and how they might complement one another. It is clear that both concepts describe some type of systemic reorganization in SES, but they originate in different literatures, and have been applied to different types of system reorganizations, using different analytical approaches. While the regime-shifts literature has typically focused on inadvertent ecological shifts that are generally regarded as negative, the transformations literature has focused mostly on reorganization of the social dimension of SES to a more desirable configuration (e.g. more sustainable ecosystem management), and entailing a substantive deliberate component (i.e. actors actively transform the system). In terms of management implications, both have however emphasized the need to manage feedbacks. The transformation literature has particularly highlighted the role of agency, leadership and social connectivity in facilitating change. These insights on how to envision and create the possibility for new regimes, and how to use windows of opportunity to achieve change are likely to be particularly useful in considering possibilities for social–ecological shifts to more sustainable SES governance configurations. However, the transformation literature has seldom framed or analysed transformative changes in terms of changes in slow variables and critical thresholds. The role of slow variables in influencing the strength of feedbacks, often in ways that go unnoticed, may therefore be a particularly useful contribution from the ecological regime shifts literature. At this stage, however, it is not clear whether transformations are qualitatively different phenomena from regime shifts, and the extent to which the concepts can be linked.

Fourth, we need to better understand which feedbacks are critical for stabilizing SES configurations that underpin desired ecosystem services in different contexts – or conversely, which feedbacks are key to destabilizing configurations that keep SES trapped in undesired regimes. For several well-studied regime shifts, substantial progress has been made in this regard. For instance Nyström *et al.* (2012) synthesized critical feedbacks that keep marine ecosystems trapped in degraded states, and identified strategies and windows of opportunity for breaking these feedbacks. Similarly, Olsson *et al.* (2006) and Biggs *et al.* (2010) have identified important factors and feedbacks that are key to enabling transformations in ecosystem management to more collaborative, adaptive approaches. Such syntheses across detailed individual case studies, combined with theoretical and empirical modelling, can be used to build understanding of key slow variables and feedbacks that underlie different types of regime shifts and transformations, and help identify focal variables for monitoring and management (Gordon *et al.* 2008; Mård Karlsson *et al.* 2011).

Fifth, we need a better understanding of the key drivers of undesired, unexpected ecological regime shifts. At a general level, it has been found that the likelihood of regime shifts increases when human activities (i) lead to the loss of response diversity (P1 – Diversity); (ii) substantially increase or decrease connectivity in a system (P2 – Connectivity); (iii) impact on ecosystems via emissions of waste, pollutants and climate change; and (iv) alter the magnitude, frequency and duration of disturbance regimes (Folke et al. 2004; Thrush et al. 2009). However, identifying specific human activities that are associated with an increased likelihood of various regime shifts could help identify policies and management practices to reduce the risk of regime shifts, particularly in fast-developing regions of the world. Better understanding the combined and often synergistic effects of multiple drivers on key feedbacks in SES is especially critical, as these may differ in surprising ways from the effects of individual drivers. Furthermore, there is a need to better understand possible cascading effects among different regime shifts.

Lastly, opportunities to learn about changes in slow variables and feedbacks are hampered in part because it is difficult to detect or predict a regime shift (Scheffer and Carpenter 2003). In cases where the feedbacks and slow variables underlying a regime shift are poorly understood, emerging work on early warnings of regime shifts may be helpful. Recent work has shown that as a system approaches a critical threshold, there are changes in the statistical behaviour of the system (e.g. rising variance, autocorrelation) that can provide early warning signals of a looming regime shift (Scheffer et al. 2009). Increasing variance and autocorrelation are metaphorically associated with the flattening of the 'cup' (Fig. 5.3), and are an indicator that the feedbacks that keep the system in a particular regime are becoming weaker. As such they could potentially be used as an indicator of changing resilience of a system. A challenge with this approach is that very detailed or long time series data are usually needed to detect these changes (Dakos et al. 2012). Furthermore, depending on the rate of change in key slow variables, the system may have already passed a threshold or be committed to doing so by the time these statistical changes become apparent (Biggs et al. 2009).

Governments at all scales are mostly aware of concepts such as ecosystem services, resilience, cumulative effects and tipping points, but are struggling with how these concepts relate to each other and how to manage them. One challenge is that the dynamic, systemic worldview that fosters an understanding and appreciation of CAS dynamics, such as regime shifts, runs directly counter to the reductionist worldview that underlies most Western-style governance institutions (P4 – CAS thinking). Perhaps for this reason, slow variables, feedbacks and thresholds are concepts that have seldom been unpacked and operationalized within governance and management settings. One attempt to identify thresholds associated with slow variables and feedbacks at global scales has been the identification of a set of 'planetary boundaries', which estimate thresholds of human impacts on the Earth that could lead to a shift in global-scale planetary dynamics (Rockström *et al.* 2009). However, in general, organizations trying to incorporate these concepts into governance institutions and policy responses need better guidance on how to do so. A possible example on which to build is the 'Thresholds of Potential Concern' approach used in South African National Parks (Roux and Foxcroft 2011); here, rather than assuming that there is no threshold until proven otherwise, best available knowledge is used to estimate suspected thresholds and then re-evaluate and update this information as new knowledge becomes available.

REFERENCES

Abel, N., Cumming, D. H. M., Anderies, J. M. (2006). Collapse and reorganization in social–ecological systems: questions, some ideas, and policy implications. *Ecology and Society*, 11, 17.

Abrahamson, E. (1991). Managerial fads and fashions: the diffusion and rejection of innovations. *Academy of Management Review*, 16, 586–612.

Adger, W. N., Eakin, H., Winkels, A. (2009). Nested and teleconnected vulnerabilities to environmental change. *Frontiers in Ecology and the Environment*, 7, 150–157.

Allison, H. E. and Hobbs, R. J. (2004). Resilience, adaptive capacity, and the 'lock-in trap' of the Western Australian Agricultural Region. *Ecology and Society*, 9, 3.

Anderies, J. M., Janssen, M. A., Walker, B. H. (2002). Grazing management, resilience and the dynamics of a fire-driven rangeland. *Ecosystems*, 5, 23–44.

Anderies, J. M., Ryan, P., Walker, B. H. (2006). Loss of resilience, crisis and institutional change: lessons from an intensive agricultural system in southeastern Australia. *Ecosystems*, 9, 865–878.

Anderson, R. C., Schwegman, J. E., Anderson, M. R. (2000). Micro-scale restoration: a 25-year history of a southern Illinois barrens. *Restoration Ecology*, 8, 296–306.

Beilin, R., Lindborg, R., Stenseke, M. et al. (2014). Analysing how drivers of agricultural land abandonment affect biodiversity and cultural landscapes using case studies from Scandinavia, Iberia and Oceania. *Land Use Policy*, 36, 60–72.

Bellwood, D. R., Hughes, T. P., Folke, C., Nyström, M. (2004). Confronting the coral reef crisis. *Nature*, 429, 827–833.

Bennett, E. M., Cumming, G. S., Peterson, G. D. (2005). A systems model approach to determining resilience surrogates for case studies. *Ecosystems*, 8, 945–957.

Bennett, E., Peterson, G., Gordon, L. (2009). Understanding relationships among multiple ecosystem services. *Ecology Letters*, 12, 1394–1404.

Berkes, F., Hughes, T. P., Steneck, R. S. et al. (2006). Globalization, roving bandits, and marine resources. *Science*, 311, 1557–1558.

Biggs, H. C. and Rogers, K. H. (2003). An adaptive system to link science, monitoring and management in practice. In *The Kruger Experience: Ecology and Management of Savanna Heterogeneity*. du Toit, J. T., Rogers, K. H., Biggs, H. C., eds. Washington, DC: Island Press.

Biggs, R., Carpenter, S. R., Brock, W. A. (2009). Turning back from the brink: detecting an impending regime shift in time to avert it. *Proceedings of the National Academy of Sciences USA*, 106, 826–831.

Biggs, R., Westley, F. R., Carpenter, S. R. (2010). Navigating the back loop: fostering social innovation and transformation in ecosystem management. *Ecology and Society*, 15, 9.

Biggs, R., Blenckner, T., Folke, C. et al. (2012). Regime shifts. In *Encyclopedia of Theoretical Ecology*. Berkeley, CA: University of California Press.

Bohensky, E. (2008). Discovering resilient pathways for South African water management: two frameworks for a vision. *Ecology and Society*, 13, 19.

Brock, W. A. and Durlauf, S. N. (1999). A formal model of theory choice in science. *Economic Theory*, 14, 113–130.

Carpenter, S. R. (2003). *Regime Shifts in Lake Ecosystems: Pattern and Variation*. Oldendorf/Luhe: International Ecology Institute.

Clark, N. L. and Worger, W. H. (2011). *South Africa: The Rise and Fall of Apartheid*. London: Routledge.

Common, M. (1995). *Sustainability and Policy. Limits to Economics.* Cambridge: Cambridge University Press.

Constanza, R., Mitsch, W. J., Day, J. W. (2006). A new vision for New Orleans and the Mississippi delta: applying ecological economics and ecological engineering. *Frontiers in Ecology and the Environment*, 4, 465–472.

Crépin, A. S., Biggs, R., Polasky, S., Troell, M., de Zeeuw, A. (2012). Regime shifts and management. *Ecological Economics*, 84, 15–22.

Dakos, V., Carpenter, S. R., Brock, W. A. *et al.* (2012). Methods for detecting early warnings of critical transitions in time series illustrated using simulated ecological data. *PLoS ONE*, 7, e41010.

Day, J. W., Boesch, D. F., Clairain, E. J. *et al.* (2007). Restoration of the Mississippi Delta: lessons from hurricanes Katrina and Rita. *Science*, 315, 1679–1684.

De Moor, A. P. G. and Calamai, P. (1997). *Subsidizing Unsustainable Development: Undermining the Earth with Public Funds.* San Jose, Costa Rica: The Earth Council.

DFO (2004). Fish landings and landed values. Department of Fisheries and Oceans, Ottawa, Ontario. Available at http://www.nfl.dfo-mpo.gc.ca.

Enfors, E. (2013). Social–ecological traps and transformations in dryland agro-ecosystems: using water system innovations to change the trajectory of development. *Global Environmental Change*, 23, 51–60.

Finlayson, A. C. and McCay, B. J. (1998). Crossing the threshold of ecosystem resilience: the commercial extinction of northern cod. In *Linking Social and Ecological Systems: Management Practices and Social Mechanisms for Building Resilience.* Cambridge: Cambridge University Press, pp. 311–337.

Folke, C., Carpenter, S. R., Walker, B. H. *et al.* (2004). Regime shifts, resilience and biodiversity in ecosystem management. *Annual Review of Ecology, Evolution and Systematics*, 35, 557–581.

Folke, C., Carpenter, S. R., Walker, B. H. *et al.* (2010). Resilience thinking: integrating resilience, adaptability and transformability. *Ecology and Society*, 15, 20.

Gordon, L. and Enfors, E. (2008). Land degradation, ecosystem services and resilience of smallholder farmers in Makanya catchment, Tanzania. In *Conserving Land, Protecting Water: Comprehensive Assessment of Water Management in Agriculture Series.* Wallingford: CABI.

Gordon, L. J., Peterson, G. D., Bennett, E. M. (2008). Agricultural modifications of hydrological flows create ecological surprises. *Trends in Ecology and Evolution*, 23, 211–219.

Gunderson, L. H. and Holling, C. S., eds. (2002). *Panarchy: Understanding Transformations in Human and Natural Systems*. Washington, DC: Island Press.

Harris, P. G. (2007). Collective action on climate change: the logic of regime failure. *Natural Resources Journal*, 47, 195–224.

Herrfahrdt-Pähle, E. and Pahl-Wostl, C. (2012). Continuity and change in social–ecological systems: the role of institutional resilience. *Ecology and Society*, 17, 8.

Hirota, M., Holmgren, M., van Nes, E. H., Scheffer, M. (2011). Global resilience of tropical forest and savanna to critical transitions. *Science*, 334, 232–235.

Holling, C. S. (2001). Understanding the complexity of economic, ecological, and social systems. *Ecosystems*, 4, 390–405.

Joughin, I., Smith, B. E., Medley, B. (2014). Marine ice sheet collapse potentially under way for the Thwaites glacier basin, west Antarctica. *Science*, 344, 735–738.

Knorr, W. and Schnitzler, K. G. (2006). Enhanced albedo feedback in North Africa from possible combined vegetation and soil-formation processes. *Climate Dynamics*, 26, 55–63.

Lade, S., Tavoni, A., Levin, S., Schlüter, M. (2013). Regime shifts in a social–ecological system. *Theoretical Ecology*, 6, 359–372.

MA (2003). *Ecosystems and Human Well-Being: A Framework for Assessment*. Washington, DC: Island Press.

MA (2005). *Ecosystems and Human Well-Being: Synthesis*. Washington, DC: Island Press.

Mack, M. C. and D'Antonio, C. M. (1998). Impacts of biological invasions on disturbance regimes. *Trends in Ecology and Evolution*, 13, 195–198.

Mård Karlsson, J., Bring, A., Peterson, G. D., Gordon, L. J., Destouni, G. (2011). Opportunities and limitations to detect climate-related regime shifts in inland Arctic ecosystems through eco-hydrological monitoring. *Environmental Research Letters*, 6, 014015.

Norberg, J. and Cumming, G. S., eds. (2008). *Complexity Theory for a Sustainable Future*. New York, NY: Columbia University Press.

Norström, A., Nyström, M., Lokrantz, J., Folke, C. (2009). Alternative states on coral reefs: beyond coral-macroalgal phase shifts. *Marine Ecology Progress Series*, 376, 295–306.

Nyström, M., Norström, A., Blenckner, T. et al. (2012). Confronting feedbacks of degraded marine ecosystems. *Ecosystems*, 15, 695–710.

Olsson, P., Folke, C., Hahn, T. (2004). Social–ecological transformation for ecosystem management: the development of adaptive co-management of a wetland landscape in southern Sweden. *Ecology and Society*, 9, 2.

Olsson, P., Gunderson, L. H., Carpenter, S. R. et al. (2006). Shooting the rapids: navigating transitions to adaptive governance of social–ecological systems. *Ecology and Society*, 11, 18.

Ostrom, E. (1990). *Governing the Commons: The Evolution of Institutions for Collective Action*. New York, NY: Cambridge University Press.

Otieno, V. O. and Anyah, R. O. (2012). Effects of land use changes on climate in the Greater Horn of Africa. *Climate Research*, 52, 77–95.

Raudsepp-Hearne, C., Peterson, G. D., Bennett, E. M. (2010). Ecosystem service bundles for analyzing tradeoffs in diverse landscapes. *Proceedings of the National Academy of Sciences USA*, 107, 5242–5247.

Rockström, J., Steffen, W. L., Noone, K. et al. (2009). A safe operating space for humanity. *Nature*, 461, 472–475.

Rogers, K. H. and Biggs, H. C. (1999). Integrating indicators, endpoint and value systems in the strategic management of the rivers of the Kruger National Park. *Freshwater Biology*, 41, 439–451.

Roux, D. J. and Foxcroft, L. C. (2011). The development and application of strategic adaptive management within South African National Parks. *Koedoe*, 53, 1–5.

Sankaran, M., Hanan, N. P., Scholes, R. J. et al. (2005). Determinants of woody cover in African savannas. *Nature*, 438, 846–849.

Scheffer, M. (2009). *Critical Transitions in Nature and Society*. Princeton, NJ: Princeton University Press.

Scheffer, M. and Carpenter, S. R. (2003). Catastrophic regime shifts in ecosystems: linking theory to observation. *Trends in Ecology and Evolution*, 18, 648–656.

Scheffer, M., Carpenter, S. R., Foley, J. A., Folke, C., Walker, B. H. (2001). Catastrophic shifts in ecosystems. *Nature*, 413, 591–596.

Scheffer, M., Westley, F., Brock, W. A. (2003). Slow responses of societies to new problems: causes and costs. *Ecosystems*, 6, 493–502.

Scheffer, M., Bascompte, J., Brock, W. A. et al. (2009). Early warning signals for critical transitions. *Nature*, 461, 53–59.

Schlüter, M., Leslie, H., Levin, S. (2009). Managing water-use trade-offs in a semi-arid river delta to sustain multiple ecosystem services: a modeling approach. *Ecological Research*, 24, 491–503.

Schlüter, M., Hirsch, D., Pahl-Wostl, C. (2010). Coping with change: responses of the Uzbek water management regime to socio-economic transition and global change. *Environmental Science and Policy*, 13, 620–636.

Schlüter, M. and Herrfahrdt-Pähle, E. (2011). Exploring resilience and transformability of a river basin in the face of socioeconomic and ecological crisis: an example from the Amudarya river basin, central Asia. *Ecology and Society*, 16, 32.

Sendzimir, J., Magnuszewski, P., Flachner, Z. et al. (2007). Assessing the resilience of a river management regime: informal learning in a shadow network in the Tisza river basin. *Ecology and Society*, 13, 11.

Slabbert, F. v. Z. (2006). *The Other Side of History: An Anecdotal Reflection on Political Transition in South Africa*. Johannesburg: Jonathan Ball.

Soranno, P. A., Cheruvelil, K. S., Bissell, E. G. et al. (2014). Cross-scale interactions: quantifying multi-scaled cause–effect relationships in macrosystems. *Frontiers in Ecology and the Environment*, 12, 65–73.

Staver, A. C., Archibald, S., Levin, S. (2011). The global extent and determinants of savanna and forest as alternative biome states. *Science*, 334, 230–232.

Steneck, R., Paris, C., Arnold, S. et al. (2009). Thinking and managing outside the box: coalescing connectivity networks to build region-wide resilience in coral reef ecosystems. *Coral Reefs*, 28, 367–378.

Suding, K. N., Gross, K. L., Houseman, G. R. (2004). Alternative states and positive feedbacks in restoration ecology. *Trends in Ecology and Evolution*, 19, 46–53.

Taylor, C. M., Lambin, E. F., Stephénne, N., Harding, R. J., Essery, R. L. H. (2002). The influence of land use change on climate in the Sahel. *Journal of Climate*, 15, 3615–3630.

Thrush, S. F., Hewitt, J. E., Dayton, P. K. et al. (2009). Forecasting the limits of resilience: integrating empirical research with theory. *Proceedings of the Royal Society of London B*, 276, 3209–3217.

Uchida, E., Xu, J., Rozelle, S. (2005). Grain for Green: cost-effectiveness and sustainability of China's conservation set-aside program. *Land Economics*, 81, 247–264.

Walker, B. H., Holling, C. S., Carpenter, S. R., Kinzig, A. (2004). Resilience, adaptability and tranformability in social–ecological systems. *Ecology and Society*, 9, 3.

Walker, B. H. and Meyer, J. A. (2004). Thresholds in ecological and socio-ecological systems: a developing database. *Ecology and Society*, 9, 3.

Walker, B. H. and Salt, D. (2006). *Resilience Thinking: Sustaining Ecosystems and People in a Changing World*. Washington, DC: Island Press.

Walker, B., Barrett, S., Polasky, S. et al. (2009). Looming global-scale failures and missing institutions. *Science*, 325, 1345–1346.

Walker, B. H., Carpenter, S. R., Rockström, J., Crépin, A-S., Peterson, G. D. (2012). 'Drivers', 'slow' variables, 'fast' variables, shocks, and resilience. *Ecology and Society*, 17, 30.

Ward, T. and Phillips, B., eds. (2008). *Seafood Ecolabelling: Principles and Practice*. Chichester: Wiley-Blackwell.

Young, O. R. (2010). Institutional dynamics: resilience, vulnerability and adaptation in environmental and resource regimes. *Global Environmental Change*, 20, 378–385.

6 Principle 4 – Foster complex adaptive systems thinking

Erin L. Bohensky, Louisa S. Evans, John M. Anderies, Duan Biggs and Christo Fabricius

SUMMARY

The social–ecological systems that provide ecosystem services to society can be viewed as complex adaptive systems (CAS), characterized by a high level of interconnectedness, potential for non-linear change, and inherent uncertainty and surprise. This chapter focuses on whether resilience of ecosystem services is enhanced by management based on what we refer to as 'CAS thinking', meaning a mental model for interpreting the world that recognizes these CAS properties. We present evidence that CAS thinking has contributed to change in management approaches in the Kruger National Park, Great Barrier Reef, Tisza river basin and Chile among other places. However, attempts to introduce CAS thinking may compromise resilience when complexity is not effectively communicated, when uncomfortable institutional change is required or when CAS thinking is not able to evolve with changing contexts or is not equitably shared. We suggest that CAS thinking can be fostered by the following: adopting a

Principles for Building Resilience: Sustaining Ecosystem Services in Social–Ecological Systems, eds R. Biggs, M. Schlüter and M. L. Schoon. Published by Cambridge University Press. © Cambridge University Press 2015.

systems framework; tolerating and embracing uncertainty; investigating critical thresholds and non-linearities; acknowledging epistemological pluralism; matching institutions to CAS processes; and recognizing barriers to cognitive change. Key questions for future research on this principle relate to communicating CAS thinking, the role of power, the importance of an organizational level of CAS thinking, and institutional barriers.

6.1 INTRODUCTION

The social–ecological systems (SES) that provide ecosystem services to society can be viewed as complex adaptive systems (CAS) (Walker et al. 2002; Levin et al. 2013). As discussed in Chapter 1, CAS are made up of many interacting components that are individually and collectively adaptive to change, enabling them to self-organize and evolve, and often yielding emergent properties at different scales (Norberg and Cumming 2008). Furthermore, CAS may shift between alternative regimes, often abruptly and irreversibly (Scheffer et al. 2001; Scheffer and Carpenter 2003), resulting in a system that looks, behaves and delivers ecosystem services in an entirely different way than before (P3 – Slow variables and feedbacks). These features make aspects of CAS highly uncertain, and therefore challenging to predict and control. Yet understanding and managing CAS is not inherently beyond our capabilities, and long traditions of research and practical experimentation have helped to reduce some important aspects of uncertainty (Lee 1993). However, to understand CAS is to accept that some facets of their uncertainty are irreducible due to unpredictability, incomplete knowledge or multiple knowledge frames (Levin 2003; Brugnach et al. 2008), and that this demands adaptive management approaches (Walters and Holling 1990; Lee 1993; P5 – Learning) that can account for these uncertainties.

The resilience of an SES is partly driven by decisions taken by actors – the resource users, managers and policy-makers – within the system. To understand SES therefore requires an understanding of how actors within the SES think (Jones et al. 2011). One way of understanding this is through the lens of mental models, or cognitive frameworks used to interpret and understand the world and decide on appropriate actions (Bower and Morrow 1990). Like worldviews, which describe a collection of ideas and theorems that allow one to construct a composite image of the world and understand one's experience and how one should act (Aerts *et al.* 2007; Vidal 2012), mental models are not only individually held but are also shared. This concept of shared or collective mental models (Abel *et al.* 1998) acknowledges the social aspects of individual cognition and decision-making (Jones *et al.* 2011). Furthermore, collective mental models and worldviews are culturally constructed, and function as schema (Quinn 2005) that describe and make meaning of understanding and experience among particular groups. They may be tacitly held as well as formalized and expressed through discourses, the negotiated ways through which a society apprehends the world (Dryzek 2005) through language, metaphors and power structures.

Mental models have been the subject of cognitive science and psychology research for more than 70 years (Craik 1943), but the application of mental models concepts in an SES context is relatively recent (Jones *et al.* 2011). While mental models are variously defined (Doyle and Ford 1998) there is general agreement about some key features:

- Mental models are the cognitive structures upon which reasoning, decision-making and behaviour are based. They are internal representations of external reality (Jones *et al.* 2011).
- As 'models' they describe relationships between system parts or phenomena, which distinguishes mental models from perceptions and attitudes, the focus of much behavioural research relevant to SES.
- Mental models can be thought of as 'habits of mind' (Rogers *et al.* 2013) that represent a pattern or cluster of cognitive behaviour that leads to action.
- Mental models are 'working models' and are always partial and limited views of the world. They are dynamic and context-dependent, and therefore often evolve over time. Thus, someone with a CAS mental model can have a more or less complex understanding of, and approaches to, problems in an SES, which can change in response to different prompts.

Understanding the different mental models that people have can help to delineate different conceptualizations of how a system works: the interactions between factors or components, the critical issues and the causal links (Lynam and Brown 2011). Importantly, current mental-models theory and approaches extend beyond simplistic 'information-deficit' models that assume knowledge influences awareness, which in turn influences behaviour (Kollmuss and Agyeman 2002). Mental-models thinking aligns with more sophisticated conceptualizations that posit multi-dimensional relationships between cognition (what we know), affect (what we feel) and behaviour (what we do) (e.g. Lorenzoni *et al.* 2007). Thus, a mental-models approach offers insight not only into how managers understand an SES but also how a manager might act and how he or she perceives the responsiveness of the SES to such management actions.

6.2 WHAT DO WE MEAN BY FOSTERING CAS THINKING?

This chapter is about how people, individually and collectively, *think about* and *make sense of* SES dynamics, and how this sense-making influences SES management in ways that enable society to benefit from a range of ecosystem services without undermining the SES that provide them. This way in which individual people and collective societies make sense of SES can be seen as a mental model or worldview. In particular, this chapter focuses on whether the resilience of ecosystem services is enhanced by management of SES based on CAS thinking. Management that views SES as CAS is thought to enhance the resilience of ecosystem services by emphasizing holistic (rather than reductionist) approaches, the management of multiple ecosystem services and trade-offs in an integrated way, managing at multiple temporal and spatial scales and the existence of lags and feedbacks in SES dynamics (P3 – Slow variables and feedbacks) (Holling and Meffe 1996; Pahl-Wostl 2009; Levin *et al.* 2013). A CAS approach also emphasizes the substantial uncertainties surrounding SES and, therefore, the need to continually learn and experiment (P5 – Learning), and adaptively manage uncertainty, disturbance and surprise rather than attempt to eliminate it (Gunderson et al. 2002; Chapin et al. 2009). Fostering CAS thinking therefore does not directly influence the resilience of ecosystem services but changes and adapts the cognitive foundations and paradigms that underpin management processes and decisions. That is, acknowledging that SES are based on a complex and unpredictable web of connections and interdependencies is the first step towards management actions that can foster resilience.

The characteristics of CAS thinking are perhaps easiest to grasp when they are contrasted with other mental models. Prevailing mental models of how ecosystems function have shifted over time (Table 6.1), in line with advances in education, science, technology and socio-cultural change. Religion, classical economics, politics and industrialization have each provided the intellectual foundations that through much of history have underpinned a quest to analyse, understand and control nature (van Doren 1992; Wallace et al. 1996). By controlling nature, it was believed that uncertainty could be reduced and outcomes predicted, establishing a basis for agricultural, industrial and social development (Holling et al. 2002). Mental models focused on linearity, determinism and the primacy of humans over nature remain deeply entrenched in the norms of business, academia and policy (Ludwig 2001) and are the foundation of highly mechanized resource management systems such as plantation forestry, monoculture farming and large-scale commercial fisheries (Holling and Meffe 1996). Until relatively recently, ecologists advocated an equilibrium worldview (Holling et al. 2002), which guided resource management agencies and broader society's thinking about SES. With time, it became evident that the view of nature 'in balance' and management through stabilization often led to decline in ecosystem services over the longer term.

In this chapter, we define CAS thinking as a mental model or worldview that views SES as CAS and appreciates the resulting implications for management. Key CAS properties in this regard include: a high level of interconnectedness; potential for non-linear change; inherent, and to some extent irreducible, uncertainty (which can lead

Table 6.1 *Views of ecosystems have shifted over time towards recognition of CAS properties (based on Schlüter et al. 2012)*

Conventional view of ecosystems	SES as CAS
System dynamics are linear and monotonic	System dynamics exhibit thresholds, hysteresis
Uncertainty is largely ignored: probability distributions for key drivers and decision variables are treated as known	Complexity and uncertainty of SES are explicitly considered: probability distributions for key drivers and decision variables are highly uncertain, as are outcomes; some uncertainties are irreducible
Individual elements can be treated in isolation	Complex systems of interacting entities at micro-scale from which macro-scale patterns emerge
Focus on impact of human behaviour on resource	Incorporate reflexive response of humans to forecasts and interventions
Actors are rational and have full information and computational capacity	Actors have imperfect knowledge, are boundedly rational or follow more complex decision patterns
Management objectives are based on simple reference points	Management involves complex trade-offs
Managed by a command-and-control approach, management of resource stocks and condition, not wider ecosystem	Managed for resilience and adaptive capacity, management of stabilizing and amplifying feedbacks within a broader context

to surprise); and a multiplicity of perspectives within SES. Rather than attempt to reduce uncertainty and surprise, CAS thinking embraces these as opportunities for positive motivational change (Janssen 2002; Cilliers *et al.* 2013). Other fields, such as the health-care industry, have recognized this positive impact of CAS thinking, whereby 'the attitude toward surprises can become one of approach and exploration rather than avoidance and defense' (McDaniel *et al.* 2003, p. 267). A CAS worldview acknowledges that attempts to smooth the variable rhythms of SES to achieve management objectives often result in unintended consequences. Today, SES management increasingly recognizes that one of the key challenges facing policy-makers, scholars and practitioners is to understand and anticipate the dynamic behaviour of a CAS that result in 'wicked problems' with neither a definitive formulation nor clear solutions (Ludwig 2001).

CAS thinking is not new. Aspects of CAS understanding and approaches are evident in some of the longstanding practices of small-scale farmers (Ishizawa 2006), traditional resource users (Moller et al. 2004) and nomadic herders (Fernandez-Gimez 2000). They are integral to traditional ecological knowledge systems (Berkes et al. 2000) and holistic frameworks to describe and support relationships between people and the environment (Salmón 2000; Turner et al. 2000; Walsh et al. 2013). CAS mental models are also present in some 'mainstream' natural resource management agencies that adopt adaptive management and co-management approaches. In these contexts, the process of development of the collective CAS mental model is important, as it may be critical for building mutual understanding amongst stakeholders (Abel et al. 1998; Biggs et al. 2011a; Jones et al. 2011) (P5 – Learning; P6 – Participation).

6.3 HOW DOES CAS THINKING ENHANCE THE RESILIENCE OF ECOSYSTEM SERVICES?

Much of what we assume about how CAS thinking can enhance resilience comes from cases where conventional resource management – lacking an appreciation of how CAS function – has resulted in a loss of SES resilience. A litany of examples suggest that management practices that optimize the provision of a narrow set of ecosystem services on the basis of linear, reductionist worldviews of ecosystems inadvertently undermine the ability of these systems to continue producing ecosystem services in the face of disturbance and change. The pervasiveness of ecosystem modification in the USA for many decades led Holling and Meffe (1996) to describe a 'pathology of resource management' entailing practices such as river stabilization, fire suppression and monocultural farming to the point of system collapse. Such a pathology also characterizes the Gariep basin in South Africa (Bohensky and Lynam 2005), the Western Australia wheat belt (Allison and Hobbes 2004) and the Goulburn–Broken Catchment (Walker and Salt 2006). Each SES was narrowly managed to maximize agriculture-based economic production in the short term but this management approach ignored the underlying capacity of the system to produce ecosystem services. As a consequence groundwater tables were drawn down, land was degraded and rivers were transformed and polluted. Agriculture, as the backbone of these regional economies, contributed to well-being and underpinned social development but, because it was unsustainable, it was ultimately at great ecological and social expense. Similarly, widespread mismanagement of fisheries (Mahon et al. 2008) and forests (Agrawal 2005) is partly attributed to forms of management based on technical, reductionist and one-size-fits-all approaches. This management style was not limited to production systems; protected areas too were managed as 'islands' with narrow functions of strict wildlife preservation or recreation, without considering a broader range of beneficiaries or landscape connectivity within and beyond park borders (Cundill and Rodela 2012). These cases suggest that an alternative management style based on a worldview that recognizes CAS properties may result in more resilient ecosystem services in the long term, because it considers consequences at a system level, across time, space and actors.

Though generally less visible than these management 'failures', cases exist where CAS thinking has contributed to improved social–ecological outcomes through resilient ecosystem services. Examples of transformations in ecosystem management suggest that changes in underlying mental models that acknowledge the characteristics of SES as CAS can lead to improvements in the resilience of ecosystem services. One example is the large-scale rezoning of Australia's Great Barrier Reef (Box 6.1), driven by increased recognition of the importance of connectivity, non-linear change and mult-iscale interactions in coral reef systems (Olsson

BOX 6.1 Complex enough? CAS thinking and the Great Barrier Reef

Changes in the way the Great Barrier Reef has been managed during the past several decades illustrate the evolution of CAS thinking, and its varied success in bringing about management change. One of the seven natural wonders of the world, the reef has long been an icon of conservation concern, and as concern grew over pressures on the reef so did the recognition that the cognitive basis of management needed to change. In 1975, the reef's designation as a marine park was a first step towards implementing precautionary and adaptive management: it prohibited mining on the reef and established a network of no-entry, no-take and multi-use zones (Fig. 6.1a). Nevertheless, pressures on the reef continued to increase and, in 1994, the Great Barrier Reef Marine Park Authority initiated a strategic process of organizational and institutional change for the region to 'Keep it Great' (GBRMPA 1994, p. 1). The authority was restructured around core strategic goals including resilient ecosystems (Fig. 6.1b).

In 1999, a systematic conservation planning approach called the Representative Areas Program (RAP) was initiated (Day 2002). This process involved developing a deep, adaptive understanding of the reef SES as a CAS. For instance, by the mid 1990s scientists had observed catastrophic phase shifts in coral reef systems in other parts of the world (Hughes 1994). This was followed by two notable disturbance events on the Great Barrier Reef: Tropical Cyclone Justin in March 1997 (Tobin et al. 2010) and extensive bleaching of corals in the 1997–1998 El Niño oscillation (Wilkinson 2004). These occurrences emphasized the vulnerability of the reef – previously viewed as a pristine habitat – due to high interconnectedness and non-linear change. To investigate further, scientists and managers undertook a large-scale experiment to analyse the effectiveness of the current zoning plan (Mapstone et al. 2004; Hughes et al. 2007). This involved the testing of opening and closure regimes on the reef, and the examination of the role of herbivores in preventing and reversing phase shifts from coral to algal dominance. By the late 1990s there was broad scientific and management consensus around the need to increase the extent of no-take zones on the reef to ensure resilient provision of diverse ecosystem services. In order to legitimately implement a new zoning

BOX 6.1 **Continued**

(a)

(b)

FIG. 6.1 (a) The management of the Great Barrier Reef illustrates how aspects of CAS thinking have shaped the evolution of this iconic SES, but also highlights challenges encountered by managers attempting to operationalize this principle in a multi-scale, multi-stakeholder context. (b) Resilient ecosystems are a core strategic goal around which the reef's primary management agency, the Great Barrier Reef Marine Park Authority, is structured. Photo credits: Erin Bohensky, CSIRO.

BOX 6.1 **Continued**

plan the authority then undertook an extensive process of stakeholder engagement and broader public awareness (Olsson *et al.* 2008). The new plan came into effect in 2004. It emphasizes the representation of key bioregions, the connectivity between habitats and species populations, and uncertainty. Consistent monitoring and research has supported the scientific argument for increasing the area of no-take zones from 4% to 33% to improve the biodiversity and resilience of the reef (McCook *et al.* 2010).

CAS thinking is also evident in the management approach to water-quality pollution from farming in the catchment; however, as this pollution originates outside the marine park boundaries and has diffuse sources, another set of institutions is required to manage water quality, which has achieved considerable reduction in agricultural runoff (Brodie and Waterhouse 2012; Brodie 2014). Again, reef managers recognized that interactions between threats could lead to irreversible change, and implied engagement with multiple stakeholder groups. Scenario planning has been used to support such engagement around CAS thinking, particularly to explore how different climate-change trajectories might play out for the reef (Bohensky *et al.* 2011; Evans *et al.* 2013; Fig. 6.2). However, by some estimations the greatest threat to the reef is currently posed by major port expansions being planned for the export of coal and coal seam gas (Brodie 2014). As the problem domain for the reef's managers expands to involve increasingly intractable, cross-scale issues with a set of stakeholders much removed from the impacts on the reef, it appears that CAS thinking is not expanding accordingly or being applied quickly enough (Brodie and Waterhouse 2012). The current situation raises the critical question of whether CAS thinking among the agencies responsible for the reef is sufficiently complex, and is able to evolve and address the broader-scale drivers affecting the system. It raises the question of whether, as a consequence, the CAS thinking that has guided past management can enhance resilience of all ecosystem services provided by the system, or whether trade-offs will inevitably be required in the multi-use, multi-stakeholder, multi-scale context in which the reef is situated, for instance between catchment ecosystem services and coastal ecosystem services, and

BOX 6.1 **Continued**

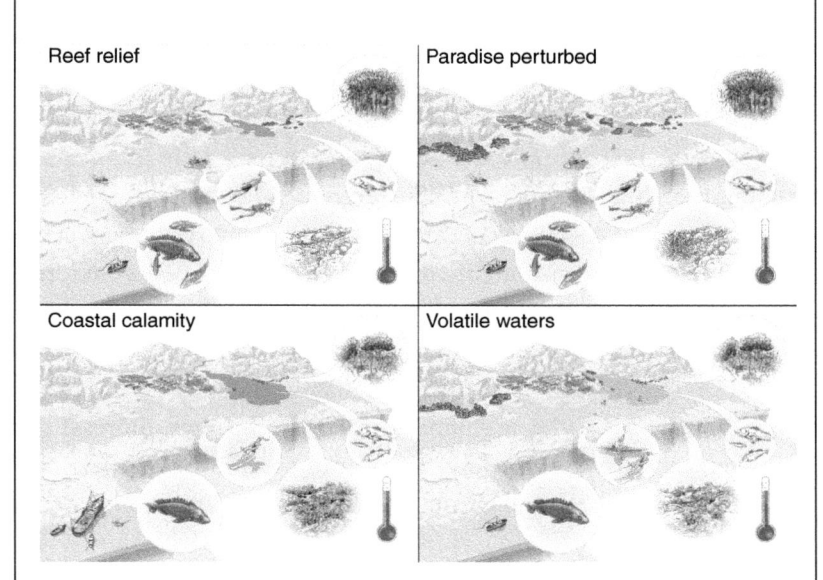

Reef relief

Paradise perturbed

Coastal calamity

Volatile waters

FIG. 6.2 Alternative future scenarios for the Great Barrier Reef (Evans et al. 2013). Scenario planning is an approach based on CAS thinking, in which participants identify key uncertainties, thresholds and non-linearities in the system.

ultimately between ecosystem services and economic growth. Does this point to the need for a CAS understanding at the broader political decision-making scales that influence outcomes for the reef, essentially redefining the boundaries of the CAS in question?

et al. 2008). The aim of the rezoning was to enact spatial restrictions on fishing and other uses to enhance the resilience of ecosystem functions to a range of perturbations including temperature anomalies and cyclones. This approach addressed CAS properties in two ways: by maintaining connectivity within the reef system and increasing the system's capacity to absorb large disturbance; and importantly, by recognizing the values and perspectives of different reef users. Ecological monitoring and experimentation indicated that the reef's marine ecosystems were more resilient to climate-change impacts where herbivorous fish assemblages are intact, thus improving the reef's ability to provide a diversity of ecosystem services (McCook et al. 2010). More recently, management is taking a more expansive view of the roles of humans in the reef system, for example by supporting a long-term monitoring programme that considers human drivers (Marshall et al. 2013). Despite this, CAS thinking within the primary management agency may be insufficient to address some of the external pressures that originate outside the marine park's boundaries, such as climate change and industrial coastal development (Bohensky et al. 2011). Thus, while CAS thinking has influenced policy in the Great Barrier Reef, the problem domain has become increasingly complex, as drivers become more multi-scale in nature and stakeholder views more factious (Brodie and Waterhouse 2012; Brodie 2014).

In South Africa's Kruger National Park, increased emphasis on the value of variation in maintaining biodiversity has led its managers, South African National Parks (SANParks), to move away from objectives that aim to keep ecosystem conditions, such as elephant populations and fire frequencies, fixed at optimal levels (Biggs et al. 2011b; Cundill and Rodela 2012). Instead, elephant numbers and fires are now allowed to fluctuate between specified boundaries (Biggs and Rogers 2003). 'Thresholds of potential concern' are developed to identify and monitor triggers of change and anticipate regime shifts, functioning as 'amber lights' that signal to managers that a component of the system (e.g. elephant numbers) is approaching a critical point. Thresholds of potential concern and strategic adaptive management are credited with making Kruger a functional adaptive management site that supports a range of ecosystem services including a greater variation in faunal diversity, fire regimes, vegetation and river flows (Biggs and Rogers 2003). This shift has reduced the human investment needed to manage ecosystems and has increased the variety of ecosystem and habitat types, as well as the opportunities for specialist species that support particular ecosystem services. SANParks has also recognized the need to incorporate human preferences, behaviour and institutional responses more explicitly into the thresholds of potential concern concept (Biggs *et al.* 2011b). However, as in the Great Barrier Reef case, SANParks' approach is unable to entirely mitigate impacts on biodiversity that originate beyond its borders, such as extraction from rivers upstream.

In Europe, water-management bodies are embracing CAS thinking. Projects such as NeWater (New methods for adaptive Water management under uncertainty) sought to improve the scientific foundations of adaptive and integrated water-resource management and support transitions from historical management regimes (Pahl-Wostl *et al.* 2009). For example, in Hungary, NeWater studied how a shadow network of scientists and local activists in the internationally shared Tisza river basin evolved over several decades around a set of dialogues about alternative river management in response to extreme flooding, water-quality decline and lost productivity (Sendzimir *et al.* 2008). Using participatory system-dynamics modelling tools in its dialogues to develop a CAS understanding and incorporate multiple views into river-management practices, the shadow network sought to understand what factors have obstructed or enabled transformation of the current river-management regime from one focused on transport and flood mitigation to one able to maintain biodiversity and land-management practices. In this way, a participatory forum (P6 – Participation) was key to the development of a shared CAS worldview. These dialogues also learned from the experiences of Germany and the Netherlands, where a CAS approach initiated a new governance paradigm termed 'living with the river', which encourages the reallocation of land for floodplains, to allow water to ebb and flow across space and time (Sendzimir *et al.* 2008).

Despite the above examples that demonstrate that CAS thinking contributes to ecosystem-service resilience, there is scant evidence that enhanced resilience can be directly attributed to CAS mental models. This is in part due to the indirect influence of CAS thinking on management and, subsequently, changes in resilience. That is, it must be demonstrated first that CAS thinking exists among the relevant actors, and second that it influences current management practices and subsequently effects a positive change in resilience. Much of the science underpinning contemporary CAS thinking only emerged in the late 1970s, and began guiding management even more recently. In many cases it is too early to assess the extent to which CAS thinking is guiding management or catalysing change. Some evidence shows that CAS thinking can trigger a change in management approaches but has not yet had demonstrable effects on the resilience of ecosystem services, or only limited change in some ecosystem services. Such an outcome seems to apply in the Great Barrier Reef and Kruger cases, where broader-scale drivers are beyond the influence of the key agency. In other cases a CAS approach is helping to build shared understanding and, by incorporating multiple perspectives, is creating social capital, such as in the Tisza river basin through the shadow network dialogues, but is yet to lead to management changes (Sendzimir et al. 2008).

6.4 UNDER WHAT CONDITIONS MAY RESILIENCE OF ECOSYSTEM SERVICES BE COMPROMISED?

While CAS thinking in itself may not compromise resilience, *attempts to foster* CAS thinking may compromise resilience in SES. For scientists and managers, communicating and applying the concepts of CAS in ways that do not create a sense of bewilderment and paralysis remains a key challenge in practical ecosystem management settings (Cilliers *et al.* 2013). Managers may be motivated by political expediency, and tried and tested 'simple' approaches may appear less risky than those that are unfamiliar, run against the grain of agency practice and threaten the status quo (Gunderson *et al.* 2002). Moreover, 'complexity' can be interpreted in ways which do not reflect an appreciation of the fundamental properties of CAS. For example, complexity sometimes implies all dimensions of a system that are not yet understood (Holling 2001).

When combined with reductionist views about the need to eliminate uncertainty before taking action, such interpretations may lead managers to invest heavily in monitoring and data collection for variables and relationships thought to be important, rather than encourage the use of adaptive approaches that allow for experimentation and the probing of boundaries as a mechanism to address uncertainty (Walters and Holling 1990). In these situations, management styles and problems that erode resilience may persist, sometimes amid the belief that complexity is being addressed.

Second, attempts to foster CAS thinking may also compromise resilience because a CAS framework implies a more integrated approach that is difficult to address across governance units that are often separate (e.g. departments of water and land). Successful integration seems to require significant investment in multi-agency coordination and sometimes new institutional arrangements that enable CAS thinking and practice to thrive (Bohensky and Lynam 2005). In addition, a CAS approach often implies a change in a management paradigm from a focus on causality and control within short timeframes, to a focus on coping with change and uncertainty over longer timescales. Such a management shift may be difficult to operationalize in contexts that focus on accountability and meeting targets (Pahl-Wostl 2009). Such changes may threaten the incentive structures that agents have learned to navigate, creating new uncertainty and anxiety. These challenges may be long-enduring (e.g. inequitable distribution of costs and benefits across society) and ultimately detrimental to ecosystem-service resilience. Transitions to new management paradigms may also involve temporary, albeit uncomfortable, 'excursions into lowered resilience to cross to another ... stability domain' (Sendzimir *et al.* 2007, p. 602). For instance, Sendzimir *et al.* (2007) describe how the transition from intensive to organic agriculture in the Tisza river basin involved a seven-year lag before financial benefits were realized.

Third, attempts to foster CAS thinking can compromise resilience when a CAS mental model is deliberately or inadvertently treated as static, intended to assist transition to a new management paradigm, which is seen as the end point. The implications of this are that continued knowledge-building, experimentation and adaptation are not pursued. Gelcich *et al.* (2010) observed such a situation in Chile following a transition to a national benthic fisheries policy, the Management and Exploitation Areas for Benthic Resources (MEABR). Though the new policy – by redefining rights to fish for the socially and economically important artisanal fishing sector – was lauded as 'transformative', avenues for continued experimentation and social learning were not maintained, thereby limiting the potential for future adaptations or transformations. A CAS worldview did not continue to evolve alongside the ever-changing SES, highlighting the importance of a supportive institutional environment for fostering CAS thinking. The Chilean case is not unique; such an outcome has also been reported in the Tisza river basin (Sendzimir *et al.* 2010).

Finally, ineffective attempts to introduce CAS thinking can erode the resilience of particular agents or groups within the system if CAS mental models are not widely shared, and fail to promote distributive justice; that is, CAS thinking may result in the same trade-offs and inequities as those experienced under more conventional management systems, or even create new trade-offs and inequities, all while being hailed as a CAS approach. These issues are discussed more in Chapter 2.

6.5 HOW CAN CAS THINKING BE OPERATIONALIZED AND APPLIED?

CAS thinking can represent system complexity, and can be developed, fostered and applied in different ways (Table 6.2). As highlighted earlier in the chapter, CAS worldviews have been present in many traditional societies who are highly dependent on ecosystem services for their livelihoods. They have also been purposefully fostered in some contemporary governance approaches. In both cases it appears that the context and process of learning matter (P5 – Learning). Among some traditional societies, variability in environmental conditions and

Table 6.2 *Applications of CAS thinking discussed in this chapter*

Case	Problem description and approach	Further reading
Great Barrier Reef (Australia)	Management of the Great Barrier Reef has evolved from a focus on species to broader ecosystem-based management, and encompasses ideas of building resilience to multiple perturbations and adaptive management. Scenario planning involving stakeholders has highlighted the multi-scale nature of drivers of change and responses.	Olsson *et al.* 2008; McCook *et al.* 2010; Bohensky *et al.* 2011; Evans *et al.* 2013
Kruger National Park (South Africa)	Thresholds of potential concern are linked to clear, nested objectives to define measurable variables, to allow for system variability in fire, elephant populations, vegetation and river flows, for example. More recent thinking includes incorporating social values and preferences and how changes in these can be incorporated into Kruger's strategic adaptive management system.	Biggs and Rogers 2003; Biggs *et al.* 2011b; Van Wilgen and Biggs 2011
Tisza river basin (Hungary)	In parallel with political change, a 'shadow network' of government agents, local activists and scientists engaged in dialogue to explore how to transition from conventional to more adaptive river management based on a paradigm of 'living with the river' and ensuring the river basin supports a range of ecosystem services on which biodiversity and agriculture rely. System-dynamics modelling tools were used to explore barriers and bridges to transformation of the river management regime and to build capacity for participatory science and learning.	Sendzimir *et al.* 2007, 2008, 2010

Table 6.2 (*Cont.*)

Case	Problem description and approach	Further reading
Benthic fisheries management (Chile)	Fisheries management in Chile has undergone a transformation following stock depletion, and now emphasizes scientific knowledge of the ecology and resilience of targeted species and their role in ecosystem dynamics. Demonstration-scale experimental trials have identified new management pathways, and improved cooperation among scientists and fishers, by integrating knowledge and establishing trust. Political turbulence and resource stock collapse provided a window of opportunity that triggered the transformation, supported by new, enabling legislation that allocates user rights and responsibilities to fisher collectives. However, current discussion in Chile centres on the rigidity of the new legislation, which may poise it to fail because it undermines adaptation to ongoing change.	Gelcich *et al.* 2010

supplies of ecosystem services, and the long-term perspectives captured in knowledge systems passed from generation to generation, have fostered CAS thinking (Berkes *et al.* 2000). In contemporary cases, the alternative paradigms of linked SES, resilience and complexity thinking have converged in response to evidence that linear mental models were not adequately explaining system dynamics or securing sustainable production of ecosystem services (Berkes and Folke 1998). These paradigms suggest that fostering CAS thinking requires long timeframes, a multi-scale approach and explicit attention to the key properties of CAS including: a high level of interconnectedness; potential for non-linear change; uncertainty; and a multiplicity of perspectives within a system.

The examples and analysis above highlight some general guidelines for operationalizing and applying CAS thinking and approaches, primarily at the collective level:

- **Develop an uncertainty-tolerant culture**. CAS thinking embodies a broad acceptance of uncertainty, variability and change, which conventional resource-management paradigms avoid. Scenario planning has been remarkably effective as an approach to illuminate and embrace uncertainty in SES and develop robust responses, all while fostering CAS thinking (Biggs *et al.* 2010). Scenario planning is a structured process of exploring and evaluating future complexity and uncertainty by identifying alternative development pathways, assessing unintended consequences of decisions and even recognizing opportunities. It has proven powerful in a wide range of SES settings, including tropical forest communities, lakeshore management in the United States, and in the navigation of political change in South Africa (Wollenberg *et al.* 2000; Peterson *et al.* 2003; Tompkins *et al.* 2008). Accepting change and uncertainty in SES dynamics is also part of adaptive management and monitoring approaches (Lindenmayer and Likens 2009). Case studies suggest that a change in the cultural attitude towards uncertainty that enables CAS thinking often evolves from long-term monitoring and experimentation articulated through both scientific and local knowledge systems (Olsson *et al.* 2008; Gelcich *et al.* 2010).
- **Start with a systems framework**. A framework can help people to articulate and organize their thinking about interconnected concepts and

relationships; many traditional societies have used systems-based frameworks over generations, and continue to do so where traditional practice remains strong (Holmes and Janpijinpa 2013). Cilliers *et al.* (2013) argue that it is only possible to have knowledge of a CAS in terms of a certain framework. Frameworks based on elements of CAS thinking include the Millennium Ecosystem Assessment (MA 2005) with its emphasis on multiple scales and knowledge systems, the SES Diagnosis Framework (Ostrom 2007) to foster widespread understanding of resource-use systems as coupled and dynamic SES and the Management Transition Framework (Sendzimir *et al.* 2010) used to analyse regime change; while the Resilience Workbooks (Resilience Alliance 2010) offer guidance on how to apply these frameworks in practice. In some cases, those wishing to collaboratively build CAS thinking might prefer to build a systems model or mind map from the ground up.

- **Acknowledge epistemological pluralism as a source of complexity**. As we noted at the beginning of this chapter, some facets of uncertainty in SES arise from multiple knowledge frames: individuals represent diverse epistemologies or knowledge systems, social values and preferences. Reflecting our discussion in Section 6.4 and the issues of power and representation (Chapter 2), CAS thinking must acknowledge the knowledge traditions of diverse stakeholders if the aim is to build resilient ecosystem services in the long term. Therefore, fostering CAS thinking generally needs to be grounded in a collaborative knowledge-building process, involving managers, scientists and resource users (Fig. 6.3) Participatory methods to achieve this include scenario planning, as noted above, and approaches discussed in other chapters (P5 – Learning; P6 – Participation). However, while collective CAS thinking often emerges in social learning and stakeholder-engagement processes, it is often not the primary goal, and how these processes contribute to developing CAS thinking needs to be better understood.
- **Investigate critical thresholds and non-linearities**. Not all change processes in SES are characterized by discontinuities or thresholds. However, where non-linear change does occur it has important implications for managers and resource users because of the high social and ecological costs of surprise events and the prospect of hysteresis – effective irreversibility. Central to fostering CAS thinking is therefore to at least consider and explore system boundaries and thresholds. The thresholds of potential concern approach,

FIG. 6.3 Engaging multiple stakeholders and knowledge systems is a key component of fostering CAS thinking in practice. (a) Participatory mapping of cultural ecosystem services in Milne Bay, Papua New Guinea (Bohensky et al. 2009). (b) Discussing drivers of change as part of a scenario planning workshop on Erub Island in the Torres Strait, Australia. Photo credits: Erin Bohensky, CSIRO.

for example, is used by managers in the Kruger National Park to build a CAS understanding to manage fire regimes and elephant populations within a variable range that accounts for 'natural' uncertainty (Biggs and Rogers 2003; Biggs *et al.* 2011b; Van Wilgen and Biggs 2011). Similarly, fishers and managers in the Pacific and West Africa have trialled participatory threshold dashboards that account for ecological and social thresholds, producing stakeholder-defined and socially-relevant metrics to learn about, monitor and manage their small-scale fisheries (Béné *et al.* 2011; Schwarz *et al.* 2011).

- **Match institutions to CAS processes**. In practice it appears that institutional change at some level may be needed to foster, and sustain the evolution of, CAS thinking at appropriate scales. Though opportunities to revamp existing institutions only arise periodically, CAS thinking can be fostered through the design of research and governance approaches such as spatial management (e.g. the Kruger National Park, Great Barrier Reef and Chilean benthic fisheries) and the 'living with the river' floodplain management paradigm in Europe. Catchment management agencies are another example of integrated governance capable of dealing with system processes across multiple interconnected ecosystem services, as opposed to historical management on a resource-by-resource basis, and thus may be more amenable to CAS thinking. It must also be remembered that CAS often resist being clearly bounded (Cilliers *et al.* 2013), and external drivers of change need to be explicitly accounted for, for example by framing coastal SES as having 'porous' system boundaries at the land–sea interface. In some situations institutional change will be beyond the agency of actors in the system, but cross-scale networks can help to foster CAS thinking about processes 'outside' the SES (P7 – Polycentricity).

- **Recognize the many barriers to cognitive change**. Human understanding is dynamic, changing over time through experience and learning (Jones *et al.* 2011). Research in psychology suggests that deliberately changing mental models, as distinct from updating or adding to them, implies the unknown – unknown risks and requirements for time, energy, skills and knowledge (Costa and Kallick 1995). As such, individuals or groups invested in a particular *modus operandi* may believe they can improve outcomes by simply doing things better, rather than doing things differently. Those benefiting from existing regimes of ecosystem management may, therefore, resist adopting CAS thinking and accepting its implications for the status quo.

6.6 KEY RESEARCH AND APPLICATION GAPS

We have presented some empirical evidence to suggest that fostering CAS thinking can facilitate the management of SES to enhance the resilient provision of ecosystem services, mainly through the choice of management approaches that recognize interconnectedness, non-linear change, uncertainty and multiple perspectives. Much of this evidence comes from examples in which a lack of CAS thinking has eroded the resilience of ecosystem services. It remains unclear to what extent CAS thinking can be credited for the adoption of management approaches to enhance resilience of ecosystem services. Two problems help explain this: (i) CAS thinking can take many forms, and it is not always clear – for those not involved in the management – what constitutes CAS thinking; (ii) CAS thinking is only one of many interacting components, types and scales of decision-making in an SES, making its contribution to resilience difficult to clarify.

The above evidence points to the following gaps in our current appreciation of how fostering CAS thinking is likely to enhance the resilience of ecosystem services, and how it can be applied in practice in a range of different contexts:

- How do we communicate complexity so that CAS thinking can be fostered and mobilized into action? To avoid bewilderment and gridlock that may stem from a perception of overwhelming complexity, participatory processes such as scenario planning have shown themselves to be helpful tools. Yet a key research gap lies in understanding how such processes can be most effective (P6 – Participation) in communicating complex concepts so that understanding and mental models can be shifted (Étienne et al. 2008; Bohensky et al. 2011; Cundill et al. 2012) and not simply lead to 'endless learning' (Fabricius and Cundill 2014). Further research can help identify which participatory processes best strengthen CAS thinking among managers, noting that many managers already have a long-evolved understanding of systems as CAS but expressed more often through the language of practice.
- How does power influence the use of a CAS approach? Whose understanding of CAS matters and how can conflicting views be reconciled?

These questions underscore that decision-making about how to apply CAS thinking (i.e. the direction and intent of institutional change and which ecosystem service should be made resilient to which disturbance events) is a political rather than purely academic exercise (see Chapter 2), and raises questions sometimes seen as absent from the resilience literature (Nadasdy 2007).

- There is a need to understand the relative importance of fostering CAS thinking at individual as opposed to collective (social and organizational) levels. Research has shown the importance of influential individuals in catalysing SES change (Olsson *et al.* 2006), but is CAS thinking among their constituents at the coalface equally if not more critical? We suggest there is a role for research on how a CAS framework might be extended to incorporate normative issues related to the distribution of power within an SES. In this context, and following from the first two questions, are there participatory and decision-making processes for the co-construction of a CAS understanding that are more likely to lead to CAS-informed decisions than others (e.g. Barnaud *et al.* 2008; Barnaud *et al.* 2010)?

- How can institutional barriers to CAS thinking and path dependency be overcome? Institutional design, including legal structures and accounting and auditing systems, stem from a worldview based on reductionist thinking, and a command-and-control approach to management (Ebbesson 2010). Even when mental models shift, the artefacts of previous administration systems sometimes linger as historical legacies. Thus, this problem pervades even those organizations that are considered world-leaders in the institutionalization of CAS thinking in management such as SANParks (Biggs *et al.* 2011a). A key research gap is therefore to understand which aspects of CAS thinking can be institutionalized and implemented within the current legal and auditing structures (Ebbesson 2010).

REFERENCES

Abel, N., Ross, H., Walker, P. (1998). Mental models in rangeland research, communication and management. *Rangeland Journal*, 20, 77–91.

Aerts, D., Apostel, L., De Moor, B. *et al.* (2007). *World Views. From fragmentation to Integration. Internet Edition 2007*. Originally published in 1994 by VUB Press, Brussels. Internet edition by Clément Vidal and Alexander RieglerVUB Press, Brussels.

Agrawal, A. (2005). *Environmentality: Technologies of Government and the Making of Subjects.* Durham, NC: Duke University Press.

Allison, H. E. and Hobbs, R. J. (2004). Resilience, adaptive capacity, and the 'Lock-in Trap' of the Western Australian agricultural region. *Ecology and Society*, 9, 3.

Barnaud, C., Bousquet, F., Trebuil, G. (2008). Multi-agent simulations to explore rules for rural credit in a highland farming community of northern Thailand. *Ecological Economics*, 66, 615–627.

Barnaud, C., van Paassen, A., Trébuil, G., Promburom, T., Bousquet F. (2010). Dealing with power games in a companion modelling process: lessons from community water management in Thailand highlands. *Journal of Agricultural Education and Extension*, 16, 55–74.

Béné, C., Evans, L., Mills, D. et al. (2011). Testing resilience thinking in a poverty context: experience from the Niger river basin. *Global Environmental Change*, 12, 1173–1184.

Berkes, F. and Folke, C., eds. (1998). *Linking Social and Ecological Systems.* Cambridge: Cambridge University Press.

Berkes, F., Colding, J., Folke, C. (2000). Rediscovery of traditional ecological knowledge as adaptive management. *Traditional Ecological Knowledge*, 10, 1251–1262.

Biggs, H. C. and Rogers, K. H. (2003). An adaptive system to link science, monitoring and management in practice. In *The Kruger Experience: Ecology and Management of Savanna Heterogeneity.* Washington, DC: Island Press, pp. 59–80.

Biggs, R., Diebel, M. W., Gilroy, D. et al. (2010). Preparing for the future: teaching scenario planning at the graduate level. *Frontiers in Ecology and the Environment*, 8, 267–273.

Biggs D., Abel N., Knight A. T. et al. (2011a). The implementation crisis in conservation planning: could 'mental models' help? *Conservation Letters*, 4, 169–183.

Biggs, H., Ferreira, S., Freitag-Ronaldson, S., Grant-Biggs, R. (2011b). Taking stock after a decade: does the thresholds of potential concern concept need a socio-ecological revamp? *Koedoe*, 53, 1002.

Bohensky, E. and Lynam, T. (2005). Evaluating responses in complex adaptive systems: insights on water management from the Southern African Millennium Ecosystem Assessment (SAfMA). *Ecology and Society*, 10, 119.

Bohensky, E. L., Butler, J., Mitchell, D. (2009). Scenarios as models for knowledge integration: ecotourism futures in Milne Bay, Papua New Guinea. *MODSIM 2009 International Congress on Modelling and Simulation.* Modelling and Simulation Society of Australia and New Zealand, July 2009.

Bohensky, E., Butler, J., Costanza, R. et al. (2011). Future makers or future takers? A scenario analysis of climate change and the Great Barrier Reef. *Global Environmental Change*, 21, 876–893.

Bower, G. H and Morrow, D. G. (1990). Mental models in narrative comprehension. *Science*, 247, 44–48.

Brodie, J. and Waterhouse, J. (2012). A critical review of environmental management of the 'not so Great' Barrier Reef. *Estuarine, Coastal and Shelf Science*, 104, 1–22.

Brodie, J. (2014). Dredging the Great Barrier Reef: use and misuse of science. *Estuarine, Coastal and Shelf Science*, 142, 1–3.

Brugnach, M., Dewulf, A., Pahl-Wostl, C., Taillieu, T. (2008). Toward a relational concept of uncertainty: about knowing too little, knowing too differently, and accepting not to know. *Ecology and Society*, 13, 30.

Chapin, F. S., Kofinas, G. P., Folke, C., eds. (2009). *Principles of Ecosystem Stewardship: Resilience-Based Natural Resource Management in a Changing World*. New York, NY: Springer.

Cilliers, P., Biggs, H. C., Blignaut, S. et al. (2013). Complexity, modeling, and natural resource management. *Ecology and Society*, 18, 1.

Costa, A. L. and Kallick, B. O., eds. (1995). *Assessment in the Learning Organization Shifting the Paradigm*. Alexandria, VA: Association for Supervision & Curriculum Development.

Craik, K. (1943). *The Nature of Explanation*. Cambridge: Cambridge University Press.

Cundill, G. and Rodela, R. (2012). A review of assertions about the processes and outcomes of social learning in natural resource management. *Journal of Environmental Management*, 113, 7–14.

Cundill, G., Cumming, G. S., Biggs, D., Fabricius, C. (2012). Soft systems thinking and social learning for adaptive management. *Conservation Biology*, 26, 13–20.

Day, J. C. (2002). Zoning-lessons from the Great Barrier Reef Marine Park. *Ocean and Coastal Management*, 45, 139–156.

Doyle, J. K. and Ford, D. N. (1998). Mental models concepts for system dynamics research. *System Dynamics Review*, 14, 3–29.

Dryzek, J. S. (2005). *The Politics of the Earth: Environmental Discourses*. Oxford: Oxford University Press.

Ebbesson, J. (2010). The rule of law in governance of complex socio-ecological changes. *Global Environmental Change*, 20, 414–422.

Étienne, M., Du Toit D., Pollard S. (2008). ARDI: a co-construction method for participatory modelling in natural resources management. Conference Proceedings, International Congress on Environmental Modelling and

Software, International Environmental Modelling and Software Society, 4th Biennial meeting, Ottawa.

Evans, L. S., Hicks, C. C., Fidelman, P., Tobin, R, C., Perry, A. L. (2013). Future scenarios as a research tool: investigating climate change impacts, adaptation options and outcomes for the Great Barrier Reef, Australia. *Human Ecology*, 41, 841–857.

Fabricius, C. and Cundill, G. (2014). Learning in adaptive management: insights from published practice. *Ecology and Society*, 19, 29.

Fernandez-Gimenez, M. E. (2000). The role of Mongolian nomadic pastoralists' ecological knowledge in rangeland management. *Ecological Applications*, 10, 1318–1326.

GBRMPA. (1994). *Year Strategic Plan for the Great Barrier Reef World Heritage Area, 1994–2019*. Townsville: Great Barrier Reef Marine Park Authority.

Gelcich, S., Hughes, T. P., Olsson, P. *et al.* (2010). Navigating transformations in governance of Chilean marine coastal resources. *Proceedings of the National Academy of Sciences USA*, 107, 16794–16799

Gunderson, L. H., Holling, C. S., Peterson, G. D. (2002). Surprises and sustainability: cycles of renewal in the everglades. In *Panarchy: Understanding Transformations in Human and Natural Systems*. Washington, DC: Island Press, pp. 315–332.

Holling, C. S. (2001). Understanding the complexity of economic, ecological, and social systems. *Ecosystems*, 4, 390–405.

Holling, C. S. and Meffe, G. K. (1996). Command and control and the pathology of natural resource management. *Conservation Biology*, 10, 328–337.

Holling, C. S., Gunderson, L. H., Ludwig, D. (2002). In quest of a theory of adaptive change. In *Panarchy: Understanding Transformations in Human and Natural Systems*. Washington, DC: Island Press, pp. 3–24.

Holmes, M. C. C. and Jampijinpa, W. S. P. (2013). Law for country: the structure of Warlpiri ecological knowledge and its application to natural resource management and ecosystem stewardship. *Ecology and Society*, 18, 19.

Hughes, T. P. (1994). Catastrophes, phase-shifts, and large-scale degradation of a Caribbean coral reef. *Science*, 265, 1547–1551.

Hughes, T. P., Rodrigues, M. J., Bellwood, D. R. *et al.* (2007). Regime-shifts, herbivory and the resilience of coral reefs to climate change. *Current Biology*, 17, 360–365.

Ishizawa, J. (2006). Cosmovisions and environmental governance: the case of *in situ* conservation of native cultivated plants and their wild relatives in Peru. In *Bridging Scales and Knowledge Systems: Concepts and Applications in Ecosystem Assessment*. Washington, DC: Millennium Ecosystem Assessment and Island Press, pp. 207–224.

Janssen, M. A. (2002). A future of surprises. In *Panarchy: Understanding Transformations in Human and Natural Systems*. Washington, DC: Island Press, pp. 241–260.

Jones, N. A., Ross, H., Lynam, T., Perez, P., Leitch, A. (2011). Mental models: an interdisciplinary synthesis of theory and methods. *Ecology and Society*, 16, 46.

Kollmuss, A. and Agyeman, J. (2002). Mind the gap: why do people act environmentally and what are the barriers to pro-environmental behavior? *Environmental Education Research*, 8, 239–260.

Lee, K. N. (1993). *Compass and Gyroscope: Integrating Science and Politics for the Environment*. Washington, DC: Island Press

Levin, S. A. (2003). Complex adaptive systems: exploring the known, the unknown and the unknowable. *Bulletin of the American Mathematical Society*, 40, 3–19.

Levin, S., Xepapadeas, A., Crepin, A-S. et al. (2013). Social-ecological systems as complex adaptive systems: modeling and policy implications. *Environment and Development Economics*, 18, 111–132.

Lindenmayer, D. B. and Likens, G. E. (2009). Adaptive monitoring: a new paradigm for long-term research and monitoring. *Trends in Ecology and Evolution*, 24, 482–486.

Lorenzoni, I., Nicholson-Cole, S., Whitmarsh, L. (2007). Barriers perceived to engaging with climate change among the UK public and their policy implications. *Global Environmental Change*, 17, 445–459.

Ludwig, D. (2001). The era of management is over. *Ecosystems*, 4, 758–764.

Lynam, T. and Brown, K. (2011). Mental models in human–environment interactions: theory, policy implications, and methodological explorations. *Ecology and Society*, 17, 24.

MA (2005). *Ecosystems and Human Well-Being: Synthesis*. Washington, DC: Island Press.

Mahon, R., McConney, P., Roy, R. N. (2008). Governing fisheries as complex adaptive systems. *Marine Policy*, 32, 104–112.

Mapstone, B. D., Davies, C. R., Little, L. R. et al. (2004). *The Effects of Line Fishing on the Great Barrier Reef and Evaluations of Alternative Potential Management Strategies*. CRC Reef Research Centre Technical Report No 52. Townsville: CRC Reef Research Centre.

Marshall, N., Bohensky, E., Goldberg, J. et al. (2013). *The Social and Economic Long Term Monitoring Program (SELTMP) 2012, Social and Economic Conditions Great Barrier Reef. Report to the National Environmental Research Program*. Cairns: Reef and Rainforest Research Centre Limited.

McCook, L. J., Ayling, T., Cappo, M. et al. (2010). Adaptive management of the Great Barrier Reef: a globally significant demonstration of the benefits of networks of marine reserves. *Proceedings of the National Academy of Sciences USA*, 107, 18278–18285.

McDaniel, R. R., Jordan, M. E., Fleeman, B. F. (2003). Surprise, surprise, surprise! A complexity science view of the unexpected. *Health Care Management Review*, 28, 266–278.

Moller, H., Berkes, F., Lyver, P. O., Kislalioglu, M. (2004). Combining science and traditional ecological knowledge: monitoring populations for co-management. *Ecology and Society*, 9, 2.

Nadasdy, P. (2007). Adaptive co-management and the gospel of resilience. In *Adaptive Co-Mangement: Collaboration, Learning, and Multi-Level Governance*. Toronto: University of British Columbia Press, pp. 208–227.

Norberg, J. and Cumming, G. S., eds. (2008). *Complexity Theory for a Sustainable Future*. New York, NY: Columbia University Press.

Olsson, P., Gunderson, L. H., Carpenter, S. R. *et al.* (2006). Shooting the rapids: navigating transitions to adaptive governance of social–ecological systems. *Ecology and Society*, 11, 18.

Olsson P, Folke C, Hughes T.P. (2008). Navigating the transition to ecosystem-based management of the Great Barrier Reef, Australia. *Proceedings of the National Academy of Sciences USA*, 105, 9489–9494.

Ostrom, E. (2007). A diagnostic approach for going beyond panaceas. *Proceedings of the National Academy of Sciences USA*, 104, 15181–15187.

Pahl-Wostl, C. (2009). A conceptual framework for analysing adaptive capacity and multi-level learning processes in resource governance regimes. *Global Environmental Change*, 19, 354–365.

Pahl-Wostl, C., Sendzimir, J., Jeffrey, P. (2009). Resources management in transition. *Ecology and Society*, 14, 46.

Peterson, G. D., Cumming, G. S., Carpenter, S. R. (2003). Scenario planning: a tool for conservation in an uncertain world. *Conservation Biology*, 17, 358–366.

Quinn, N. (2005). How to reconstruct schemas people share. In *Finding Culture in Talk: A Collection of Methods*. New York, NY: Palgrave Miller, pp. 33–81.

Resilience Alliance (2010). Assessing resilience in social–ecological systems: workbook for practitioners. Version 2.0. Online. Available at http://www.resalliance.org/3871.php.

Rogers, K. H., Luton, R., Biggs, H. *et al.* (2013). Fostering complexity thinking in action research for change in social–ecological systems. *Ecology and Society*, 18, 31.

Salmón, E. (2000). Kincentric ecology: indigenous perceptions of the human-nature relationship. *Ecological Applications*, 10, 1318–1326.

Scheffer, M. and Carpenter, S. R. (2003). Catastrophic regime shifts in ecosystems: linking theory to observation. *Trends in Ecology and Evolution*, 18, 648–656.

Scheffer, M., Carpenter, S., Foley, J. A., Folke, C., Walker, B. (2001). Catastrophic shifts in ecosystems. *Nature*, 413, 591–596.

Schlüter, M., McAllister, R. R. J., Arlinghaus, R. et al. (2012). New horizons for managing the environment: a review of coupled social–ecological systems modeling. *Natural Resource Modelling*, 25, 219.

Schwarz, A. M., Bene, C., Bennett, G. et al. (2011). Vulnerability and resilience of remote rural communities to shocks and global changes: empirical analysis from Solomon Islands. *Global Environmental Change*, 21, 1128–1140.

Sendzimir, J., Magnuszewski, P., Balogh, P., Vari, A. (2007). Anticipatory modeling of biocomplexity in the Tisza river basin: first steps to establish a participatory adaptive framework. *Environmental Modeling and Software*, 22, 599–609.

Sendzimir, J., Magnuszewski, P., Flachner, Z. et al. (2008). Assessing the resilience of a river management regime: informal learning in a shadow network in the Tisza river basin. *Ecology and Society*, 13, 11.

Sendzimir, J., Flachner, Z., Pahl-Wostl, C., Knieper, C. (2010). Stalled regime transition in the upper Tisza river basin: the dynamics of linked action situations. *Environmental Science and Policy*, 13, 604–619.

Tobin, A., Schlaff, A., Tobin, R. et al. (2010). *Adapting to Change: Minimising Uncertainty About the Effects of Rapidly-Changing Environmental Conditions on the Queensland Coral Reef Fin Fish Fishery*. Townsville: James Cook University.

Tompkins, E. L., Few, R., Brown, K. (2008). Scenario-based stakeholder engagement: incorporating stakeholders preferences into coastal planning for climate change. *Journal of Environmental Management*, 88, 1580–1592.

Turner, N. J., Ignace, M. B., Ignace, R. (2000). Traditional ecological knowledge and wisdom of aboriginal peoples in British Columbia. *Ecological Applications*, 10, 1275–1287.

Van Doren, C. (1992). *A History of Knowledge: Past, Present, and Future*. New York, NY: Ballantine Books.

Van Wilgen, B. W. and Biggs, H. C. (2011). A critical assessment of adaptive ecosystem management in a large savanna protected area in South Africa. *Biological Conservation*, 144, 1179–1187.

Vidal, C. (2012). Metaphilosophical criteria for worldview comparison. *Metaphilosophy*, 43, 306–347.

Walker, B. H and Salt, D. (2006). *Resilience Thinking: Sustaining Ecosystems and People in a Changing World*. Washington, DC: Island Press.

Walker, B., Carpenter, S., Anderies, J. *et al.* (2002). Resilience management in social-ecological systems: a working hypothesis for a participatory approach. *Conservation Ecology*, 6, 14.

Wallace, M. G., Cortner, H. J., Moote, M. A., Burke, S. (1996). Moving toward ecosystem management: examining a change in philosophy for resource management. *Journal of Political Ecology*, 3, 1–36.

Walsh, F. J., Dobson, P. V., Douglas, J. C. (2013). *Anpernirrentye*: a framework for enhanced application of indigenous ecological knowledge in natural resource management. *Ecology and Society*, 18, 18.

Walters, C. J. and Holling, C. S. (1990). Large-scale management experiments and learning by doing. *Ecology*, 71, 2060–2068.

Wilkinson, C., ed. (2004). *Status of Coral Reefs of the World*. Townsville: Australian Institute of Marine Science.

Wollenberg, E., Edmunds, D., Buck, L. (2000). Using scenarios to make decisions about the future: anticipatory learning for the adaptive co-management of community forests. *Landscape and Urban Planning*, 47, 65–77.

7 Principle 5 – Encourage learning

Georgina Cundill, Anne M. Leitch, Lisen Schultz, Derek Armitage and Garry Peterson

SUMMARY

Knowledge of social–ecological systems is always partial and incomplete. Efforts to enhance the resilience of ecosystem services must therefore be supported by continuous learning processes. Towards this end, learning can be fostered in a variety of ways, including through processes of experimentation and monitoring, and through knowledge co-production and collaboration. Evidence suggests that all of these learning processes can enhance the resilience of ecosystem services in important ways, primarily through an influence on governance and decision-making. Learning can, however, be undermined by failing to take into account asymmetrical power relations, the appropriate scale for learning activities and the human and financial costs involved. Effective learning can be supported through long-term monitoring, diverse participation, appropriate facilitation, sufficient financial and human resources and social networking. Important research gaps, however, remain, including what types of learning are most appropriate under different conditions, and

Principles for Building Resilience: Sustaining Ecosystem Services in Social–Ecological Systems, eds R. Biggs, M. Schlüter and M. L. Schoon. Published by Cambridge University Press. © Cambridge University Press 2015.

how new technologies can be harnessed in support of broader societal engagement in learning.

7.1 INTRODUCTION

The recognition of complexity in social–ecological systems (SES) brings with it an assumption that knowledge of SES is always partial, and that knowledge requires continual renewal otherwise it will become obsolete as the system it represents changes. Hence, there is a constant need to revise existing knowledge to enable adaptation to change in SES, as well as to maintain valued ecosystem services in the face of disturbance and change (Walker and Salt 2006; Chapin *et al.* 2009). This change also requires that there is a process of creating new knowledge, re-evaluating values, and articulating and evaluating alternative understandings of a system. This process of revising existing, and creating new, knowledge is referred to as learning.

There are three key approaches to managing SES that explicitly aim to support learning: adaptive management, adaptive co-management and adaptive governance. All three approaches recognize that knowledge is incomplete, and that uncertainty, change and surprise are inevitable in managing SES. Learning is therefore fundamental to all three, although the approach to learning, and the desired outcomes, tend to differ between them (Table 7.1).

Learning in adaptive management is based on the scientific approach of articulating alternative hypotheses, experimentation and hypotheses evaluation. Ongoing management actions are viewed as deliberate, large-scale experiments, and explicit alternative hypotheses are formulated about SES dynamics and the potential outcomes of different management actions (Walters 1986; Walters and Holling 1990). Active adaptive management integrates the testing of these hypotheses into environmental management, considering learning as one of the outcomes of management. This approach can lead to more proactive management approaches that introduce variation and allow scientists to resolve differences between alternative hypotheses and policies by, for example, allowing higher levels of fishing or creating

Table 7.1 Approaches to learning in the management of SES (adapted from Cundill and Rodela 2012)

	Why an interest in learning?	Processes that support learning	The outcomes of learning	Key source references
Adaptive management	Ecological complexity; management uncertainty	Articulation of alternative hypotheses; deliberate experimentation; ongoing monitoring; joint actions; reflective practice	Improved decision-making; increase in social–ecological understanding; improved problem-solving capacity; assessment of likelihood of alternative social–ecological hypotheses	Holling 1978; Walters 1986; Lee 1993
Adaptive co-management	Social–ecological complexity; management uncertainty	Long-term self-organizing process; experience of crises; iterative reflection; knowledge sharing	Improved decision-making; changes in perceptions, values and norms; collective action; direct social–ecological systems on desirable pathways	Olsson et al. 2004; Folke et al. 2005; Armitage et al. 2007; Armitage et al. 2009
Adaptive governance	Social–ecological complexity; management uncertainty; recognition that management is shaped by governance and needs to respond to changes at multiple scales, including the global scale	Flexible and responsive institutions at multiple levels; policy experiments; knowledge sharing across multiple levels of decision-making	Improved decision-making; changes in perceptions, values, norms and rules; collective action; direct social–ecological systems on desirable pathways	Folke et al. 2005, Pahl-Wostl 2007

an experimental flood. Adaptive management therefore emphasizes learning-by-doing, the design of monitoring systems, and the continual creation, evaluation and comparison of alternative working hypotheses (Holling 1978). Adaptive management typically involves transdisciplinary teams of scientists, environmental managers and policy-makers in support of learning how to better manage SES to achieve multiple goals (Holling 1978; Walters 1986; Fernandez-Gimenez et al. 2008).

Adaptive co-management emerged in the early 2000s as an approach that married adaptive management's focus on learning through experimentation and monitoring with co-management's focus on learning through sustained interactions between multiple stakeholders (Ruitenbeek and Cartier 2001; Olsson et al. 2004; Armitage et al. 2007). Co-management refers to a variety of power-sharing processes involving multiple actors including local communities, the state and non-governmental stakeholders (Carlsson and Berkes 2005). In adaptive co-management, while the interest in learning is cognisant of social–ecological complexity, the focus of learning expands beyond experimentation to include knowledge sharing between multiple actors. Some of the desired outcomes of these learning processes include changes in values and norms, and collective action around common environmental concerns (Armitage et al. 2009).

More recently, the related concept of adaptive governance has gained recognition as a framework for managing SES in which learning is equally considered central (Folke et al. 2005; Gunderson and Light 2006; Olsson et al. 2007). However, in adaptive governance a key focus of learning tends to include knowledge sharing across scales. This cross-scale focus of learning is pursued because approaches to adaptive governance tend to emphasize the development of social norms and cooperation (Levin 2006; Vincent 2007), nested organizational structures (Folke et al. 2005; Folke et al. 2007) and also the role of bridging organizations in matching the scale of decision-making to the scale of ecological processes (Olsson et al. 2007).

The purpose of learning, and the processes through which learning is pursued, thus differ in important ways depending on the management paradigm that dominates attempts to increase the resilience of valued ecosystem services. These differences are important to understand as they significantly influence practical approaches that are designed to support learning in these contexts, and are summarized in Table 7.1.

7.2 WHAT DO WE MEAN BY 'LEARNING'?

Learning is a multifaceted phenomenon and includes: (1) acquiring information and increasing knowledge; (2) memorizing; (3) acquiring facts, skills and methods; (4) making sense or abstracting meaning; and (5) interpreting and understanding reality in a different way by reinterpreting knowledge (Säljö 1979). Two complementary forms of learning are believed to enhance the resilience of ecosystem services: loop learning and social learning.

Single-loop learning comprises a change in skills, practices or actions to meet existing goals and expectations. This learning focuses on the question, 'are we doing things right?' In contrast, double-loop learning actively questions the assumptions that underlie action by asking, 'are we doing the right things?' (Flood and Romm 1996). For example, a study of US community-based forestry organizations found that collaborative monitoring activities led to single-loop learning (recommendations for optimal treatment of invasive weed species that threaten forests) and double-loop learning (realization of the impact of salvaging timber) (Fernandez-Gimenez et al. 2008). Triple-loop learning involves a more deep-seated questioning of values and norms that underlie institutions and actions by asking, 'how do we know what the right thing to do is?' (Flood and Romm 1996). Triple-loop learning can result in the restructuring of beliefs and values, underlies transformations in worldviews and may prompt changes in ecosystem governance and management approaches (Pahl-Wostl 2009; Biggs et al. 2010) (P4 – CAS thinking).

Social learning refers to 'a change in understanding that goes beyond the individual to become situated within wider social units or communities of practice through social interactions between actors within social networks' (Reed et al. 2010: r1). Social learning is generally regarded to take place in two key ways (see Cundill and Rodela 2012 for a review): through deliberative processes involving ongoing interaction between individuals and the sharing of knowledge and perspectives in a trusting environment (Daniels and Walker 1996; Roling 2002; Schusler et al. 2003; Standa-Gunda et al. 2003; Selin et al. 2007; Kendrick and Manseau 2008), and through deliberate experimentation and reflection involving shared activities such as monitoring (Lee 1993; Steyaert et al. 2007; Fernandez-Gimenez et al. 2008; Kuper et al. 2009). Social learning can take place through intentional, facilitated processes (Mostert et al. 2007); or it can be an emergent outcome of social interaction (Olsson et al. 2004).

While loop learning is most concerned with, and defined by, *what* is learned (e.g. new skills and practice, or new values and assumptions), social learning tends to be defined by *how* learning takes place (e.g. through social interaction). Although often confused in the literature, these two approaches to learning therefore potentially complement one another in useful ways in the context of resilience in SES.

7.3 HOW DOES LEARNING ENHANCE THE RESILIENCE OF ECOSYSTEM SERVICES?

Since knowledge of complex systems is always partial and becoming out-dated (Chapter 1), enhancing the resilience of ecosystem services requires continuous learning about the SES that provides these services (Holling 1978; Walker and Salt 2006; Chapin et al. 2009). Learning can support the resilience of ecosystem services primarily through influencing decision-making processes and governance. Such learning in support of decision-making is achieved through a variety of both planned and unplanned processes, including active experimentation and monitoring, multi-actor collaboration and through intergenerational interactions with the environment.

Adaptively creating, testing and designing experiments to explore alternative management options is an important means to support learning and enhance the resilience of ecosystem services.

Experimentation and monitoring provide information about changes in the availability of ecosystem services (Bellamy et al. 2001; Boyle et al. 2001), and can also be used to resolve uncertainty about how the world works. The use of monitoring to evaluate competing models of the world is an example of passive adaptive management in which monitoring can be planned to take advantage of 'natural' experiments or expected shocks to a system, such as policy changes, droughts or floods. Experimentation, or active adaptive management, involves the purposeful, structured manipulation of particular SES processes and structures to observe and compare outcomes (Walters and Holling 1990). Experimentation can highlight trade-offs associated with building resilience of one aspect of a system versus building general system resilience, thereby providing better information to support decision-making.

One of the main contributions that scientists can make in such contexts is to expand the range of hypotheses (or models) that are considered for a given system. Often a practical barrier to learning is the lack of plausible alternatives to a dysfunctional status quo. Experimental management is a way to explore the dynamics of the system being managed in cases where when there seems to be an opportunity to improve management and where available information does not allow new policies to be evaluated. Although management experiments are rare, some have occurred. In the Colorado River experimental floods were carried out to assess ideas about water flow and river geomorphology and food webs (Cross et al. 2011). Such experiments are very difficult to implement for social, political and financial reasons (Walters 2007), and the difficulties that many large-scale environmental problems present for experimentation suggest that adaptive management may not be possible in many situations (Allen and Gunderson 2011).

Although specialist agencies and scientists often carry out monitoring and experimentation, and therefore learn during the process, there is growing recognition of the importance of broader participation and its role in supporting the resilience of ecosystem services through learning (Danielsen et al. 2005) (P6 – Participation). A study of five US community-based forestry organizations involved in collaborative ecological monitoring programmes found that co-monitoring activities led to single-loop learning, which identified changes in recommendations for optimal treatment of invasive weed species, and double-loop learning (through the realization of the significance and need for sustainable harvesting of mushrooms), which together altered social attitudes and assumptions. In another example – the case of transformative change in the Chilean benthic fisheries governance – Gelcich et al. (2006) attribute the development of the innovative territorial user-rights policy to learning processes among fishers, scientists and managers and demonstration-scale experimental trials that identified new management pathways. The territorial user-rights policy has led to the recovery of some highly valuable benthic species following collapse of these fisheries in the 1980s.

Collaborative processes can also support learning and therefore decision-making by helping to make the values regarding different ecosystem services explicit. For example, participatory modelling as described by Bousquet et al. (2002) can assist actors in sharing multiple representations of SES, or mental models, thus enabling collective decision-making on a systemic level that take diverse values into account. Such processes can shift governance towards more ecosystem-based, integrative approaches (P4 – CAS thinking). For example, in Kristianstads Vattenrike, when local inhabitants and politicians changed their perception of local wetlands from being water-logged swamps of low value to water-rich areas for recreation of high value, the habitats were restored and associated ecosystem services maintained, contrary to the overall trend of disappearing wetlands in Europe (Olsson et al. 2004). Similarly, in the Great Barrier Reef, the change of perceptions among politicians and the public from seeing the reef as pristine to seeing it as severely threatened paved the way for stronger protection of the reef and its associated ecosystem services (Olsson et al. 2008). Both of these shifts in perceptions occurred through processes of learning. These experiences therefore simultaneously highlight the role of learning in potentially supporting the resilience of ecosystem services, and also the fact that not all the learning required to achieve such shifts can be planned for.

Indeed, many learning processes that support the resilience of ecosystem services are not planned for or facilitated. Practices that underpin the generation, accumulation and transmission of knowledge and institutions for responding to and managing ecosystem services, i.e. learning, have been found in many traditional societies, particularly those with high levels of dependence on local resources (Berkes et al. 2000; Gadgil et al. 2003). Examples include management of multiple species and landscape patchiness, which enable comparison of, and learning about, responses of different species or vegetation communities to different management practices. Traditional learning-based approaches also include mechanisms for cultural internalization of new practices and the adaptation of worldviews and cultural values. For example, in the traditional caribou-hunting Cree society, an event of extreme overhunting that resulted in the disappearance of caribou in the early 1900s triggered the development of a more conservationist approach that then became encoded in the ethical and cultural beliefs of the Cree (Berkes et al. 2000).

In the case of co-management in the Canadian Arctic (Box 7.1), experience suggests that knowledge sharing and co-production may indeed be the underlying mechanisms that facilitate social learning. Further insight into such mechanisms is offered by a study of transborder polar bear and walrus management in the Bering Strait (Meek et al. 2008), which has shown how supportive institutional arrangements (such as interlocal linkages that enable local communities to share a decision-making framework) have enabled learning, particularly relearning of traditional wildlife management practices, to occur at the community level despite slow or absent international funding or legal agreements. This points to the importance of cross-scale learning to support ecosystem services resilience, meaning the linking of actors across scales (vertically and horizontally), which one tends to see in adaptive co-management arrangements.

BOX 7.1 **Learning and collaborative management build resilience of Arctic ecosystem services**

A seasonally ice-free Arctic is projected within the next several decades (ACIA 2005; AMAP 2011). Such changes will have profound implications for ice-adapted Arctic marine mammals (e.g. narwhal, beluga) and the indigenous communities whose social well-being and culture have long-standing connections to Arctic ecosystems, such as the Inuit and Inuvialuit (Fig. 7.1). However, evidence is starting to emerge that social learning processes associated with flexible collaborative management (co-management) arrangements can help to transform how indigenous communities, managers and scientists cope with social–ecological change and uncertainty and, in turn, build the resilience of desired ecosystem services. For example, evidence from Canada's Arctic shows how marine-mammal co-management can support shared understanding and sense-making, increased dialogue among harvesters and government decision-makers, can distribute control and shared responsibility for management actions, and provide conditions for individual and group learning (Dale and Armitage 2010; Armitage *et al.* 2011). Specifically, the linking and learning attributes of these Arctic marine-mammal co-management experiences can help to build resilience of ecosystem services by: (1) creating opportunities to co-produce knowledge about ecosystem conditions and interpretations of ecosystem change; and (2) linking actors across scales in decision-making networks, thus leading to better social and ecological outcomes.

In a rapidly changing Arctic, knowledge about ecosystem conditions (e.g. sea ice) and marine-mammal stocks (location, number, trends) is insufficient, while historic top-down management approaches (e.g. harvest allocation and quota setting) have been contested (Armitage 2005). However, the institutionalization through enabling legislation (i.e. land claims) of processes to incorporate different forms and types of knowledge – or knowledge co-production – has emerged as an important mechanism or trigger for learning. Knowledge co-production is the collaborative process of bringing a plurality of knowledge sources and types together to address a defined problem and build an integrated or systems-oriented understanding of that problem. These processes are most successful when catalysed by regular cycles of community-based and regional workshops, repeated interactions between harvesters, managers

BOX 7.1 **Continued**

and scientists and a recognition that management plans are 'living' documents (i.e. adaptable). The transaction costs are high and the processes are often slow (nor are they always successful), but knowledge co-production and social learning processes are generating positive social outcomes (e.g. increased trust, willingness to experiment and share risk) and helping to build ecosystem resilience

(a)

(b)

FIG. 7.1 (a) Qikiqtarjuaq, Nunavut where changes in ecosystem services attributable to sea-ice loss are creating new pressures for the community to learn through change. Photo credit: Derek Armitage. (b) Travelling under increasingly uncertain ice conditions means hunters must adapt to unexpected ecosystem changes. Photo credit: Aaron Dale.

(e.g. improved stock conditions through changes in harvest practices, new monitoring and enforcement conditions, greater local control on harvest decisions) (Dale and Armitage 2010; Armitage *et al.* 2011).

Experience with marine-mammal co-management in Canada's Arctic also points to the relationship between learning and the emergence of multi-level institutional arrangements that link social actors vertically and horizontally (P7 – Polycentricity). Vertical and horizontal linkages in co-management can lead to the emergence of new social networks, and are supported by 'bridging organizations' (see Schultz 2009). Co-management boards in Canada's Arctic – like the Nunavut Wildlife Management Board or the Fisheries Joint Management Commission – serve as crucial bridging organizations to connect local, regional and federal actors and contribute to learning processes. Evidence from marine--mammal co-management (Armitage *et al.* 2011) illustrates how social networks supported by bridging organizations have become more meaningful through time, and have led to changes in understanding ecosystem conditions that are situated within wider social networks, such as increased appreciation among scientists about the importance of traditional knowledge, and the need to reconsider stock estimates in the light of the local knowledge of resource harvesters (Dale and Armitage 2010).

Learning through co-management is no panacea for rapid ecosystem change. There are deeply embedded and historical power relationships in Canada's Arctic that influence how indigenous people connect with their lands and participate in decision-making, and which act as barriers to trust building. Moreover, significant time is required to build co-management arrangements and, in the case of the Arctic, it is unclear if knowledge co-production and learning processes will be sufficiently quick to address predicted sea-ice loss, accompanying perturbations to wildlife stocks and biodiversity, and the potential loss of cultural practices and knowledge gained from everyday interactions with ecosystems. Despite the challenges, learning and experimentation through adaptive and collaborative management contexts in the Arctic is an important mechanism for building resilience of ecosystem services: it leads to changes in worldviews, ensures different types and sources of knowledge are valued, leads to greater willingness to experiment and take risk and fosters an enabling policy context for long-term sustainability.

In summary, experience has shown that learning can enhance the resilience of ecosystem services primarily through its influence on governance and decision-making processes associated with such ecosystem services. Such learning may be either planned for, for example through carefully thought-out experimentation and monitoring, or it can be unplanned, as was the case in the changing mental models of the wetlands in Kristianstads Vattenrike in Sweden. Where such processes are planned it is vital also to create spaces for ongoing interactions that support knowledge sharing and co-production, as discussed in Section 7.5.

7.4 UNDER WHAT CONDITIONS MAY RESILIENCE OF ECOSYSTEM SERVICES BE COMPROMISED?

The evidence in support of learning does not tend to systematically demonstrate what type of learning is most appropriate or inappropriate to build resilient ecosystem services and under what conditions (Biggs *et al.* 2012). Nevertheless, there is increasing recognition that learning can be ineffective, or worse, maladaptive, and that the design of the learning process is crucial. Muro and Jeffrey (2008) reference a number of studies of deliberate learning processes in which participants fail to reach agreement or consensus, conflict intensifies, participants develop negative perceptions of others, or 'mistaken learning' occurs. In the latter example, participants internalized some misinformation provided by other stakeholders involved in the learning process and repeated it as misconceived evidence of a deeper understanding (Schusler *et al.* 2003). In such cases the resilience of ecosystem services may be compromised and effective governance may require sustained processes of un-learning.

Maladaptive or dysfunctional learning can lead more directly to beliefs and behaviour that threaten the function of an SES. For example, the systematic anti-environmental campaigning outlined in Naomi Oreskes and Erik Conway's book *Merchants of*

Doubt (2010) set out to deliberately undermine environmental science by emphasizing uncertainty and manufacturing 'debate'. This sense of unresolved scientific consensus, while inaccurate, successfully created a grand narrative that influenced the worldviews of individuals, governance organizations and networks globally, and helped to stimulate a range of maladaptive decisions from the stalling of environmental policy to active promotion of industries contributing to issues such as acid rain, the ozone hole and global warming. A number of factors have been identified as potential challenges for effective and legitimate social learning and adaptive governance, including power relations, scale and cost.

Power dynamics can influence how learning takes place, including who is learning, the linkages between learners, what type of learning takes place, whose knowledge is included and integrated or discarded, and what is monitored (Maarleveld and Dabgbegnon 1999; Armitage *et al*. 2009). There are numerous examples of scientific knowledge being prioritized for learning and management above other knowledge systems, in particular traditional or local ecological knowledge, to the eventual detriment of ecosystem-service resilience (Moller *et al*. 2004) (Chapter 2). An iconic example was the collapse of the Canadian cod fishery, where local fishers raised serious concerns about cod stocks but these concerns were ignored (Finlayson 1994).

Power asymmetries can be enshrined in both people and structures. For instance, relatively more powerful stakeholders can dominate poorly implemented learning processes and assert the standing and influence of their own knowledge, thereby co-opting or misrepresenting other voices within communities (Béné *et al*. 2009). Similarly, power concentrated in organizations such as national governments can stifle the potential contribution of learning and innovation at the local scale (Marin and Berkes 2010). As Blaikie (2006, p. 1945) notes, it is assumed that local ecological change 'can be addressed by local experience and experimentation, adaptive agricultural practice … and forest use, local farmer networks, etc.' but that 'it is acknowledged that there are formidable problems to negotiating these knowledges at the interface with development organizations'. Such mismatch between local and bureaucratic knowledge can range from disagreements over matters of fact, such as the maximum number of pups a polar bear can have in a year, to what is important to learn about, to how to run meetings and discuss issues (Houde 2007).

Effective monitoring requires that monitoring be linked to management problems or decisions. While such a goal might seem easy in theory it is often not so easy in practice, as the management dilemmas and problems vary with scale and across groups. Large-scale monitoring that is not tied to specific management questions is often of little use for improving management decisions. For example, large-scale forest monitoring may be useful for the management of timber supply, but is inadequate for managing logging impacts on trap lines, because key information on trapping activities, animal populations and forest animal interactions are not being monitored (Houde 2007). Consequently, monitoring programmes that are implemented to monitor the species or forests often fail to adequately monitor key processes or enable managers to resolve key uncertainties they grapple with in their decision-making.

Monitoring or experimentation applied at the wrong scale, for example over short timescales or limited spatial scales, can also fail to provide an adequate basis for decision-making or can lead to inappropriate management decisions (Olsson et al. 2004). Global climate models, for instance, often lack sufficient detail for action or decision-making at the sub-national level (Kates et al. 2001). In the Goulburn–Broken Catchment in Australia, Walker et al. (2004) argue that learning has been unevenly distributed spatially and sectorally, focusing on pollution control in the irrigation region but neglecting the drylands region. In this case, learning and experimentation have also been directed at maintaining the status quo and keeping the SES within its current 'production' regime, with multi-scale and long-term ecological and economic consequences.

Lindemayer and Likens (2009) argue that monitoring programmes should address clearly articulated socially defined questions, should be designed so that monitoring can answer the questions and should be based on a model of how the SES may work. These prescriptions are designed to deal with three serious and common ecological monitoring problems. The first is that monitoring is often planned without explicitly articulating the goals of the process. The second is that there is often a lack of adequate experimental design to determine whether the monitoring will be able to detect changes and trends. The third, which often drives the first two problems, is that monitoring is often politically mandated and imposed prior to an analysis of the objectives and questions behind the monitoring. Strategic adaptive management, which has been successfully used in Kruger National Park in South Africa, and applied across South Africa's national parks, appears to offer a practical framework for updating and revising monitoring in light of learning and social preferences (Biggs and Rogers 2003; Roux and Foxcroft 2011).

By its nature, experimentation in SES is risky and requires leadership, trust, networks and resources. When the social capital of a community is so eroded that the community cannot afford to make mistakes, social capital might have to be built up or supported through external intervention before experimentation can be considered (Cundill and Fabricius 2010). In addition, long-term monitoring and other learning processes can be costly in terms of human and financial resources. In some cases, these costs may exceed the value of the SES under improved governance. This is particularly so where the benefits derived from an SES are relatively small, for instance in the case of a small-stock, low-value fishery (acknowledging the focus on provisioning services) (Garcia et al. 2008), or where resilience of an SES is already so eroded and under high anthropogenic pressure that significantly increased benefits are unlikely (Garcia et al. 2008). The high cost of learning processes relative to perceived benefits is demonstrated by the lack of sustained engagement in participatory monitoring programmes by communities when external funding support lapses (Garcia and Lescuyer 2008).

Overall, experience suggests that, to be effective, the process of monitoring, experimentation and learning needs to be collaborative and long-term, at an appropriate scale for decision-making and the SES, as well as able to withstand the impact of short-term funding cycles, politics and objectives (Barthel *et al.* 2010; Cundill and Fabricius 2010). As discussed above, enabling conditions – whether policy, institutions, resources, organizations or individuals – are important in this respect as they act as barriers as well as facilitators of learning at different levels (Armitage *et al.* 2009; Crona and Parker 2012).

7.5 HOW CAN THE PRINCIPLE OF LEARNING BE OPERATIONALIZED AND APPLIED?

Operationalizing the principle of learning depends strongly on the context in which it is applied, but it is useful to consider process-orientated guidelines to support learning (Schusler *et al.* 2003). While several scholars lament the lack of certainty around what learning mechanisms to use and when to use them (Muro and Jeffrey 2008; Armitage *et al.* 2009), several studies suggest the following, often overlapping, guidelines as important in fostering learning.

- **Support long-term social–ecological monitoring**. The collection of long-term monitoring data can provide a means to separate trends from variation in complex SES. Managing for resilience often involves the management of slowly changing variables, and observing change in these slow variables requires long-term monitoring. Such long-term monitoring programmes must monitor socially and scientifically meaningful variables, in a fashion that supports the detection of expected and unexpected changes in SES (Lindemayer and Likens 2009).
- **Provide opportunities for interaction that enable extended engagement**. Social learning requires appropriate social forums that support prolonged and frequent interaction (Webler *et al.* 1995; Schusler *et al.* 2003; Mostert *et al.* 2007). Typically, these social spaces are physical, formally organized settings where stakeholders interact face to face through workshops. They

can also occur through less direct means via social networks (Reed et al. 2010). Interventions tend to be organized from outside the community; however, they can also emerge from within the community (e.g. farmers' networks; Rist et al. 2003).
- **Enable diverse participation that considers representativeness and multiple knowledge sources as well as clarity of roles.** Broad and diverse participation representing a range of different sources of knowledge is considered important for a diversity of perspectives (P6 – Participation). Also important is the capacity of participants to engage, which can be influenced, for example, by power differentials and levels of literacy (Mostert et al. 2007; Cundill and Rodela 2012).
- **Effectively facilitate adequate conditions that foster understanding of others' perspectives and experiences.** Social learning depends on establishing a suitable social context that supports the sharing and negotiation of knowledge, beliefs and worldviews. Appropriate facilitation can help to enable the open communication required for this (Webler et al. 1995; Schusler et al. 2003; Mostert et al. 2007; Reed et al. 2010). Skilled facilitation focuses on process as much as substance and in particular supports a democratic structure, encourages open communication, manages conflict to ensure it is constructive and supports systems thinking and 'unrestrained' thinking (Schusler et al. 2003). Without competent facilitation, processes can stagnate or suffer from destructive conflict (Pahl-Wostl 2006; Muro and Jeffrey 2008) or lack sufficient information to allow experimentation (Cundill 2010).
- **Ensure sufficient resources to enable learning processes through adequate funding and a suitably skilled team.** Social learning activities tend to be time-consuming and expensive (Mostert et al. 2007). Failing to provide adequate support for learning processes or activities such as adaptive decision-making in response to monitoring has been found to limit or inhibit learning (Mostert et al. 2007). Sendzimir et al. (2007) note that not having sufficient resources to provide opportunities for people to meet and interact constrained learning and limited the emergence of a comprehensive vision of adaptive management. A lack of resources may stem in part from not having a deep understanding of the importance, potential impact or demands of learning activities. A related issue is being able to validate the expense of learning activities where the cost of supporting such activities exceeds the economic value of the resources (e.g. Walters 2007).

- **Enable networking.** One of the most meaningful ways to ensure the resilience of social learning processes is to embed them within learning networks or communities of practice. Such networks can provide sources of knowledge, interpretation and resources. In particular, such networks can be mobilized to respond to threats to SES, and they can provide opportunities to better link local activities with other actors and activities at other scales (Berkes *et al.* 2003).

There is a range of collaborative tools commonly used to foster learning that spans from deliberation tools to processes for active experimentation. For example, participatory modelling activities used by Sendzimir *et al.* (2007) in the NeWater project in Hungary primarily used causal loop diagrams, alongside field experiments, to aid social learning and so transition to more adaptive management of the region, and enhance a diversity of ecosystem services. Scenario planning can be used as part of an adaptive learning process when participatory modelling is conceptually difficult (Peterson *et al.* 2003a). For example, participatory scenarios were used to stimulate social learning in the Minnesota2050 project, where such a scenario development reinforced relationships between people, built a shared understanding of different perspectives on the issues at hand and also supported systems thinking (Johnson *et al.* 2012). Most commonly, social learning processes draw on a suite of tools. Some examples are the following: the SLIM project, which focused on the sustainable use of water, and employed mapping and diagramming techniques based on systems approaches; media technologies like geographic information systems (GIS); intermediary objects and concepts; and performance arts such as theatre events and metaphor exploration (Steyaert and Jiggins 2007).

7.6 KEY RESEARCH AND APPLICATION GAPS

A long-held assumption in SES management is that learning, supported through experimentation, monitoring and collaboration, is fundamental to managing SES as it provides a basis for adapting management to ensure continued provision of ecosystem services in the face of disturbance and change. However, the evidence in support of learning and experimentation does not indicate what type of learning works and under what conditions. We know, however, that learning can play a key role in changing worldviews (P4 – CAS thinking). We also know that the design of learning processes is key to avoid learning traps. The participation of multiple actors in learning processes (P6 – Participation) is crucial to guard against maladaptive learning and domination of the learning process by powerful subgroups. A broad consideration of alternative system dynamics is also essential to avoid perceptions that present conditions are always optimal, without an awareness of more desirable, achievable alternative SES configurations (Peterson et al. 2003b).

However, how learning can be harnessed to promote resilience of ecosystem services needs to be much better understood. Particularly important areas for future research include: a better understanding of different types of learning and of how institutions enable and supress learning; a better integration of different knowledge systems; and how to better combine management, monitoring and learning. First, there is a need for greater empirical scrutiny and conceptual clarity on what loop learning and social learning are, and therefore how they contribute to the resilience of ecosystem services. Towards this end, there is a need to develop and test methods for assessing learning processes and outcomes in the field (Reed et al. 2010; Cundill and Rodela 2012). Second, there is a need to better understand the conditions and institutions that support learning to inform the facilitation of learning processes in practice. This includes a better understanding of the influence and negotiation of power asymmetries in the learning process as well as the development of methods to monitor and evaluate whether (and what) learning has taken place. A third gap relates to how different types of knowledge can be integrated to facilitate learning, including within and across scales. Fourth, the grand challenge of adaptive management is to better integrate management, monitoring and learning, as repeated efforts have demonstrated that there are substantial social barriers to making learning a focus of management (Walters 2007), and to maintain long-term monitoring (Lindemayer and Likens 2010). Greater knowledge of these barriers to the integration of learning and management is required, but even more important are strategies that overcome these barriers to enable learning-based management.

Looking towards the future, major technological advances offer the potential to fundamentally rethink how we understand and pursue collaborative monitoring and learning. The advent of widespread cell phones, especially smart phones, cheap remote sensing and mapping technologies, such as Google Earth™, offer great potential to develop new forms of citizen science, and there are numerous examples of just such initiatives worldwide (see the *Frontiers* 2012 special issue on citizen science). The challenge these technologies present is how to tie social learning processes, which produce new forms of understanding and knowledge, to these new sources of monitoring data, so that learning is not drowned in a sea of confusing and contradictory data. The challenge will be to build novel approaches to sense-making to enable more participatory and robust learning processes that enhance the resilience of ecosystem services.

REFERENCES

ACIA (2005). *Arctic Climate Impact Assessment.* Cambridge: Cambridge University Press.

Allen, C. R. and Gunderson, L. H. (2011). Pathology and failure in the design and implementation of adaptive management. *Journal of Environmental Management,* 92, 1379–1384.

AMAP (2011). *Snow, Water, Ice and Permafrost in the Arctic (SWIPA) Report.* Oslo: Arctic Council.

Armitage, D. (2005). Community-based narwhal management in Nunavut, Canada: change, uncertainty and adaptation. *Society and Natural Resources,* 18, 715–731.

Armitage, D., Berkes, F., Doubleday, N., eds. (2007). *Adaptive Co-Management: Collaboration, Learning, and Multi-Level Governance.* Vancouver: University of British Columbia Press.

Armitage, D., Plummer, R., Berkes, F. *et al.* (2009). Adaptive co-management for social–ecological complexity. *Frontiers in Ecology and Envronment,* 7, 95–102.

Armitage, D., Berkes, F., Dale, A. et al. (2011). Co-management and the co-production of knowledge: learning to adapt in Canada's Arctic. *Global Environmental Change*, 21, 995–1004.

Barthel, S., Folke, C., Colding, J. (2010). Social–ecological memory in urban gardens: retaining the capacity for management of ecosystem services. *Global Environmental Change*, 20, 255–265.

Bellamy, J., Walker, D., McDonald, G., Syme, G. (2001). A systems approach to the evaluation of natural resource management initiatives. *Journal of Environmental Management*, 63, 407–423.

Béné, C., Belal, E., Baba, M. O. et al. (2009). Power struggle, dispute and alliance over local resources: analyzing 'democratic' decentralization of natural resources through the lenses of Africa inland fisheries. *World Development*, 37, 1935–1950.

Berkes, F., Colding, J., Folke, C. (2000). Rediscovery of traditional ecological knowledge as adaptive management. *Ecological Applications*, 10, 1251–1262.

Berkes, F., Colding, J., Folke, C., eds. (2003). *Navigating Social-Ecological Systems: Building Resilience for Complexity and Change*. Cambridge, UK: Cambridge University Press.

Biggs, H. and Rogers, K. (2003). An adaptive system to link science, monitoring and management in practice. In *The Kruger Experience: Ecology and Management of Savanna Heterogeneity*. Washington, DC: Island Press, pp. 59–80.

Biggs, R., Westley, F., Carpenter, S. (2010). Navigating the back loop: fostering social innovation and transformation in ecosystem management. *Ecology and Society*, 15, 9.

Biggs, R., Schlüter, M., Biggs, D. et al. (2012). Towards principles for enhancing the resilience of ecosystem services. *Annual Review of Environment and Resources*, 37, 421–448.

Blaikie, P. (2006). Is small really beautiful? Community based natural resource management in Malawi and Botswana. *World Development*, 34, 1942–1957.

Bousquet, F., Barreteau, O., d'Aquino, P. et al. (2002). Multi-agent systems and role games: collective learning processes for ecosystem management. In *Complexity and Ecosystem Management: The Theory and Practice of Multi-Agent Approaches*. Cheltenham: Edward Elgar Publishing, pp. 248–285.

Boyle, M., Kay, J., Pond, B. (2001). Monitoring in support of policy: an adaptive ecosystem approach. In *Encyclopedia of Global Environmental Change*. New York, NY: Wiley, pp. 116–137.

Carlsson, L. and Berkes, F. (2005). Co-management: concepts and methodological implications. *Journal of Environmental Management*, 75, 65–76.

Chapin, F. S., Kofinas, G. P., Folke, C., eds. (2009). *Principles of Ecosystem Stewardship: Resilience-Based Natural Resource Management in a Changing World*. New York, NY: Springer.

Crona, B. and Parker, J. (2012). Learning in support of governance: theories, methods, and a framework to assess how bridging organizations contribute to adaptive resource governance. *Ecology and Society*, 17, 32.

Cross, W., Colden, V., Baxter, K. et al. (2011). Ecosystem ecology meets adaptive management: food web response to a controlled flood on the Colorado River, Glen Canyon. *Ecological Applications*, 21, 2016–2033.

Cundill, G. (2010). Monitoring social learning processes in adaptive comanagement: three case studies from South Africa. *Ecology and Society*, 15, 28.

Cundill, G. and Fabricius, C. (2010). Monitoring the governance dimension of the adaptive co-management of natural resources. *Ecology and Society*, 15, 15.

Cundill, G. and Rodela, R. (2012). A review of assertions about the processes and outcomes of social learning in natural resource management. *Journal of Environmental Management*, 113, 7–14.

Dale, A. and Armitage, D. (2010). Marine mammal co-management in Canada's Arctic: knowledge co-production for learning and adaptive capacity. *Marine Policy*, 35, 440–449.

Daniels, S. and Walker, G. (1996). Collaborative learning: improving public deliberation in ecosystem-based management. *Environmental Impact Assessment Review*, 16, 71–102.

Danielsen, F., Burgess, N., Balmford A. (2005). Monitoring matters: examining the potential of locally-based approaches. *Biodiversity Conservation*, 14, 2507–2542.

Fernandez-Gimenez, M., Ballard, H., Sturtevant, V. (2008). Adaptive management and social learning in collaborative and community-based monitoring: a study of five community-based forestry organizations in the western USA. *Ecology and Society*, 13, 4.

Finlayson, A. C. (1994). *Fishing for Truth: A Sociological Analysis of Northern Cod Stock Assessments from 1977 to 1990*. St Johns, Newfoundland: ISER.

Flood, R. and Romm, N. (1996). *Diversity Management: Triple Loop Learning*. Chicester: Wiley.

Folke, C., Hahn, T., Olsson, P., Norberg, J. (2005). Adaptive governance of social–ecological systems. *Annual Review of Environment and Resources*, 30, 441–473.

Folke, C., Pritchard, L. Jr, Berkes, F., Colding, J., Svedin, U. (2007). The problem of fit between ecosystems and institutions: ten years later. *Ecology and Society*, 12, 30.

Gadgil, M., Olsson, P., Berkes, F., Folke, C. (2003). Exploring the role of local ecological knowledge in ecosystem management: three case studies. In *Navigating Social–Ecological Systems: Building Resilience for Complexity and Change*. Cambridge: Cambridge University Press, pp. 189–209.

Garcia, C. A. and Lescuyer, G. (2008). Monitoring, indicators and community based forest management in the tropics: pretexts or red herrings? *Biodiversity and Conservation*, 17, 1303–1317.

Garcia, S., Allison, E., Andrew, N. *et al.* (2008). Towards integrated assessment and advice in small-scale fisheries: principles and processes. In *FAO Fisheries and Aquaculture Technical Paper No. 515*. Rome: FAO.

Gelcich, S., Edwards-Jones, G., Kaiser, M., Castilla, J. (2006). Co-management policy can reduce resilience in traditionally managed marine ecosystems. *Ecosystems*, 9, 951–966.

Gunderson, L. and Light, S. (2006). Adaptive management and adaptive governance in the Everglades ecosystem. *Policy Science*, 39, 323–334.

Holling, C. (1978). *Adaptive Environmental Assessment and Management*. London: Wiley.

Houde, N. (2007). The six faces of traditional ecological knowledge: challenges and opportunities for Canadian co-management arrangements. *Ecology and Society*, 12, 34.

Johnson, K. A., Dana, G., Jordan, N. *et al.* (2012). Using participatory scenarios to stimulate social learning for collaborative sustainable development. *Ecology and Society*, 17, 9.

Kates, R., Clark, W., Corell, R. *et al.* (2001). Sustainability science. *Science*, 292, 641–642.

Kendrick, A. and Manseau, M. (2008). Representing traditional knowledge: resource management and Inuit knowledge of barren-ground Caribou. *Society and Natural Resources*, 21, 404–418.

Kuper, M., Dionnet, M., Hammani, A. *et al.* (2009). Supporting the shift from state water to community water: lessons from a social learning approach to designing joint irrigation projects in Morocco. *Ecology and Society*, 14, 19.

Lee, K. (1993). *Compass and Gyroscope: Integrating Science and Politics for the Environment*. Washington, DC: Island Press.

Levin, S. (2006). Learning to live in a global commons: socioeconomic challenges for a sustainable environment. *Ecological Research*, 21, 328–333.

Lindenmayer, D. and Likens, G. (2009). Adaptive monitoring: a new paradigm in long-term studies. *Trends in Ecology and Evolution*, 24, 482–486.

Lindenmayer, D. and Likens, G. (2010). The science and application of ecological monitoring. *Biological Conservation*, 143, 1317–1328.

Maarleveld, M. and Dabgbegnon, C. (1999). Managing natural resources: a social learning perspective. *Agriculture and Human Values*, 16, 267–280.

Marın, A. and Berkes, F. (2010). Network approach for understanding small-scale fisheries governance: the case of the Chilean coastal co-management system. *Marine Policy*, 34, 851–858.

Meek, C., Lovecraft, A., Robards, M., Kofinas, G. (2008). Building resilience through interlocal relations: case studies of polar bear and walrus management in the Bering Strait. *Marine Policy*, 32, 1080–1089.

Moller, H., Berkes, F., Lyver, P. O. B., Kislalioglu, M. (2004). Combining science and traditional ecological knowledge: monitoring populations for co-management. *Ecology and Society*, 9, 2.

Mostert, E., Pahl-Wostl, C., Rees, Y. et al. (2007). Social learning in European river-basin management: barriers and fostering mechanisms from 10 river basins. *Ecology and Society*, 12, 19.

Muro, M. and Jeffrey, P. (2008). A critical review of the theory and application of social learning in participatory natural resource management. *Journal of Environmental Planning and Management*, 51, 325–344.

Olsson, P., Folke, C., Berkes, F. (2004). Adaptive co-management for building resilience in socialecological systems. *Environmental Management*, 34, 75–90.

Olsson, P., Folke, C., Galaz, V., Hahn, T., Schulze, L. (2007). Enhancing the fit through adaptive co-management: creating and maintaining bridging functions for matching scales in Kristianstads Vattenrike biosphere reserve, Sweden. *Ecology and Society*, 12, 28.

Olsson, P., Folke, C., Hughes, T. P. (2008). Navigating the transition to ecosystem-based management of the Great Barrier Reef, Australia. *Proceedings of the National Academy of Sciences USA*, 105, 9489–9494.

Oreskes, N. and Conway, E. (2010). *Merchants of Doubt: How a Handful of Scientists Obscured the Truth on Issues from Tobacco Smoke to Global Warming*. New York, NY: Bloomsbury Press.

Pahl-Wostl, C. (2006). The importance of social learning in restoring the multi-functionality of rivers and floodplains. *Ecology and Society*, 11, 10.

Pahl-Wostl, C. (2007). The implications of complexity for integrated resources management. *Environmental Modelling and Software*, 22, 561–569.

Pahl-Wostl C. (2009). A conceptual framework for analysing adaptive capacity and multi-level learning processes in resource governance regimes. *Global Environmental Change*, 19, 354–365.

Peterson, G., Cumming, G., Carpenter, S. (2003a). Scenario planning: a tool for conservation in an uncertain world. *Conservation Biology*, 17, 358–366.

Peterson, G., Carpenter, S., Brock, W. (2003b). Uncertainty and the management of multistate ecosystems: an apparently rational route to collapse. *Ecology*, 84, 1403–1411.

Reed, M., Evely, A., Cundill, G. *et al.* (2010). What is social learning? *Ecology and Society*, 15, 1.

Rist, S., Delgado Burgoa, F., Wiesman, U. (2003). The role of social learning processes in the emergence and development of Aymara land use systems. *Mountain Research and Development*, 23, 263–270.

Roling, N. (2002). Beyond the aggregation of individual preferences: moving from multiple to distributed cognition in resource dilemmas. In *Wheelbarrows Full of Frogs: Social Learning in Rural Resource Management*. Assen: Koninklijke Van Gorcum, pp. 25–48.

Roux, D. and Foxcroft, L. (2011). The development and application of strategic adaptive management within South African National Parks. *Koedoe*, 53, 1–5.

Ruitenbeek, J. and Cartier, C. (2001). *The Invisible Wand: Adaptive Co-Management as an Emergent Strategy in Complex Bio-Economic Systems.* Bogor, Indonesia: CIFOR.

Säljö, R. (1979). Learning in the learner's perspective: some common-sense conceptions. *Reports from the Institute of Education, University of Gothenburg*, 76.

Schultz, L. (2009). Nurturing resilience in social–ecological systems: lessons learned from bridging organizations. Doctoral Thesis, Stockholm: Stockholm University.

Schusler, M. T., Decker, J. D., Pfeffer, J. M. (2003). Social learning for collaborative natural resource management. *Society and Natural Resources*, 15, 309–326.

Selin, S., Pierskalla, C., Smaldone, D., Robinson, K. (2007). Social learning and building trust through a participatory design for natural resource planning. *Journal of Forestry*, 105, 421–425.

Sendzimir, J., Magnuszewski, P., Flachner, Z. *et al.* (2007). Assessing the resilience of a river management regime: informal learning in a shadow network in the Tisza river basin. *Ecology and Society*, 13, 11.

Standa-Gunda, W., Mutimukuru, T., Nyirenda, R. *et al.* (2003). Participatory modelling to enhance social learning collective action and mobilization among users of the Mafungautsi Forest, Zimbabwe. *Small-Scale Forestry*, 2, 313–326.

Steyaert, P. and Jiggins, J. (2007). Governance of complex environmental situations through social learning: a synthesis of SLIM's lessons for research, policy and practice. *Environmental Science and Policy*, 10, 575–586.

Steyaert, P., Barzman, M., Billaud, J. *et al.* (2007). The role of knowledge and research in facilitating social learning among stakeholders in natural resources management in the French Atlantic coastal wetlands. *Environmental Science and Policy*, 10, 537–550.

Vincent, J. (2007). Spatial dynamics, social norms, and the opportunity of the commons. *Ecological Research*, 22, 3–7.

Walker, B. and Salt, D. (2006). *Resilience Thinking: Sustaining Ecosystems and People in a Changing World*. Washington, DC: Island Press.

Walker, B., Holling, C., Carpenter, S., Kinzig, A. (2004). Resilience, adaptability and transformability in social–ecological systems. *Ecology and Society*, 9, 5.

Walters, C. (1986). *Adaptive Management of Renewable Resources*. New York, NY: Macmillan.

Walters, C. (2007). Is adaptive management helping to solve fisheries problems? *AMBIO*, 36, 304–307.

Walters, C. and Holling, C. (1990). Large-scale management experiments and learning by doing. *Ecology*, 71, 2060–2068.

Webler, T., Kastenholz, H., Renn, O. (1995). Public participation in impact assessment: a social learning perspective. *Environmental Impact Assessment Review*, 15, 443–463.

8 Principle 6 – Broaden participation

Anne M. Leitch, Georgina Cundill, Lisen Schultz and Chanda L. Meek

SUMMARY

Participation refers to the active engagement of relevant stakeholders in the management and governance process. Participation can range from simply informing stakeholders to complete devolution of power. It may occur in various or all stages of a management process: from identifying problems and goals to implementing policy, monitoring results or evaluating outcomes. Participation can play a role in supporting transparency, knowledge sharing, trust building, the legitimacy of decisions, and learning. These mechanisms can promote understanding of system dynamics and enhance the capacity of a management system to detect and interpret shocks and disturbances, which is central to facilitating the collective action required to respond to change in social–ecological systems. Examples are presented of how participation can support or undermine resilience of ecosystem services with cases showing both successful and unsuccessful participation in management of ecosystem services.

Principles for Building Resilience: Sustaining Ecosystem Services in Social–Ecological Systems, eds R. Biggs, M. Schlüter and M. L. Schoon. Published by Cambridge University Press. © Cambridge University Press 2015.

8.1 INTRODUCTION

Participation is considered fundamental to initiatives which aim to build social–ecological resilience (Walker et al. 2002). The participation of a diversity of stakeholders (P1 – Diversity) is thought to build trust and relationships which, in turn, improve legitimacy of the knowledge base and decision-making; to promote understanding of system dynamics; and to improve the capacity of a management system to detect and interpret shocks and disturbances (e.g. Ostrom 1990; Lee 1993; Folke et al. 2005). These attributes and factors are key to facilitating the collective action required to respond to change and disturbance in social–ecological systems (SES) (Lebel et al. 2006).

The spectrum of participation ranges from simply informing stakeholders to complete devolution of power (e.g. Arnstein 1969; Rowe and Frewer 2005). Participation can help to initiate and build relationships, but to do this effectively requires a nuanced understanding of the value of multiple perspectives relating to managing ecosystem services, of when participation is appropriate and of how participation should take place (Reed 2008). Participation can also mean involvement in different stages of the management cycle (from identifying problems and goals to implementing policy, monitoring results and evaluating outcomes; Stringer et al. 2006), the engagement of different groups (from inviting whole communities to targeting strategically selected partners; Kok et al. 2007) and different participatory methods and processes (Lynam et al. 2007).

In general, participation is considered by the ecosystem-service management literature for mainly pragmatic reasons rather than ideological reasons (such as supporting democratic rights). The ecosystem-service literature has a primary focus on stakeholders, who have an active interest in the management of ecosystem services or have relevant local or scientific knowledge (Olsson et al. 2004). Similarly, participatory processes generally target actors who can contribute in some way to the management of ecosystem services by providing knowledge or services such as information, monitoring capacities, management practices, funding or political support. Participation in ecosystem-service management tends to bring together stakeholders with different ideals and knowledge but it can also exacerbate inequities in power leading to conflict and restricting input from some groups (Arnold et al. 2012). Discussions in the ecosystem-service literature often gloss over aspects of agency relevant to participation such as conflict and power inequities between stakeholders. There have been calls for a more critical description and reflection of participation, particularly regarding issues of power and marginality (Leeuwis 2000; Arnold et al. 2012; Cook et al. 2013).

Different strands of participatory processes are emerging for ecosystem services such as adaptive co-management, which combines the learning-by-doing approach of adaptive management with the collaborative approach of co-management (Olsson et al. 2004; Armitage et al. 2007). Adaptive co-management emphasizes two types of stakeholder participation: the participation of actors with different types of ecosystem knowledge (both scientific knowledge and experiential, e.g. local, traditional and indigenous knowledge) and that of actors working at different ecological scales and levels of decision-making (e.g. both managers and policy-makers at local and national levels) (Olsson et al. 2004; Charles 2007). There is also an emerging interest in 'citizen-science' types of participation, particularly in monitoring ecosystem services whereby volunteers collect and or analyse data for ecosystem research especially where large data sets are required (e.g. Fernandez-Gimenez et al. 2008; Silvertown 2009; Devictor et al. 2010; Shirk et al. 2012).

8.2   WHAT DO WE MEAN BY PARTICIPATION?

Participation refers to the active engagement of relevant stakeholders in the management and governance process (Stringer et al. 2006). Participation can occur in all or some stages of an ecosystem services process: from identifying problems and goals to implementing policy and monitoring results, to evaluating outcomes. Generally, a prescriptive definition of participation is avoided in the resilience literature because who participates, and what they contribute, is context specific and should be revised throughout the adaptive management cycle (Stringer *et al.* 2006). Participative approaches – whereby 'individuals, groups and organizations choose to take an active role in making decisions that affect them' – have emerged and evolved through a series of phases since the 1960s and have featured a gradual devolution of power and gradual inclusion of different types of knowledges (Reed 2008, p. 2418).

8.3 HOW DOES PARTICIPATION ENHANCE THE RESILIENCE OF ECOSYSTEM SERVICES?

For ecosystem services to be resilient, a diversity of stakeholders need to be involved in their management to improve legitimacy, to expand the depth and diversity of knowledge, and to help detect and interpret perturbations. These elements are also interdependent and iterative.

First, participation can improve legitimacy of ecosystem-service management through establishing processes that are deliberative and support forming or developing relationships (Chapter 2). These relationships have the potential to build trust and shared understanding as a basis for collective action around approaching thresholds, developing innovative solutions or facilitating learning or shared experiences (Lebel *et al.* 2006). An example of effective participation which contributed to enhanced resilience of ecosystem services – in urban water planning in Indonesia – through improved decision-making and trust is described through a case study (see Box 8.1). In Makassar, Indonesia, a participation regime which effectively engaged and invested in a wide spectrum of stakeholders from the local water sector was able to dramatically improve relationships across the water domain (Kirono *et al.* 2013).

Second, participation can also promote the understanding of the system through increased knowledge. If a variety of actors participate, including those with non-scientific or experiential knowledge, it can promote understanding of the SES dynamics by providing a range of

BOX 8.1 **Urban water planning in Makassar, Indonesia**

Being resilient to a changing climate requires the security of natural resources such as urban water-supply systems. This necessitates an understanding of current and future water-resource-related issues as well as participation of the diverse range of actors and agencies involved in planning and managing the resource. In Indonesia, regional governments are encouraged to consider and integrate the risks of climate change into regional development planning. Indonesia's Mamminasata region in South Sulawesi Province has been earmarked by the Indonesian national government to become a model metropolitan region and an exemplar of urban development. Water security is just one factor required to support sustainable urban development of this region. Achieving the millennium development goals (MDG) for water and sanitation access is a key challenge for authorities, with the provision of clean water being the first of six priority programmes for the Mamminasata region.

In 2010–2012, a research project, Climate Adaptation through Sustainable Urban Development (SUD), was undertaken in the Mamminasata region in South Sulawesi by researchers from Australia's Commonwealth Scientific and Research Organisation (CSIRO), in collaboration with Indonesia's Hasanuddin University (UNHAS). Using a sustainable urban development framework (Kirono et al. 2013) the project aimed to inform policy development to improve access to clean water and to manage impacts of development and climate change in the main city of Makassar (Fig. 8.1a). With a population of 1.27 million people in 2009, Makassar was already experiencing pressure from urbanization, population growth and limited economic resources, as well as uncertainties in the future water supply due to a changing climate together with complex institutional structures and informal networks within the water domain.

Central to the SUD project was an effective participation regime, which involved the engagement of a wide spectrum of stakeholders such as policy-makers and managers in the local water domain. This participation aimed to facilitate a clear consensus and shared understanding of the problems facing the region and the city among cross-institutional stakeholders and build the capacity of these stakeholders

BOX 8.1 **Continued**

to plan for a changing climate. Throughout the project there was considerable investment in planning, undertaking and evaluating the various engagement activities. By the conclusion of the project more than 500 people from government organizations and academia had been involved in project discussions to enable input of local knowledge of the Makassar water system and its management. This was through knowledge sharing and training activities in both Makassar and Australia (detailed in Larson et al. 2012) (Fig. 8.1b, c).

Effective participation depends on getting the right people involved and supporting their continued engagement through relevant phases. The SUD project began by identifying champions from two key institutions in Indonesia and in South Sulawesi Province to assist project scoping. The latter involved a comprehensive identification of key stakeholder groups through stakeholder workshops, a review of government documents and interviews with government representatives. A stakeholder engagement plan (Larsen et al. 2012) helped ensure that the participation of stakeholders was effectively planned, resourced, monitored and evaluated. Designed as a living document, the engagement plan was updated continuously to note progress and outputs of engagement activities.

Participation often aims to build relationships and facilitate collective action. In this project, stakeholders identified the main focus-decided to be the reliability of water supply – via a workshop which involved 30 high-level representatives from a variety of governmental agencies (at national, provincial and city levels), non-government organizations, business enterprises, donor agencies and researchers. The research team assessed and modelled the water supply system and then identified adaptation options through a series of participatory workshops, thus incorporating both science and local knowledge. These potential adaptation options were presented at a subsequent stakeholder workshop (Tjandraatmadja et al. 2012).

Undertaking participative research processes challenges research organizations because a lack of predetermined processes and outcomes requires flexibility and understanding from research managers and funders. Important for this project was the flexibility of the composition of the research team. Once the project focus was identified it was

BOX 8.1 **Continued**

(a)

(b)

FIG. 8.1 (a) With a population of 1.27 million in 2009, the city of Makassar in Indonesia is already experiencing pressure from urbanization, population growth and limited economic resources, as well as uncertainties in future water supply due to a changing climate. Photo credit: Dewi Kirono, CSIRO. (b) Workshop participants discussed the problems facing the Makassar city and the broader Mamminasata region. Photo credit: Dewi Kirono, CSIRO. (c) Field trips presented a valuable opportunity for shared learning among stakeholder organizations. Photo credit: Anne Leitch, CSIRO.

BOX 8.1 **Continued**

(c)

FIG. 8.1 (Cont.)

used to guide the research-team composition and process. For instance, the final team comprised a central core of CSIRO and UNHAS researchers with additional expertise drawn from UNHAS students, environmental managers, urban managers, and practitioners trained in more than a dozen biophysical and social disciplines. Researchers were also required to have experience in facilitation. Building of local research capacity was enhanced through training in climate or water modelling of eight researchers at Hasanuddin University's Centre of Climate Change Response (CCCR) and the Bureau of Meteorology, Climatology and Geophysics (BMKG).

Evaluating and learning from participation can be difficult to do affordably and effectively. Effectiveness of the participation was evaluated throughout the Makassar project, with stakeholders at each project event being surveyed about what they had learned from the specific event and the broader project. In addition, the project and engagement process were evaluated by the project beneficiates (seven agencies) at the end of the first and second year of the project. These evaluations identified that the project was perceived as being extremely relevant and useful to stakeholders' work (Larson et al. 2012).

BOX 8.1 **Continued**

Outputs from the project are being used by the Makassar City Public Work Agency to develop a new water and sanitation masterplan. Local partners are also using the data generated for further research by Hasanuddin University such as the development of regional erosion maps, as well as the application of the methodology to water shortages in nearby regions. Benefits have also carried into the next generation of researchers, with an increase of postgraduate students researching climate change from three in 2010 to seventeen in 2012.

ecological, social and political perspectives that may not be acquired through more traditional scientific processes (Armitage et al. 2009; Folke et al. 2005). For instance, in a marine protected area (MPA) in Italy, Micheli and Niccolini (2013) found that successful participation by a diversity of stakeholders – categorized by their interaction with and influence over the MPA – resulted in a widely shared and implemented vision for the MPA. A critical element needed to galvanize involvement by key actors was the leadership provided early on by a small group of committed individuals. Subsequently, a highly effective director ensured strong awareness and support for the MPA and its mission, which also improved its legitimacy.

Third, participation can help to strengthen the link between information-gathering and decision-making, thus enabling responses to ecosystem change (Danielsen et al. 2005; Evans and Guariguata 2008). Where participation is specifically targeted at monitoring social–ecological change a number of specific outcomes have been shown to support the resilience of ecosystem services. In China, participatory monitoring was able to promote learning processes (P5 – Learning) that created opportunities for consensus-building, collective sense-making, and action (Rijsoort and Jinfeng 2005). After just one year of the implementation of the participatory monitoring programme in Yunnan, all villagers reported that they were better able to manage their resources. Both villagers and government staff reported increased communication and understanding between the two groups resulting in jointly developed management solutions to problems identified. In the Philippines, participatory monitoring of reef protected areas improved transparency of decision-making, which enhanced relationships between project stakeholders as well as resulting in the improved comprehension and perceived validity of information and its use in decision-making by local people (Uychiaoco et al. 2005; Evans and Guariguata 2008) While participatory monitoring led to better management of the marine ecosystem the authors report the most significant outcome was collaboration over practical management goals and strategies.

Experiences in Ecuador and elsewhere show that participatory processes, including participatory monitoring, can facilitate a shift in perceptions and attitudes (P4 – CAS thinking; Danielsen et al. 2005), which can strengthen the ability of management systems to respond to observed ecosystem-service change. Such a shift in perceptions and attitudes can lead to a questioning of existing institutions and decision-making, which may facilitate transitions to more appropriate governance arrangements that enhance the resilience of ecosystem services (Pahl-Wostl et al. 2007). Such transformative learning takes time, however, and there is little empirical evidence of it occurring: published studies tend to report on learning related to practice rather than on deeper reflection (e.g. Everly et al. 2011).

An example of participation which supports collective action in response to approaching thresholds is found in Australia. An extensive public participation and consultancy process was initiated in an effort to raise awareness about threats to the Great Barrier Reef, and to assist with new zoning plans to protect the reef (Olsson et al. 2008). Through greater awareness of the threats facing the Great Barrier Reef, the public participation process was able to achieve both broad public support for the final zoning plans as well as the alteration of marine park zoning plans, in order to incorporate the concerns of some groups. Similar experiences were reported in the water governance sector, where public participation was found to broaden the range of interests considered in ecosystem-service management (Lebel et al. 2006).

8.4 UNDER WHAT CONDITIONS MAY RESILIENCE OF ECOSYSTEM SERVICES BE COMPROMISED?

Although ample evidence suggests that participation can contribute to enhanced resilience of ecosystem services, actual attainment of this enhanced resilience depends on factors such as the participants, the process and the social and institutional environment (Stringer et al. 2006). These factors are interdependent and also context-dependent and, if not well thought out, executed, supported or resourced, can then undermine or compromise resilience.

The participants are crucial to the governance process because of their role in determining what ecosystem services are desired from a landscape and what should be the focus for resilience building (Chapter 2). Resilience of ecosystem services can be compromised through participation that fails to engage the appropriate individuals and groups with significant agency relating to understanding or governance; or if it fails to consider the context-specific nature of the participation or the need to review and revise participation during the policy process or the adaptive management cycle (Stringer et al. 2009). This is true particularly in cases of ecosystem services that are changing due to physical, ecological or social forcing events or trends. For instance, when migratory species begin to change their long-term movement patterns due to climate change, additional stakeholders may need to be part of any new stewardship action (Meek 2011). In the case of polar bears in many parts of the Arctic, sea-ice loss has driven bears on shore for longer periods of time, where they are more likely to have negative interactions with people. This change has required collective action at the community scale, rather than primarily amongst subsistence hunters, as was previously the case (Meek 2011).

The processes of participation are also important for ecosystem-service management, which suggest that degradation of ecosystem services can ensue through failing to have participatory strategies that successfully build social capital or that fail to effectively link to natural systems. For example, Buscher and Schoon (2009) show how transfrontier conservation areas, promoted as 'peace parks', often lead to competition and conflict between stakeholders instead of the envisioned collaboration and mutual understanding needed for successful conservation efforts. Similarly, participation of groups focused on short-term gains rather than long-term resilience can degrade rather than enhance the resilience of ecosystem services (Robards et al. 2011).

Participation can also enhance the influence of some stakeholders at the expense of others, by increasing their power or influence within the system (Blaikie 2006; Robards et al. 2011). For instance, participation can increase connectivity among different actors in the system, which can compromise resilience if stakeholders use the information gained through these peer networks to overexploit the resource. Increased exploitation then acts as a positive feedback loop, encouraging more exploitation and potentially degrading resilience. For example, Satake et al. (2008) built a model to compare the actions of two groups of forest owners: those who harvest their forest resources either under conditions of social learning or under conditions of 'perfect' information. When forest regeneration is fast, owners in both groups harvest the resource because they anticipate high profits with high recovery rates. When forest regeneration is slow, forest owners who benefit from social learning do not harvest their forests because they remember the long regeneration time. However, forest owners who work from a simulated 'perfect' information base continue to use the market and to harvest trees at the highest market rate without concern for future returns (P2 – Connectivity).

Resilience may also be degraded by participation if it exacerbates negative stakeholder relationships that, in turn, undermine existing networks or further weaken the capacity to share information or take appropriate action. For instance, where the legal or political authorities to act are unclear, the use of a participatory strategy to manage a resource that is contested may create antagonistic relationships between a government and resource users. Davis (2009) describes the work of the Long Beach Model Forest in Clayoquot Sound, British Columbia. This is a participatory research programme which was established in the midst of a complex system without a mandate to research social, cultural and political change that was largely driving the system. The lack of jurisdiction to implement ideas, as well as federal directives to consider only the technological problems of forest management, created participatory fatigue among stakeholders and led to a weakening of social capital. Similarly, experiences in Botswana and Malawi demonstrate that participatory approaches may weaken resilience in locations that do not have recent experience with democratic governance, or the capacity to protect resource users with little political power. In these cases participatory processes may weaken linkages between people, the existing regulatory system and the environment through corruption or rent-seeking by elites and newly powerful actors within the system (Blaikie 2006). A further example in Poland showed how limited experience of democracy, and a lack of leadership commitment to power devolution, meant that attempts at participation tended to reinforce existing power relations and therefore resource inequities (Niedziałkowski et al. 2012).

Participation processes may also compromise ecosystem-service management if they do not have a supportive social or institutional environment. In such cases, while individual participatory activities may be successful they will not foster resilience – and may even undermine it – if they are not nested within a supportive institutional setting. For example, weak forms of co-management that promote the devolution of responsibility to local resource users, without the authority to act to protect resources, may degrade the resilience of ecosystem services. In Chilean fisheries and elsewhere, formalized co-management institutions were found to undermine previously strong local resource management institutions (Gelcich et al. 2006). Gelcich and collaborators found that co-management policy in Chile, which was ostensibly used as a means to better achieve government management goals, added a layer of bureaucratic management institutions between resource users and the resource. This weakened local capacity to respond quickly to changes in the resource base. A similar situation has been reported in British Columbia, Canada where a government-driven participatory strategy was overlaid on unrecognized indigenous rights and hastened resource extraction as a way of asserting government over indigenous sovereignty (Charles 2007).

Finally, too many participatory schemes may unwittingly lead to degradation of the resilience of ecosystem services if communities experience 'consultation fatigue'. This is especially true in the case of poorly run processes which fail to tailor the approach to the needs to the community or fail to deliver change; or, for example, in small communities where representatives are required to assume many stakeholder roles. For example, Carter (2010) – in considering participation expectations of indigenous communities in Australia – stresses the need for appropriate representation and place-based approaches to replace the current situation of often unrealistic and uncoordinated demands for indigenous effort in engagement forums.

In contrast, Agrawal (2005) demonstrates how strong participation in Indian forest management can create a psychology of stewardship, or environmental subjectivity, which strengthens community stewardship of forests. Turnhout *et al.* (2010) argue that concepts of citizenship as an identity can be shaped as well as expressed through performing participatory governance, with positive and negative results, depending on the 'script'. In the case of ecosystem services, variations of inclusion and exclusion of perspectives, knowledge and preferences cannot be said to enhance nor degrade resilience a priori.

8.5 HOW CAN THE PRINCIPLE OF PARTICIPATION BE OPERATIONALIZED AND APPLIED?

The quality of the participation process has a strong influence over the ecosystem-service outcomes including social outcomes (increased understanding and trust) as well as environmental outcomes (changes on the ground). Operationalizing the principle of participation depends on the context in which it is applied but several overlapping factors contribute to effective participation.

- **Clarity of goals and expectations**. There is a need to be clear about which participative methodology is appropriate, as well as being clear throughout the participative process in terms of goals, roles and expectations (Lynam et al. 2007; Barreteau et al. 2010).
- **Involvement**. This includes getting the 'right' people participating (Brody 2003), retaining people in the process or engendering support for long-term commitment. Knowing who are the 'right' stakeholders and how to (and who should) identify them is challenging. Undertaking a systematic and thoughtful stakeholder analysis can clarify the diversity of stakeholder interests, which can help to ensure that appropriate stakeholders are involved as well as facilitating learning (Reed et al. 2009). Who participates depends on factors related to project design, such as inclusive or restrictive approaches, as well as on participant motivation, which is influenced by perceptions of the potential for personal benefit, success and power imbalances (de Vente et al., in review). A related issue is how to reward participation with a consideration of whether participants are rewarded for their involvement through direct payment, cost recovery or through less tangible rewards such as access to information or training. For example, Constantino et al. (2012) found in the ecosystem-service monitoring schemes in Brazil and Namibia that payment of local people for monitoring services was closely linked to psychological, social and political empowerment. Poor experiences with participative processes may inhibit involvement in future processes (Barreteau et al. 2010).
- **Facilitation and leadership**. Inspired and motivated leaders are essential to facilitate participation (Shannon 1991; Leach and Pelkey 2001; Olsson et al. 2004; Lebel et al. 2006). For example, effective leadership can support innovation, flexibility and adaptive decision-making to deal with ecosystem change through participation that builds trust, manages conflict, links actors, initiates partnerships among groups and mobilizes broad support for change (Folke et al. 2005). Facilitation also refers to developing and implementing effective processes for participation, which requires specialist skills especially in managing conflict, although not necessarily consensus (e.g. Arnold et al. 2012). Facilitators need to work hard to ensure that they are impartial, open and approachable. A competent facilitator

should be able to manage group dynamics including conflict, to draw out reticent participants, to encourage participants to question assumptions and positions, and to withstand short-term failure (Reed et al. 2008; Méndez et al. 2012). Participatory processes with skilled facilitators tend to have greater success through greater information-sharing and learning between participants, better conflict resolution and more equitable outcomes (de Vente et al., in review). A lay person should be able to build some level of competency for facilitation through leadership-skill development.

- **Capacity building.** Capacity building of participants may be required as the skills required to engage in participatory processes may not exist or may be overtaken by other priorities (Wollenberg et al. 2008; Berglund et al. 2013). Capacity-building objectives, such as social learning, are increasingly a primary goal of participation (Blackstock et al. 2007; Cundill et al. 2012; Muro and Jeffrey 2012) (P5 – Learning).
- **Power.** Managing ecosystem services is a political process and requires sensitivity in how it is acknowledged and addressed (see Chapter 2). Across a community, power differentials can determine who can participate, whereas during group processes power differentials and levels of literacy amongst participants can influence how they interact (Mostert et al. 2007; Cundill and Rodela 2012). Conflict, often the result of such power differentials, is also important to acknowledge and address (Young et al. 2013).
- **Resourcing.** Participatory processes are demanding in terms of resources, such as financial resources, time and effort (e.g. Berghöfer et al. 2008), as well as skills, expertise and flexibility (e.g. institutional flexibility in timeframes, allowing time for learning or failure; Enfors et al. 2008; Fernandez-Gimenez et al. 2008; Wollenberg et al. 2008, Méndez et al. 2012).

More generally, participatory tools are ideally used within long-term relationships in which all actors build relationships, develop trust and learn (Reed et al. 2008). Determining the most appropriate participatory tools is challenging; there have been a number of reviews of participatory tools (e.g. van Asselt Marjolein and and Rijkens-Klomp 2002; Rowe and Frewer 2005; Lynam et al. 2007; Tippet et al. 2007). Participatory tools can be described in terms of their goals, process as a means or output – for example to increase democracy, to enrich through increased knowledge or options, as decision support or decision-making processes – or to test novel alternatives (van Asselt

Marjolein and Rijkens-Klomp 2002). Lynam *et al.* (2007) recommend general-purpose tools that they believe are better suited in the early stages of analysis with more contextual tools applied later to narrow the focus. They also caution about the tools becoming ends in themselves, particularly computer-mediated tools.

While participation can be included at any phase in management of ecosystem services it is suggested to be particularly useful in the start-up phase; local knowledge can be particularly helpful for an early and broad view or to inform project design, which may help to ensure that local priorities are met (Enfors *et al.* 2008; Reed *et al.* 2008). Similarly, local commitment to place, or other galvanizing factors, can help to build unity early on (Childs *et al.* 2013). Participatory monitoring projects involving a diverse cross-section of affected communities in all phases of a monitoring programme are found to be most successful in achieving many of the above outcomes. However, it is a major challenge to achieve such broad-based participation in long-term programmes (Fernandez-Gimenez *et al.* 2008). Successful participation requires that participants feel that they are included and have a meaningful role. For example, in the Arctic, resource users' perceptions of inclusion were enhanced through the development of public policy that was aligned with local social patterns and networks (Meek 2012).

Common pitfalls found in operationalizing participatory processes include: insufficient consideration being given to participatory methodology, choice of methods in research, describing methods in research outputs or evaluating participation against objectives (van Asselt Marjolein and Rijkens-Klomp 2002); insufficient resources to fund successful participation (Sendzimir *et al.* 2007); insufficient training in communication and facilitation skills (Berglund *et al.* 2013); lack of clarity on the roles or rules of participation (Lynam *et al.* 2007); stakeholders becoming involved too late in the process to have meaningful impact (Reed *et al.* 2008); drawn-out processes stalling or delaying action (Brody 2003; Sendzimir *et al.* 2007; Reed *et al.* 2008); processes that become dominated by locally driven issues, ignoring more global drivers, particularly when local people have limited education or experience of other places (Enfors *et al.* 2008); and when there is an overreliance on volunteers, particularly in the implementation phase, which is insufficient (Schultz *et al.* 2011). In reality, meaningful participation is often restricted to a few stakeholders who have the resources such as persistence or creativity to work within often restrictive guidelines and practices (Turnout *et al.* 2010).

8.6 KEY RESEARCH AND APPLICATION GAPS

The role of participation in ecosystem management is well accepted (Schreiber *et al.* 2004; Armitage *et al.* 2007). Participation appears to function mainly as a facilitating mechanism that promotes the capacity for learning (P5 – Learning) and collective action in response to SES change. Evidence supporting this principle – i.e. that resilience will be enhanced through broadening participation – is equally matched with evidence highlighting situations in which inappropriate application of participatory management approaches may undermine the resilience of ecosystem services. Therefore it is essential to develop a nuanced understanding of who participates, under what conditions participation is appropriate and how participation takes place. The participation of stakeholders is usually necessary but not sufficient for resilience of ecosystem services. Despite a plethora of studies of participation in managing ecosystem services there are still a number of theoretical and practical knowledge gaps.

A key gap in current knowledge is the understanding of how participatory processes support resilience under different conditions, such as different institutional settings (e.g. institutionally polycentric or monocentric settings such as Huitema *et al.* 2009), resource-poor versus resource-rich contexts (e.g. Fabricius and Cundill 2010) and urban (e.g. Ernstson *et al.* 2008) versus rural systems (e.g. Smajgl *et al.* 2009). Although there has been a recent research focus on empirical studies of the influence of different participation arrangements to support ecosystem services (e.g. Muro and Jeffrey 2012; Berglund *et al.* 2013) we require more case studies to be able to better understand the influences of such broader contextual factors on effective participation.

A significant practical challenge remains the lack an understanding of the most effective processes for participation, including who should be involved (Stringer *et al.* 2006), who decides who should be involved and who excludes themselves. Other important considerations include the timing, approaches and tools for participative processes in different contexts (Lebel *et al.* 2006; Reed 2008) and how to balance process with outcomes (Berglund *et al.* 2013). Related issues are leadership, representativeness, power and accountability. These have been intensively studied across many domains, and we know these are important in ensuring that participatory processes are effective. However, they are often difficult to manage or measure in practice. We continue to need specific case studies (e.g. Micheli and Niccolini 2013) that demonstrate empirically how leadership contributes to successful ecosystem-service management.

An additional challenge remains that there are very few empirical studies that demonstrate the outcomes of participatory processes for resilience of ecosystem services. There are also very few examples in the literature of failed studies, which would provide important learning for others (Lynam *et al.* 2007). One of the reasons for the paucity of data is the difficulty in assigning causality, i.e. being able to say with certainty that a particular participatory process led to specific outcomes in terms of resilience of ecosystem services. This can be important to secure the long-term funding required to pursue participatory approaches. Key gaps relate to the identification of indicators or other metrics to evaluate both the outcomes of participatory tools and processes and also the implications of these for ecosystem-service resilience.

Despite these challenges participation is becoming increasingly entrenched in the management of ecosystem services. The emerging picture is that, while not a panacea, participation that enhances learning, trust and opportunities for monitoring resource condition, is likely to lead to improved resilience of ecosystem services. However, there still remain big questions around many practical concerns of processes, tools and the evaluation of participation.

REFERENCES

Agrawal, A. (2005). *Environmentality: Technologies of Government and the Making of Subjects.* Durham, NC: Duke University Press.

Arnold, J. S., Koro-Ljungberg, M., Bartels, W. L. (2012). Power and conflict in adaptive management: analyzing the discourse of riparian management on public lands. *Ecology and Society*, 17, 19.

Arnstein, S. R. (1969). A ladder of citizen participation. *Journal of the American Institute of Planners*, 35, 216–224.

Armitage, D., Berkes, F., Doubleday, N., eds. (2007). *Adaptive Co-Management: Collaboration, Learning, and Multi-Level Governance.* Vancouver: UBC Press.

Armitage, D., Plummer, R., Berkes, F. et al. (2009). Adaptive co-management for social–ecological complexity. *Frontiers in Ecology and Environment*, 7, 95–102.

Barreteau, O., Bots, P. W. G., Daniell, K. A. (2010). A framework for clarifying 'participation' in participatory research to prevent its rejection for the wrong reasons. *Ecology and Society*, 15, 22.

Berghöfer, A., Wittmer, H. F., Rauschmayer, F. (2008). Stakeholder participation in ecosystem-based approaches to fisheries management: a synthesis from European research projects, *Marine Policy*, 32, 243–253.

Berglund, B., Hallgren L., Aradóttir, A. L. (2013). Cultivating communication: participatory approaches in land restoration in Iceland. *Ecology and Society*, 18, 35.

Blackstock, K. L., Kelly, G. J., Horsey, B. L. (2007). Developing and applying a framework to evaluate participatory research for sustainability. *Ecological Economics*, 60, 726–742.

Blaikie, P. (2006). Is small really beautiful? Community-based natural resource management in Malawi and Botswana. *World Development*, 34, 1942–1957.

Brody, S. D. (2003). Measuring the effects of stakeholder participation on the quality of local plans based on the principles of collaborative ecosystem management. *Journal of Planning Education and Research*, 22, 407–419.

Buscher, B. and Schoon, M. L. (2009). Competition over conservation: collective action and negotiating transfrontier conservation in southern Africa. *Journal of International Wildlife Law and Policy*, 12, 33–59.

Carter, J. (2010). Protocols, particularities, and problematising indigenous 'engagement' in community-based environmental management in settled Australia. *Geographical Journal*, 176, 199–213.

Charles, A. T. (2007). Adaptive co-management for resilient resource systems: some ingredients and the implications of their absence. In *Adaptive*

Co-Management. Collaboration, Learning, and Multi-Level Governance. Vancouver: University of British Columbia Press, pp. 83–102.

Childs, C., York, A. M., White, D., Schoon, M. L., Bodner, G. S. (2013). Navigating a murky adaptive comanagement governance network: Agua Fria Watershed, Arizona, USA. *Ecology and Society*, 18, 11.

Constantino, P. D. A. L., Carlos, H. S. A., Ramalho, E. E. *et al.* (2012). Empowering local people through community-based resource monitoring: a comparison of Brazil and Namibia. *Ecology and Society*, 17, 22.

Cook, B. R., Kesby, M., Fazey, I., Spray, C. (2013). The persistence of 'normal' catchment management despite the participatory turn: coproduction and consultation framings. *Social Studies of Science*, 43, 754–779.

Cundill, G. and Rodela, R. (2012). A review of assertions about the processes and outcomes of social learning in natural resource management. *Journal of Environmental Management*, 113, 7–14.

Cundill, G., Cumming, G. S., Biggs, D., Fabricius, C. (2012). Soft systems thinking and social learning for adaptive management. *Conservation Biology*, 26, 13–20.

Danielsen, F., Burgess, N., Balmford, A. (2005). Monitoring matters: examining the potential of locally-based approaches. *Biodiversity and Conservation*, 14, 2507–2542.

Davis, E. J. (2009). The rise and fall of a model forest. *BC Studies: The British Columbian Quarterly*, 161, 35–57.

de Vente, J., Reed, M., Stringer, L. C. *et al.* (in review). How does the context and design of participatory decision-making processes affect their outcomes? Evidence from sustainable land management in global drylands. *Journal of Environmental Management*.

Devictor, V., Whittaker, R. J., Beltrame, C. (2010). Beyond scarcity: citizen science programmes as useful tools for conservation biogeography. *Diversity and Distributions*, 16, 354–362.

Enfors, E. I., Gordon, L. J., Peterson, G. D., Bossio, D. (2008). Making investments in dryland development work: participatory scenario planning in the Makanya catchment, Tanzania. *Ecology and Society*, 13, 42.

Ernstson, H., Sörlin, S., Elmqvist, T. (2008). Social movements and ecosystem services: the role of social network structure in protecting and managing urban green areas in Stockholm. *Ecology and Society*, 13, 39.

Evans, K. and Guariguata, M. R. (2008). *Participatory Monitoring in Tropical Forest Management: A Review of Tools, Concepts and Lessons Learned*. Bogor: CIFOR.

Evely, A. C., Fazey, I., Reed, M. S., Pinard, M. (2011). High levels of participation in conservation projects enhance learning. *Conservation Letters*, 4, 116–126.

Fabricius, C. and Cundill, G. (2010). Building adaptive capacity in systems beyond the threshold: the story of Macubeni, South Africa. In *Adaptive Capacity and Environmental Governance*. Berlin: Springer, pp. 43–68.

Fernandez-Gimenez, M. E., Ballard, H. L., Sturtevant, V. E. (2008). Adaptive management and social learning in collaborative and community-based monitoring: a study of five community-based forestry organizations in the western USA. *Ecology and Society*, 13, 4.

Folke, C., Hahn, T., Olsson, P., Norberg, J. (2005). Adaptive governance of social–ecological systems. *Annual Review of Environmental Resoures*, 30, 441–73.

Gelcich, S., Defeo, O., Iribarne, O. et al. (2009). Marine ecosystem-based management in the southern cone of South America: stakeholder perceptions and lessons for implementation. *Marine Policy*, 33, 801–806.

Huitema, D., Mostert, E., Egas, W. et al. (2009). Adaptive water governance: assessing the institutional prescriptions of adaptive (co-)management from a governance perspective and defining a research agenda. *Ecology and Society*, 14, 26.

Kirono, D. G. C, Larson, S, Tjandraatmadja, G. et al. (2013). Adapting to climate change through urban water management: a participatory case study in Indonesia. *Regional Environmental Change*, 14, 355–367.

Kok, K., Biggs, R., Zurek, M. (2007). Methods for developing multiscale participatory scenarios: insights from southern Africa and Europe. *Ecology and Society*, 13, 8.

Larson, S., Kirono, D. G. C., Barkey, R. A., Tjandraatmadja, G. (2012). *Stakeholder Engagement Within the Climate Adaptation Through Sustainable Urban Development in Makassar – Indonesia Project, The First Year Report*. Australia: CSIRO.

Leach, W. D. and Pelkey, N. W. (2001). Making watershed partnerships work: a review of the empirical literature. *Journal of Water Resources Planning and Management*, 127, 378–385.

Lebel, L., Anderies, J. M., Campbell, B. M. et al. (2006). Governance and the capacity to manage resilience in social–ecological systems. *Ecology and Society*, 11, 19.

Lee, K. N. (1993). *Compass and Gyroscope. Integrating Politics and Science for the Environment*. Washington, DC: Island Press.

Leeuwis, C. (2000). Reconceptualizing participation for sustainable rural development: towards a negotiation approach. *Development and Change*, 31, 931–959.

Lynam, T., De Jong, W., Sheil, D. et al. (2007). A review of tools for incorporating community knowledge, preferences, and values into decision making in natural resources management. *Ecology and Society*, 12, 5.

Meek, C. L. (2011). Putting the US polar bear debate into context: the disconnect between old policy and new problems. *Marine Policy*, 35, 430–439.

Meek, C. L. (2012). Forms of collaboration and social fit in wildlife management: a comparison of policy networks in Alaska. *Global Environmental Change*, 23, 217–228.

Méndez, P. F., Isendahl, N., Amezaga, J. M., Santamaría. L. (2012). Facilitating transitional processes in rigid institutional regimes for water management and wetland conservation: experience from the Guadalquivir estuary. *Ecology and Society*, 17, 26.

Micheli, F. and Niccolini, F. (2013). Achieving success under pressure in the conservation of intensely used coastal areas. *Ecology and Society*, 18, 19.

Mostert, E., Pahl-Wostl, C., Rees, Y. et al. (2007). Social learning in European river basin management: barriers and supportive mechanisms from 10 river basins. *Ecology and Society*, 12, 19.

Muro, M. and Jeffrey, P. (2012). Time to talk? How the structure of dialog processes shapes stakeholder learning in participatory water resources management. *Ecology and Society*, 17, 3.

Niedziałkowski, K., Paavola, J., Jędrzejewska, B. (2012). Participation and protected areas governance: the impact of changing influence of local authorities on the conservation of the Białowieża Primeval Forest, Poland. *Ecology and Society*, 17, 2.

Olsson, P., Folke, C., Berkes, F. (2004). Adaptive comanagement for building resilience in social–ecological systems. *Environmental Management*, 34, 75–90.

Olsson, P., Folke, C., Hughes, T. P. (2008). Navigating the transition to ecosystem-based management of the Great Barrier Reef, Australia. *Proceedings of the National Academy of Sciences USA*, 105, 9489–9494.

Ostrom, E. (1990). *Governing the Commons: The Evolution of Institutions for Collective Action*. New York, NY: Cambridge University Press.

Pahl-Wostl, C., Sendzimir, J. Jeffrey, P. et al. (2007). Managing change toward adaptive water management through social learning. *Ecology and Society*, 12, 30.

Reed, M. S. (2008). Stakeholder participation for environmental management: a literature review. *Biological Conservation*, 141, 2417–2431.

Reed, M. S., Dougill, A. J., Baker, T. R. (2008). Participatory indicator development: what can ecologists and local communities learn from each other. *Ecological Applications*, 18, 1253–1269.

Reed, M. S., Graves, A., Dandy, N. et al. (2009). Who's in and why? A typology of stakeholder analysis methods for natural resource management. *Journal of Environmental Management*, 90, 1933–1949.

Rijsoort, J. and Jinfeng, Z. (2005). Participatory resource monitoring as a means for promoting social change in Yunnan, China. *Biodiversity and Conservation*, 14, 2543–2573.

Robards, M. D., Schoon, M. L., Meek, C. L., Engle, N. L. (2011). The importance of social drivers in the resilient provision of ecosystem services. *Global Environmental Change*, 21, 522–529.

Rowe, G. and Frewer, L. (2005). A typology of public engagement mechanisms. *Science Technology and Human Values*, 30, 251–290.

Satake, A., Iwasa, Y., Levin, S. (2008). Comparison between perfect information and passive–adaptive social learning models of forest harvesting. *Theoretical Ecology*, 1, 189–197.

Schreiber, E. S., Bearlin, A. R., Nicol, S. J., Todd, C. R. (2004). Adaptive management: a synthesis of current understanding and effective application. *Ecological Management and Restoration*, 5, 177–182.

Schultz, L., Duit, A., Folke, C. (2011). Participation, adaptive co-management, and management performance in the World Network of Biosphere Reserves. *World Development*, 39, 662–671.

Sendzimir, J., Magnuszewski, P., Flachner, Z. et al. (2007). Assessing the resilience of a river management regime: informal learning in a shadow network in the Tisza river basin. *Ecology and Society*, 13, 11.

Shannon, M. A. (1991). Resource managers as policy entrepreneurs. *Journal of Forestry*, 89, 27–30.

Shirk, J. L., Ballard, H. L., Wilderman, C. C. et al. (2012). Public participation in scientific research: a framework for deliberate design. *Ecology and Society*, 17, 29.

Silvertown, J. (2009). A new dawn for citizen science. *Trends in Ecological Evolution*, 24, 467–471.

Smajgl, A., Leitch, A. M., Lynam, T., eds. (2009). *Outback Institutions: An Application of the Institutional Analysis and Development (IAD) Framework to Four Case Studies in Australia's Outback. DKCRC Report 31*. Alice Springs, Australia: Desert Knowledge Cooperative Research Centre.

Stringer, L. C., Dougill, A. J., Fraser, E. et al. (2006). Unpacking 'participation' in the adaptive management of social–ecological systems: a critical review. *Ecology and Society*, 11, 39.

Stringer, L. C., Dyer, J. C., Reed, M. S. et al. (2009). Adaptations to climate change, drought and desertification: local insights to enhance policy in southern Africa. *Environmental Science and Policy*, 12, 748–765.

Tippett, J., Handley, J. F., Ravetz, J. (2007). Meeting the challenges of sustainable development: a conceptual appraisal of a new methodology for participatory ecological planning. *Progress in Planning*, 67, 9–98.

Tjandraatmadja, G., Larson, S., Kirono, D. et al. (2012). *Climate Adaptation Through Sustainable Urban Development: Developing Adaptation Options to Improve Future Water Security in Makassar City: A Report*. Australia: CSIRO

Turnhout, E., Van Bommel, S., Aarts, N. (2010). How participation creates citizens: participatory governance as performative practice. *Ecology and Society*, 15, 26.

Walker, B., Carpenter, S., Anderies, J. M. *et al.* (2002). Resilience management in social ecological systems: a working hypothesis for a participatory approach. *Conservation Ecology*, 6, 14.

Wollenberg, E., Campbell, B., Dounias, E. *et al.* (2008). Interactive land-use planning in Indonesian rain-forest landscapes: reconnecting plans to practice. *Ecology and Society*, 14, 35.

Uychiaoco, A. J., Arceo, H. O., Green, S. J. *et al.* (2005). Monitoring and evaluation of reef protected areas by local fishers in the Philippines: tightening the adaptive management cycle. *Biodiversity and Conservation*, 14, 2775–2794.

van Asselt Marjolein, B. A., Rijkens-Klomp, N. (2002). A look in the mirror: reflection on participation in integrated assessment from a methodological perspective. *Global Environmental Change*, 12, 167–184.

Young, J. C., Jordan, A., Searle, K. R. *et al.* (2013). Framing scale in participatory biodiversity management may contribute to more sustainable solutions. *Conservation Letters*, 6, 333–340.

9 Principle 7 – Promote polycentric governance systems

Michael L. Schoon, Martin D. Robards, Chanda L. Meek and Victor Galaz

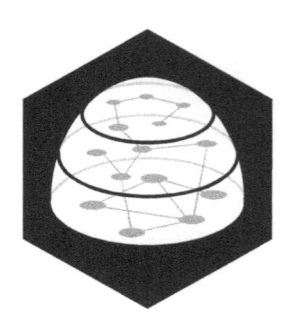

SUMMARY

Polycentricity is a governance system in which there are multiple interacting governing bodies with autonomy to make and enforce rules within a specific policy arena and geography. These governance authorities interact with others at similar scales horizontally and within nested scales vertically. Multiple governance units have been suggested to provide many institutional sources for enhancing resilience and create a mechanism enabling other resilience-enhancing factors. In theory, and in empirical cases, they have been found to create a foundation for learning and experimentation, to be a source of policy/institutional diversity, to enable broader levels of participation and to improve connectivity between groups while building in modularity and redundancy. Recent work has started to explore variance in polycentricity – notably, levels of structural inclusiveness (narrowly to more broadly representative) and degree of collaboration (type of collaborative activity). We see a need to learn more about

Principles for Building Resilience: Sustaining Ecosystem Services in Social–Ecological Systems, eds R. Biggs, M. Schlüter and M. L. Schoon. Published by Cambridge University Press. © Cambridge University Press 2015.

how inclusiveness and degree interact and how they lead to divergent outcomes in different situations, and also when polycentricity succeeds and fails, and to what extent. Studies to date in complex systems have been largely diagnostic and lacked predictive power and precision. In short, there is a lack of understanding of how to operationalize the idea of polycentricity in governance of social–ecological systems.

9.1 INTRODUCTION

Governing the human use of ecosystem services is a classic collective-action problem, in that distinct actors (i.e. individuals and organizations) can most effectively achieve mutually beneficial outcomes by working together across scales to resolve cases in which individual goals may be in conflict with societal outcomes, a classic collective-action dilemma (Olson 1965). Although there are many ways in which collective action can be achieved, polycentricity, as defined in the following section, is a form of governance system uniquely qualified to facilitate collective action towards sustaining ecosystem services in the face of disturbance and change. The ability to reach decisions and resolve collective dilemmas when confronted by a changing environment provides one aspect of how polycentricity improves governance.

Classic studies on governance for sustainability in social–ecological systems (SES) focus on sets of guiding principles for crafting long-enduring institutional arrangements (Ostrom 1990; Young 2002). Among these are basic guidelines for nested institutions, where sets of rules interact across a variety of scales to address problems or challenges confronted at different temporal and spatial scales due to systems dynamics and feedbacks occurring at these multiple scales. Nested institutions also enable the creation of rules for social engagement and collective action to 'fit' the problem they are meant to address. Further, good governance requires active engagement of individuals in the problems that directly affect them and allows them to participate, share their knowledge and resolve social and environmental dilemmas in their lives through participation in collective-choice arrangements.

Polycentricity directly addresses many of these good-governance concepts. One of the key principles of polycentricity is that better governance outcomes are the result of congruence between the institutional arrangements and a particular problem that they attempt to resolve. In effect, polycentricity attempts to match governance levels to the scale of the problem (McGinnis 1999a). This aspect of polycentricity equates with the notion of 'fit' as described in other policy literature, in which fit refers to mismatches between system properties and institutional attributes (Young 2002). It is thus particularly relevant to resources such as ecosystem services that have strong multi-scale aspects. This parallels the panarchical structure of nested systems (Gunderson and Holling 2002). Polycentric systems in principle allow for experimentation across multiple authorities at a given level as well as learning across them (P5 – Learning). What fails at one level may be rebuilt from broader levels that remained in place, and what works at one level may be extrapolated to other levels. Note that this 'experimentation' is often not planned or coordinated in advance as much as providing a process or mechanism of independent exploration and learning from other governance bodies. In cases of governance failure at one level, others can learn from it and reduce their own losses as well as innovate with broader levels and, in turn, facilitate renewal.

9.2 WHAT DO WE MEAN BY POLYCENTRICITY?

Polycentricity consists of multiple governing authorities that interact across different levels of the policy process (Ostrom *et al.* 1961). Here, governance refers to the exercise of deliberation and decision-making among groups of people in the act of self-ordering their relationships. Each governing authority – whether a state regulator, a national government or a regional management group – has the autonomy to make and enforce rules within a circumscribed policy arena for a specific geography (Ostrom 2005). For instance, while national government agencies have the legitimate authority to make rules that are binding on all citizens, a regional management group (such as a borough or watershed management authority) may have autonomy to self-organize within its own domain. In an ideal polycentric system, each individual governing body interacts and links with other authorities both horizontally and vertically to achieve a balance of collaboration and autonomy.

Theoretical work on polycentricity often confronts two areas of confusion, neither of which has a universally accepted solution. The first concerns the differentiation between various types or versions of multi-authority governance. These include the concepts of subsidiarity, multi-level governance (Hooghe and Marks 2003), decentralization (Furniss 1974; Ribot 2002), network governance (Jones *et al.* 1997), policy networks (van Waarden 1992), co-management (Carlsson and Berkes 2005), adaptive governance (Folke *et al.* 2005) and many others. These types of governance structures all include some aspects of polycentricity – finding congruence between scale of governance and scale of the governance challenge, governing at multiple scales or building connections between governance authorities. However, none of these emphasize the core components of multiple overlapping entities across scales that facilitate experimentation at multiple levels, some level of connection across multiple levels as well as between authorities at a common level, and potentially different authorities for unique issue arenas. Nor do many of these alternative governance structures consider governance as an activity beyond formal governments that includes interactions and relationships, including non-governmental organizations (NGOs), civil society, the private sector and public–private partnerships. Thinking in terms of structural properties, policy networks and polycentric networks could be considered classes of governance networks, with the former concerned with particular issue areas and their articulation into public policy (e.g. fisheries policy) and the latter describing a governance system responsible for achieving outcomes (e.g. multi-jurisdictional landscape cooperatives). Polycentric systems can be described not only through their degrees of connectivity, however; they also feature elements of modularity and redundancy important for fostering resilience to shocks (P1 – Diversity and Redundancy, P2 – Connectivity). We discuss this further in the following section.

The second area of confusion stems from the assessment of polycentricity in a system. Frequently, the literature suggests a binary, polycentric or monocentric division in governance (Ostrom and Parks 1999). Other literature suggests that everything is polycentric to some extent, which brings the challenge of identifying causal variables to evaluate outcomes between governance systems. There have been very few efforts to distinguish gradations of polycentricity, although Galaz *et al.* (2012) is a notable exception. In the current text, we examine polycentricity along two gradients. First, we see a continuum of structures from a monocentric, top-down centralized government to a highly decentralized, polycentric governance system with gradations along the number and diversity of governance bodies – what we term 'breadth of inclusion'. In the past this concept has been termed the system's 'diffusiveness'; however, the connotation of dispersion and movement through a medium alludes to something different than our aims (Aligica and Tarko 2012). Second, we also see a continuum regarding the type of activities between authorities in a polycentric system, which Galaz *et al.* (2012) term the degree of polycentricity. Here, collaboration ranges from information-sharing to coordination (weak polycentrism) to problem-solving and, ultimately, internal conflict resolution (strong polycentrism), which we also refer to as 'collaborative degree'. In our conceptualization, degree also encompasses the amount of modularity (P2) and connectivity (P2) of the governance system, ranging from anarchy, in which collaborating governance bodies are non-hierarchical as in international agreements, to nested legal authorities within a federalist system.

In this chapter, we see the shift of governance agents towards increasing breadth of inclusion as contributing to the resilient provision of ecosystem services from an SES. We also see benefit from examining the collaborative degree of polycentricity to further assess resilience, although, as detailed in Section 9.6, these points still need empirical testing.

9.3 HOW DOES POLYCENTRICITY ENHANCE THE RESILIENCE OF ECOSYSTEM SERVICES?

Polycentric governance, in contrast to more monocentric strategies, is believed to enhance the resilience of ecosystem services in several fundamental ways (common in all systems), all of which link with other principles in this book: (i) providing opportunities for enhanced learning and experimentation (P5); (ii) enabling broader levels of participation (P6); (iii) improving connectivity (P2) in governance; (iv) creating modularity (P2); (v) improving the potential for response diversity (P1); (vi) building in redundancy (P1) that can minimize and correct errors in governance; and (vii) increasing accountability and improving fit between resources and institutions (P6). See Table 9.1 for examples. We discuss how each of these varies based on breadth of inclusion and collaborative degree.

First, a broadly inclusive system with governance at multiple smaller scales provides opportunities for experimentation at more localized levels, creating natural experiments for trying different policies (Brondizio et al. 2009). Such processes are essential for learning. An example includes the collaboration between local fishing fleets and state governmental units in the lobster fisheries of Maine (Acheson 1988). Local communities have crafted multiple individualized, context-specific rules, often building on innovations from neighbouring groups. Other examples include: the interplay between local ejidos, the state and the national government in Mexican forest governance; the importance of nested cross-scale linkages with higher levels of governance in the Seri fisheries of the Gulf of California (Basurto and Ostrom 2009); and co-management systems for protected areas (Reid et al. 2004). In all of these examples, a more inclusive system, with multiple centres of authority, provides laboratories for institutional arrangement trials. These systems vary in their collaborative degree of polycentricity depending on the specific nature of the problem, ranging from information-sharing in the case of the Mexican forest governance to coordination and problem-solving in

Table 9.1 Mechanisms by which polycentricity enhances resilience of ecosystem services

Mechanism	Example	Source
Provides opportunities for enhanced learning and experimentation (P5)	Collaboration between local organizations and state governmental units in the lobster fisheries of Maine	Acheson 1988
Broadens participation across scales (P6)	Local and regional water governance where polycentric institutions and/or organizations facilitate participation by a broad range of actors and the incorporation of local, traditional and scientific knowledge	Neef 2009; Murtinho and Hayes 2012
Improves connectivity in governance (P2)	Nested cross-scale linkages with higher levels of governance in the Seri fisheries of Gulf of California	Basurto and Ostrom 2009

Creates modularity (P2)	Linked but separate legal systems in former British colonies allow for a common evolution of the recognition of aboriginal rights while rooted in each context by each country's legal institutions	Havemann 2001
Improves the potential for response diversity (P1)	Where institutional failure occurs at the national and international level, local-level conservation actions can provide functional redundancy by, for instance, protecting species through assisted migration, protection of migration corridors and other place-based actions	Rohlf 2001
Builds in redundancy that can minimize and correct errors in governance (P1)	The United States federal government's capacity to protect endangered species in cases where local efforts prove ineffectual	Nagle and Ruhl 2002

the case of some co-management cases (Schoon 2012) to stronger collaborative polycentricity in other cases such as in federal land management (Galaz et al. 2012) and subsistence whaling in Alaska (Meek 2013).

Second, by increasing the breadth of inclusion, a polycentric system can capitalize on scale-specific knowledge (e.g. traditional and local knowledge) to aid learning through sharing information, experience and knowledge across cultures and scales (Olsson et al. 2004), while also providing an opportunity for broader participation. Local levels with more direct linkages to resource provision and use provide institutional diversity from which successes can be shared with others (Folke et al. 1998). This is particularly evident in local and regional water governance where polycentric institutions and/or organizations have facilitated participation by a broad range of actors and the incorporation of local, traditional and scientific knowledge (Neef 2009; Murtinho and Hayes 2012). Furthermore, this decentralized design often serves to increase the legitimacy of the governance system at a given level with more scale-specific input into decision-making (Engle and Lemos 2010). Increasing legitimacy and accountability through pushing the decision-making authority (and responsibility) down to the lowest level possible further benefits monitoring and enforcement of (locally designed and implemented) rules. Monitoring and enforcing rules are two factors of critical importance to the creation and maintenance of sustainable institutional arrangements (Ostrom 1990). The maintenance of long-enduring institutions, in turn, has been documented to be a necessary precursor to the resilient provision of ecosystem services (Ostrom 1990).

Further, a polycentric approach has been suggested to confer connectivity, modularity, response diversity and functional redundancy that can foster preservation of key SES elements in the face of disturbance and change. These characteristics of resilient governance may in turn change in scope with increasingly collaborative degrees of polycentricity. An illustration of the effects of connectivity and modularity can be found when broader levels of governance step in after local levels collapse and fail. Examples include the United States federal government's capacity to protect endangered species in cases where local efforts prove ineffectual (Nagle and Ruhl 2002). On the other hand, where institutional failure occurs at the national and international level, local-level conservation actions can provide functional redundancy by, for instance, protecting species through assisted migration, the protection of migration corridors and other place-based actions (Rohlf 2001). The modularity of a system allows governance bodies to reduce exposure to failures and losses of collaborators through a degree of independence. For instance, the inclusion of NGOs in a governance system may provide a diversity of ideological positions and policy ideas that are less directly affected by changes in a country's elected leadership than are governmental agencies (Schoon and York 2011). As described in the introduction to polycentricity above, these notions of modularity and redundancy through polycentric centres of authority provide opportunities for successful experimentation to spread and failures to remain isolated. Functional redundancy and response diversity also emerge from the multiple arenas, and the chance for experimentation. Studies of decentralization highlight how pushing authority to lower, more problem-oriented levels enables a diversity of approaches, comparable to the concept of response diversity within an ecosystem.

9.4 UNDER WHAT CONDITIONS MAY RESILIENCE OF ECOSYSTEM SERVICES BE COMPROMISED?

Polycentric governance raises three key challenges, which if not resolved may lead to degradation of ecosystem services at one or more scales. The first is that of the need to balance redundancy and experimentation, the benefits of which are described above, with inefficiencies resulting from both overlapping authority and increasing transaction costs (Parks and Ostrom 1999). In effect, the transaction costs may rise due to the accelerating needs for coordination with other centres of authority, both horizontally and vertically, as well as problems emerging from a lack of coordination, unnecessary overlapping of authority and escalating communication and information costs in general (also see P1 – Diversity and redundancy). Ecosystem services are produced at a wide range of scales, from local provision of food to global climate regulation, so that trying to match levels of governance to the scale of different ecosystem services may call for a very large number of governance arrangements. Additionally, the costs of maintaining polycentric governance structures must include that of overlap and redundancy beyond the increasing transaction costs. These transaction costs also include the challenge of addressing the capacity of governments and civil society to create governance providers at multiple scales. While these may often include NGOs and other groups beyond formal government, the overlap may often prove overwhelming, particularly in a developing world context. Additionally, the inclusion of non-state and non-democratically elected actors raises questions of legitimacy, transparency and accountability (Black 2008). In such cases, a reduced 'fit' may counterbalance the required capacity to do the task adequately. For instance, South Africa's National Water Act advocates integrated water resource management and working towards improved institutional fit, yet it acknowledges the need to manage adaptively based on system constraints and uncertainty in complex systems (Pollard and du Toit 2008). The benefits of increasing breadth must be compared to the costs. On the other hand, where a mismatch exists between the scale of governance and a particular ecosystem services lack of understanding, enforcement and resources at the appropriate scale may lead to failures, as, for example, in the lack of institutions governing global marine fisheries (Berkes *et al.* 2006; see also Box 9.1). Of course, institutions covering increased breadth without the funds or capacity to accomplish their goals may preclude any potential benefits.

A second challenge is that of negotiating trade-offs between various ecosystem-service users (Rodriguez *et al.* 2006; Robards *et al.* 2011). Trade-offs may occur when impacts are incurred by those not affecting or benefiting from an ecosystem service (Chapin *et al.* 2006), or between conflicting goals and needs among users of current or potential ecosystem services (Søreng 2006). In such cases, a polycentric approach may lead to degradation of ecosystem services at some scales if powerful elites can externalize trade-offs from their area of interest (e.g. constituency; see Chapter 2). An example of this phenomenon is the trade-off between domestic energy security and mitigating climate change when countries determine oil and gas development policy (Chalvatzis and Hooper 2009). Encouraging domestic oil and gas production, especially under conditions which require carbon-intensive extraction methods, prioritizes energy security over environmental or other considerations. Nelson *et al.* (2009) also provide examples of biodiversity conservation and ecosystem-service trade-offs in the Wilamette Valley of Oregon, which shows potential trade-offs under a variety of scenarios. The challenge is not only one of political struggle between competing groups, however. It may also occur between groups at a given level or between levels that are uncoordinated (due to collective-action problems or lack of social–ecological understanding), with the potential for conflicting or contradictory actions. Theoretically, the likelihood for this problem increases as a system moves from a monocentric, top-down system to a more polycentric system. At the same time, as the collaborative degree of polycentricity moves from weaker to stronger, the problem alleviates at the expense of an increase in transaction costs.

Trade-offs between and across both scales and user groups links to a third challenge: politics, or the process of resolving conflict and making collective decisions over how to allocate trade-offs. One of the largest problems in SES governance arises from the issue of who bears the costs and who benefits from enhancing resilience in favour of particular ecosystem services (Lebel *et al.* 2006; Robards *et al.* 2011). Polycentric governance systems enable those dissatisfied with politics at one scale to go 'scale-shopping' for a more favourable political venue in which to frame a specific issue, as when local NGOs who are dissatisfied with their national government's policies advocate for international regimes over the same issue. Likewise, this trade-off can be mitigated in the movement from a weakly polycentric system to one with a more collaborative degree of polycentricity, with an increasing focus on collective problem-solving and conflict resolution. Finally, political problem-solving over allocation of resources can also be affected by the collaborative degree of polycentricity in terms of connectivity (P2) and modularity (P2). For instance, in former British colonies such as Canada, New Zealand and Australia, legal rulings relating to aboriginal rights (i.e. land rights, self-governance rights, etc.) in one jurisdiction may affect other jurisdictions through the shared system of British Common Law (Havemann 2001). As a result, the political power of indigenous peoples in governing ecosystem services rests in no small part on the extent to which their property rights to ecosystem services are recognized in other countries governed by this common law. In some jurisdictions, the protection of aboriginal rights through domestic law and/or constitutional provisions provides some level of modularity from the effects of British Common Law (Robards and Lovecraft 2010).

Evidence further suggests that polycentric governance structures are most effective in securing resilience of ecosystem services in cases where groups have open communication, accountability for actions and time to work together in order to build trust and social capital (Lebel *et al.* 2006; also see P6 – Participation). In effect, increasing polycentricity coincides with what has been coined 'collaborative resilience' (Goldstein 2011). This corresponds with the shift from weak collaborative degrees to stronger forms. An example is the traditional management of provisioning services in the Chisasibi First Nation of Cree (Berkes 1999). Where those conditions are not met, as in the management of the Everglades for a variety of regulating services, polycentric governance is less or not effective (Gunderson 2000).

One additional caveat on polycentric approaches to governing ecosystem services is that polycentricity is just one aggregate form of governance. Under some situations, particularly short timescales or crises where coordination across scales impedes necessary action, there may be other tools (including top-down coercion or market approaches) that alone may accomplish specific goals more effectively than through a polycentric system (Imperial and Yandle 2005; Hilborn et al. 2006). For instance, in some disaster or crisis situations, top-down governmental edicts may facilitate more rapid recovery, as there is the capacity to lead from the centre, and thus benefit from hierarchical bureaucratic structures. However, see Galaz et al. (2011) for an explanation of the superior performance of *ad hoc* coordination of networks. Centralized control comes with its own set of risks, but it may facilitate rebound and recovery. One instance of this top-down governance 'working' is in the Great Barrier Reef Marine Park, where the large size of the resource system (350 000 km^2) led to a single large governing body at the 'scale of the problem' (Evans et al. 2014). Additionally, in situations where high levels of conflict exist, more monocentric, autocratic systems may have the capacity to act faster than democratic systems, at the clear expense of the benefits of polycentricity highlighted above. This 'advantage' has been featured in conservation debates and the preservation of highly endangered species (Woodruffe et al. 2005).

9.5 HOW CAN THE PRINCIPLE OF POLYCENTRICITY BE OPERATIONALIZED AND APPLIED?

One of the key shortcomings regarding the principle of polycentricity lies in the lack of understanding of how it can be operationalized. Often the literature on polycentric governance in SES focuses on the concept as a 'good' idea due to the proposed resilience-enhancing principles that it facilitates. However, current research is beginning to look at how variation in polycentric order – both its breadth of inclusion and collaborative degree, as discussed above – affects governance outcomes in different contexts. Rather than thinking in dichotomous concepts of monocentricity versus polycentricity, we can instead look to Fig. 9.1 and explore how different polycentric orders interact in different situations.

York and Schoon (2011a) highlight a number of collaborations in Arizona that, taken together, can be treated as a moderately inclusive

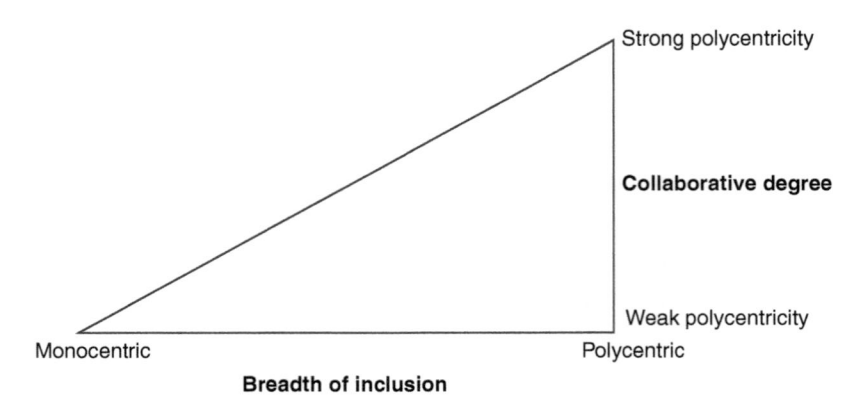

FIG. 9.1 The two continua of polycentricity: breadth of inclusion and degree of collaboration.

polycentric system for environmental management in Cochise County, with 20+ collaborative groups comprised of overlapping organizational actors making decisions. By degree, the various collaborations range from weakly collaborative polycentrism, as in the Sonoran Joint Venture or Northern Jaguar Project, where actors share information and are building trust, to others with higher degrees of collaboration. The Chiricahua Firescape planning, an example of polycentric coordination, shares information and has begun to create informal networks linking the various actors together. The Upper San Pedro Partnership goes further and coordinates monitoring and joint investment (polycentric ordering). On the same landscape, the Malpai Borderlands, representing a strongly polycentric system, is a tight-knit group of trusting relationships built over decades for monitoring rangeland conditions (York and Schoon 2011b). In aggregate, these multiple collaborative networks form a polycentric system of environmental management that is coordinated, with shadow networks emerging between and across collaborations at a broader landscape scale. These provide examples of how, using case studies, social network analyses and ethnographies, researchers can utilize the concepts of breadth of inclusion and collaborative degree to assess polycentric systems. However, missing in this analysis is still any attempt to assess how these variants affect governance outcomes.

Galaz et al. (2012) begin to do this by outlining an example of polycentricity in the form of a hybrid governance system created by international organizations, non-profits-making organizations and scientists to coordinate action, share information and gain international attention for issues related to ocean acidification and marine biodiversity, monitoring of the state of the world's oceans. As highlighted in Box 9.1, different network configurations represent different collaborative degrees of polycentricity with implications for the governance systems' resilience-enhancing capacity and the ramifications on governance outcomes. Finally, as described in the concluding section, polycentricity cannot be designed for but needs to be fostered by creating an accommodating social context.

9.6 KEY RESEARCH AND APPLICATION GAPS

Polycentricity has been suggested to contribute to the resilience of ecosystem services by providing a governance structure that facilitates other key resilience-enhancing principles, especially learning and experimentation (P5), participation (P6), modularity (P2), connectivity (P2), response diversity (P1) and functional redundancy (P1). However, simply establishing polycentric institutions is insufficient; the social processes enabling polycentric governance are essential to its success. These social processes include building trust and social capital, maintaining or developing strong leadership, social learning and bridging scales, through use of explicit strategies (Folke et al. 2005; Olsson et al. 2006). In short, we still need research to assess how polycentricity varies based on these other variables and how these interactions affect the resilience of ecosystem services, assuming that they are designed to protect or foster particular systems or bundles of ecosystem services. Additionally, coordination among scales and governance units, and negotiating trade-offs amongst ecosystem-service users at different scales, are critical to effective

> BOX 9.1 **Networks and polycentricity in international ocean governance**
>
> Governance at the international level has always been characterized by fragmentation due to institutional and actor complexity. Ocean governance is an illuminating example of this (Fig. 9.2). It entails complex multi-sectoral issues, actor diversity (ranging from nation states to private companies and NGOs) and the lack of an effective overarching institutional framework. This setting creates serious collective-action challenges, and multiple 'problems of fit' as existing modes of governance are unable to cope with rapid technological, social and ecological change (such as ocean acidification, overfishing, eutrophication).
>
> These severe governance challenges, however, do not imply anarchy. The work of Galaz et al. (2012) is an attempt to apply theories about polycentric governance at the international level with a special emphasis on international networks and their attempts to deal with multiple stresses posed by ocean acidification, loss of marine biodiversity and climate change. The authors differentiate between different degrees of polycentric coordination, separated by different levels of information-sharing, coordination and problem-solving (Fig. 9.3). As the article elaborates, coordination of this type evolves over time, and can shift between different modes depending on internal and external factors – such as the interests of the participating actors, and external political 'windows of opportunity'. These patterns of collaboration are not necessarily non-hierarchic. On the contrary, it requires one or several organizations able to keep the network together over time.
>
> Galaz et al. (2012) note that international organizations such as United Nations agencies play a key role as coordinators of information-sharing and action at multiple levels of governance, and across sectors such as science–industry–food security. While this coordination across multiple levels clearly indicates a possibility for learning and experimentation between governance entities, it also poses continuous challenges due to a lack of financial resources, negative interactions with other related institutions and potential legitimacy conflicts as key actors attempt to act more effectively in international policy arenas. Despite these weaknesses, however,

PRINCIPLE 7 – PROMOTE POLYCENTRIC GOVERNANCE SYSTEMS 243

BOX 9.1 **Continued**

(a)

(b)

FIG. 9.2 (a) A tuna market in Japan shows the products from the high seas fishing fleets. An estimated 85% of ocean fisheries are fully or overexploited according to the US Food and Agriculture Organization. Much of this problem stems from open-access conditions with little enforceable regulation. Photo credit: A. Maslennikov/Azote. (b) Several international regimes and other international governance initiatives, such as the International Commission for the Conservation of Atlantic Tuna (ICCAT) are working to address the lack of ocean governance, both directly and as part of polycentric governance systems. Photo credit: Deirdre Warner-Kramer/CC BY-NC-SA 2.0.

BOX 9.1 **Continued**

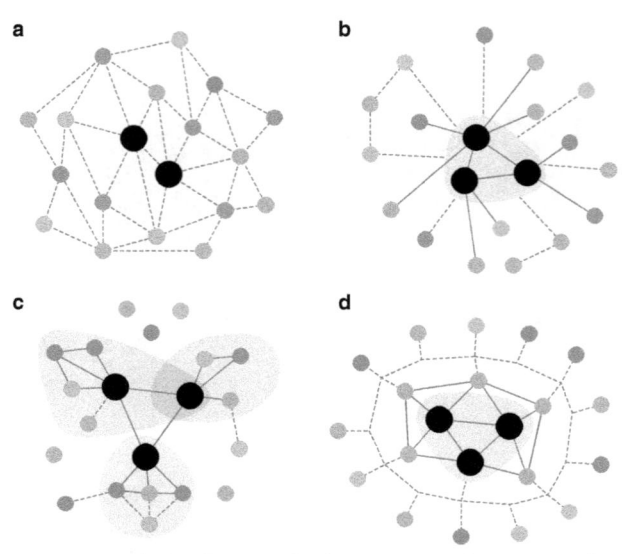

FIG. 9.3 Different degrees of polycentric coordination can be differentiated by different levels of information-sharing, coordination and problem-solving (Galaz et al. 2012). The first degree, communication, shown in (a), illustrates a simple communication network that allows for mutual adjustment in multi-actor settings. The second diagram (b) illustrates a stronger form of coordination as it combines communication linkages (dotted lines), with formal partnership arrangements (regular lines). Example (c) denotes polycentric problem-solving, a stronger form of polycentricity involving tangible joint projects/experiments between actors (shaded areas), which often overlap. The fourth degree of polycentricity (d) includes conflict resolution and is the strongest form of polycentric order; it involves strong formal ties between key actors as well as a suite of joint projects and the evolution of rules. Some external communication linkages to peripheral actors (dotted lines) co-exist with this stronger form of polycentric order. Figure based on Galaz et al. 2012.

patterns of collaboration of this sort can complement or support the *enforcement* of existing international institutions, as well as create the endogenous and exogenous pressure needed to induce changes in international institutions.

polycentric governance. Future work can assess how these trade-offs affect or change the 'effectiveness' or 'appropriateness' of different polycentric arrangements – the differences of collaborative degree and breadth of inclusion of polycentricity.

Key knowledge gaps with respect to polycentricity and its role in enhancing resilience of ecosystem services revolve around the implementation of polycentric governance and monitoring progress over time. Specifically, to what extent can polycentricity be designed, and what are the key indicators for measuring polycentricity? We have posited two measures of variation in polycentric systems and have defined our research along these gradients (Fig. 9.1). However, other types of variation in polycentric systems may prove more important in general or for specific cases. There is also a need to better understand how polycentricity functions in different contexts and at various scales, and whether it is appropriate in all societal contexts. In cases where polycentricity has failed, there is a need to better understand the mechanisms of failure – is it due to polycentricity, poor implementation of polycentric principles or some other cause? Comparative analysis of different polycentric systems could greatly advance our understanding in this respect.

The majority of case studies in the literature focus on the development of polycentricity as a consequence of a failure of single-level governance or of a shock to the resource or governance system. While many studies demonstrate failures of single-level governance, few studies have looked for failures in polycentric structures. The absence of such comparative studies means that evidence for the importance of polycentric governance in the resilient provision of ecosystem services is as yet inconclusive. While we need good policy and political scientists examining this, the field would benefit even more from an interdisciplinary perspective. In addition, researchers need to study how different polycentric arrangements under varying contexts affect governance outcomes.

However, the single biggest gap in the understanding of the concept, for both its resilience-building aspects specifically and for the concept in general, is in operationalizing and then implementing it. A great deal of thought, conceptualization and empirical research went into the basic theories of polycentricity (McGinnis 1999a, b, c). Since then, very little theoretical work has occurred beyond highlighting the commonsensical ideas in case studies that demonstrate the benefits of polycentricity outlined above, with little regard for the trade-offs or drawbacks, particularly the increase in coordination costs. Empirically, very few studies have attempted to differentiate between polycentric and monocentric systems beyond description and label, typically with the former being considered a universal good and the latter as a relic of bad governance. Even fewer have attempted to diagnose any sort of gradations of polycentricity. This chapter makes a first attempt to provide mechanisms for treating polycentricity with the variation necessary for its use as an independent variable so that future studies can begin to assess how polycentricity truly affects the resilience of ecosystem services.

REFERENCES

Acheson, J. M. (1988). *The Lobster Gangs of Maine*. Hanover, NH: Upne.

Aligica, P. D. and Tarko, V. (2012). Polycentricity: from Polanyi to Ostrom, and beyond. *Governance*, 25, 237–262.

Basurto, X. and Ostrom, E. (2009). Beyond the tragedy of the commons. *Economia delle fonti di energia e dell'ambiente*, 52, 35–60.

Berkes, F. (1999). *Sacred Ecology*. Philadelphia, PA: Taylor & Francis.

Berkes, F., Hughes, T. P., Steneck, R. S. *et al.* (2006). Globalization, roving bandits, and marine resources. *Science*, 311, 1557–1558.

Black, J. (2008). Constructing and contesting legitimacy and accountability in polycentric regulatory regimes. *Regulation and Governance*, 2, 137–164.

Brondizio, E. S., Ostrom, E., Young, O. R. (2009). Connectivity and the governance of multilevel social–ecological systems: the role of social capital. *Annual Review of Environment and Resources*, 34, 253–278.

Carlsson, L. and Berkes, F. (2005). Co-management: concepts and methodological implications. *Journal of Environmental Management*, 75, 65–76.

Chalvatzis, K. J. and Hooper, E. (2009). Energy security vs. climate change: theoretical framework development and experience in selected EU electricity markets. *Renewable and Sustainable Energy Reviews*, 13, 2703–2709.

Chapin, F. S. III, Lovecraft, A. L., Zavaleta, E. S. et al. (2006). Inaugural article: policy strategies to address sustainability of Alaskan boreal forests in response to a directionally changing climate. *Proceedings of the National Academy of Sciences USA*, 103, 16637–16643.

Engle, N. L. and Lemos, M. C. (2010). Unpacking governance: building adaptive capacity to climate change of river basins in Brazil. *Global Environmental Change*, 20, 4–13.

Evans, L., Ban, N., Schoon, M., Nenadovic, M. (2014). Explaining the Great in the Great Barrier Reef: the GBR Marine Park as a large-scale social–ecological system. *International Journal of the Commons*, 8, 396–427.

Folke, C., Berkes, F., Colding, J. (1998). Ecological practices and social mechanisms for building resilience and sustainability. In *Linking Social and Ecological Systems*. London: Cambridge University Press, pp. 414–436.

Folke, C., Hahn, T., Olsson, P., Norberg, J. (2005). Adaptive governance of social–ecological systems. *Annual Review of Environment and Resources*, 30, 441–473.

Furniss, N. (1974). The practical significance of decentralization. *Journal of Politics*, 36, 958–982.

Galaz, V., Moberg, F., Olsson, E. K., Paglia, E., Parker, C. (2011). Institutional and political leadership dimensions of cascading ecological crises. *Public Administration*, 89, 361–380.

Galaz, V., Crona, B., Österblom, H. et al. (2012). Polycentric systems and interacting planetary boundaries: emerging governance of climate change–ocean acidification–marine biodiversity. *Ecological Economics*, 81, 21–32

Goldstein, B. E., ed. (2011). *Collaborative Resilience: Moving Through Crisis to Opportunity*. Cambridge, MA: MIT Press.

Gunderson, L. H. (2000). Ecological resilience: in theory and application. *Annual Review of Ecology and Systematics*, 31, 425–439.

Gunderson, L. H. and Holling, C. S., eds. (2002). *Panarchy: Understanding Transformations in Human and Natural Systems*. Washington, DC: Island Press.

Havemann, P., ed. (2001). *Indigenous Peoples' Rights in Australia, Canada and New Zealand*. Auckland: Oxford University Press.

Hilborn, R., Arcese, P., Borner, M. et al. (2006). Effective enforcement in a conservation area. *Science*, 314, 1266–1266.

Hooghe, L. and Marks, G. (2003). Unravelling the central state, but how? Types of multi-level governance. *American Political Science Review*, 97, 233–243.

Imperial, M. T. and Yandle, T. (2005). Taking institutions seriously: using the IAD framework to analyze fisheries policy. *Society and Natural Resources*, 18, 493–509.

Jones, C., Hesterly, W. S., Borgatti, S. P. (1997). A general theory of network governance: exchange conditions and social mechanisms. *Academy of Management Review*, 22, 911–945.

Lebel, L., Anderies, J. M., Campbell, B. et al. (2006). Governance and the capacity to manage resilience in regional social–ecological systems. *Ecology and Society*, 11, 19.

McGinnis, M. D., ed. (1999a). *Polycentric Governance and Development – Readings from the Workshop in Political Theory and Policy Analysis*. Michigan, MI: University of Michigan Press.

McGinnis, M. D., ed. (1999b). *Polycentric Games and Institutions: Readings from the Workshop in Political Theory and Policy Analysis*. Michigan, MI: University of Michigan Press.

McGinnis, M. D., ed. (1999c). *Polycentricity and Local Public Economies: Readings from the Workshop in Political Theory and Policy Analysis*. Michigan, MI: University of Michigan Press.

Meek, C. L. (2013). Forms of collaboration and social fit in wildlife management: a comparison of policy networks in Alaska. *Global Environmental Change*, 23, 217–228.

Murtinho, F. and Hayes, T. M. (2012). Adaptation in resource-dependent communities: a call for greater methodological clarity in adaptation field research. *Society and Natural Resources*, 25, 513–522.

Nagle, J. and Ruhl, J. B. (2002). *The Law of Biodiversity and Ecosystem Management*. New York, NY: Foundation Press.

Neef, A. (2009). Transforming rural water governance: towards deliberative and polycentric models? *Water Alternatives*, 2, 53–60.

Nelson, E., Mendoza, G., Regetz, J. et al. (2009). Modeling multiple ecosystem services, biodiversity conservation, commodity production, and tradeoffs at landscape scales. *Frontiers in Ecology and the Environment*, 7, 4–11.

Olson, M. (1965). *The Logic of Collective Action: Public Goods and the Theory of Groups*. Cambridge, MA: Harvard University Press.

Olsson, P., Folke, C., Berkes, F. (2004). Adaptive comanagement for building resilience in social–ecological systems. *Environmental Management*, 34, 75–90.

Olsson, P., Gunderson, L. H., Carpenter, S. R. et al. (2006). Shooting the rapids: navigating transitions to adaptive governance of social–ecological systems. *Ecology and Society*, 11, 18.

Ostrom, E. (1990). *Governing the Commons: The Evolution of Institutions for Collective Action*. Cambridge: Cambridge University Press.

Ostrom, E. (2005). *Understanding Institutional Diversity*. Princeton, NJ: Princeton University Press.

Ostrom, E. and Parks, R. B. (1999). Neither Gargantua nor the land of Lilliputs: conjectures on mixed systems of metropolitan organization. In *Polycentricity and Local Public Economies: Readings from the Workshop in Political Theory and Policy Analysis*. Michigan, MI: University of Michigan Press, pp. 284–305.

Ostrom, V., Tiebout, C.M Warren, R. (1961). The organization of government in metropolitan areas: a theoretical inquiry. *American Political Science Review*, 55, 831–842.

Parks, R. B. and Ostrom, E. (1999). Complex models of urban service systems. In *Polycentricity and Local Public Economies: Readings from the Workshop in Political Theory and Policy Analysis*. Michigan, MI: University of Michigan Press, pp. 355–383.

Pollard, S. and du Toit, D. (2008). Integrated water resource management in complex systems: how the catchment management strategies seek to achieve sustainability and equity in water resources in South Africa. *Water SA*, 34, 671–679.

Reid, H., Fig, D., Magome, H., Leader-Williams, N. (2004). Co-management of contractual national parks in South Africa: lessons from Australia. *Conservation and Society*, 2, 377.

Ribot, J. C. (2002). *Democratic Decentralization of Natural Resources: Institutionalizing Popular Participation*. Washington, DC: World Resources Institute.

Robards, M. D. and Lovecraft, A. L. (2010). Evaluating comanagement for social-ecological fit: indigenous priorities and agency mandates for Pacific walrus. *Policy Studies Journal*, 38, 257–279.

Robards, M. D., Schoon, M. L., Meek, C. L., Engle, N. L. (2011). The importance of social drivers in the resilient provision of ecosystem services. *Global Environmental Change*, 21, 522–529.

Rodríguez, J. P., Beard, Jr, T. D., Bennett, E. M. et al. (2006). Trade-offs across space, time, and ecosystem services. *Ecology and Society*, 11, 28.

Rohlf, D. (2001). Jeopardy under the endangered species act: playing a game protected species can't win. *Washburn University Law Journal*, 41, 114–163.

Schoon, M. L. and York, A. M. (2011). Cooperation across boundaries: the role of political entrepreneurs in environmental collaboration. *Journal of Natural Resources Policy Research*, 3, 113–123.

Schoon, M. L. (2012). Governance in southern African transboundary protected areas. In *Parks, Peace, and Partnerships*. Calgary: University of Calgary Press.

Søreng, S. U. (2006). Moral discourse in fisheries co-management: a case study of the Senja fishery, northern Norway. *Ocean and Coastal Management*, 49, 147–163.

van Waarden, F. (1992). Dimensions and types of policy networks. *European Journal of Political Research*, 21, 29–52.

Woodroffe, R., Thirgood, S., Rabinowitz, A., eds. (2005). *People and Wildlife, Conflict or Co-Existence?* Cambridge: Cambridge University Press.

York, A. M and Schoon, M. (2011a). Collective action on the western range: coping with external and internal threats. *International Journal of the Commons*, 5, 388–409.

York, A. M. and Schoon, M. (2011b). Collaboration in the shadow of the wall: shifting power in the borderlands. *Policy Sciences*, 44, 345–365.

Young, O. R (2002). *The Institutional Dimensions of Environmental Change: Fit, Interplay, and Scale*. Cambridge, MA: MIT press.

10 Reflections on building resilience – interactions among principles and implications for governance

Maja Schlüter, Reinette Biggs, Michael L. Schoon, Martin D. Robards and John M. Anderies

SUMMARY

This book synthesizes and reviews the evidence in support of seven generic principles for enhancing the resilience of ecosystem services, i.e. the capacity of a social–ecological system to sustain a desired set of ecosystem services in the face of disturbance and ongoing change. Although some principles are better established than others, there is evidence that all are important. At the same time, none of the principles are universally beneficial, and all require a nuanced understanding of how, when and where they apply. Furthermore, the principles are often highly interdependent. Context matters and promoting the enhanced resilience of ecosystem services depends as much on how the individual principles are applied as on achieving an appropriate combination of principles. The nature of social–ecological systems as interdependent complex adaptive systems calls for governance and management that enhances aspects of a social–ecological system that help shape trajectories in desirable directions and enable adaptive responses to unexpected events. The principles are thus not final outcomes in themselves but rather features relevant for building resilience that should be considered when designing governance structures and management policies. More research is needed to better

Principles for Building Resilience: Sustaining Ecosystem Services in Social–Ecological Systems, eds R. Biggs, M. Schlüter and M. L. Schoon. Published by Cambridge University Press. © Cambridge University Press 2015.

understand the individual principles, how they interact and how they can be operationalized and applied in different contexts.

10.1 INTRODUCTION

The degree to which humans are shaping ecosystems at local to global scales poses significant challenges in providing for the well-being of the planet's growing number of people (MA 2005; Martin 2007). One of the critical issues is ensuring the adequate and reliable provision of essential ecosystem services, such as freshwater, food and climate regulation, to meet the needs of society in a world that is expected to continue changing rapidly over the coming century. Social–ecological resilience is one growing body of research that seeks to provide insights and understanding to help address this challenge, premised on the assumption that the functioning of ecosystems and the provision of ecosystem services cannot be understood without accounting for the actions of people who live in these systems. The resulting social–ecological systems (SES) behave as complex adaptive systems (CAS), characterized by dynamic interactions across scales, self-organization and possible abrupt changes such as regime shifts. Taking a resilience approach specifically contributes an understanding of how to build capacity to deal with change in SES, particularly unexpected and unpredictable change (Chapter 1).

This book has sought to help inform the design of governance structures for SES at local to global scales to promote development trajectories that favour a resilient supply of ecosystem services for human well-being in the face of ongoing social and ecological change. Rather than focusing on specific management actions, we have sought to uncover general underlying principles that could form the basis for developing governance arrangements and management strategies that are tailored to function within a particular SES. We have focused specifically on generic principles for enhancing the resilience of ecosystem services, which we define as the capacity of an SES to sustain a desired set of ecosystem services in the face of disturbance and ongoing change. This desired set of ecosystem services will vary between different SES contexts, and can change over time.

The seven principles we present have been derived from an extensive review of the social–ecological resilience and related literature, based on research conducted around the world over the past two to three decades, and originally summarized in Biggs *et al.* (2012). Clearly, any attempt to identify such general principles must make judgements on how to lump or split the large number of factors that researchers suggest affect resilience in SES. We grouped these into seven general principles based on extensive discussions and revisions with a large group of scholars in the resilience field (Chapter 1). However, other categorizations are clearly possible and new principles may emerge from further research. Our hope is that the principles we have identified will stimulate further discussion and research that expands and refines the principles over time, even if a definitive set of principles may never exist. At the same time, we believe there is sufficient evidence to support the current set of principles so that as they stand they can provide practical guidance that improves governance of SES and enhances resilience of ecosystem services. We also believe the principles can be applied more generally to foster resilience of other important aspects of SES, such as equity or education, although the details will clearly differ.

In this final chapter we briefly summarize the key findings and insights from each of the principles before reflecting on their interactions. When compiling this book the challenges associated with finding empirical evidence for the functioning of such general principles in SES characterized by the features of CAS, and operationalizing these principles in a given social–ecological setting, have come to the fore. Below we provide some reflections on these challenges as well as the implications for management and governance that arise from the multi-faceted, multi-causal and interacting nature of the principles and the SES of which we are part. We conclude by highlighting some future research and implementation challenges in this context.

10.2 KEY INSIGHTS FROM THE INDIVIDUAL PRINCIPLES

This book discusses seven principles that enhance the resilience of ecosystem services to disturbance and ongoing change. As the capacity of an SES to sustain desired ecosystem services in the face of disturbance and change is a central aspect of the resilience of SES in general (Chapter 1), our assessment of the principles also points to general aspects of building resilience in SES. The first three principles focus on generic social–ecological features of SES: (P1) maintain diversity and redundancy, (P2) manage connectivity and (P3) manage slow variables and feedbacks. The remaining four principles focus on key attributes of the SES governance system: (P4) foster CAS thinking, (P5) encourage learning, (P6) broaden participation and (P7) promote polycentric governance systems. We have assessed how each principle enhances the resilience of ecosystem services, but also how it might compromise resilience, and we have summarized the available evidence for its functioning across case studies and social–ecological contexts. We have further highlighted challenges for operationalization and implementation of each principle as well as key research gaps.

Although none of the principles is fully established or understood, we found evidence for the importance of all seven principles. A summary of our key findings with respect to each principle is given in Box 10.1. With respect to the generic features of SES (P1–P3), our review highlights that it is not simply diversity of SES elements such as actors and species that is important for resilience, but diversity in combination with functional redundancy (P1 – Diversity). Furthermore, we find evidence that more diversity is not always beneficial for sustaining the capacity of SES to produce desired sets of ecosystem services. Especially when it comes to the social domain, high levels of diversity can compromise the ability of society to find consensus for collectively adapting and responding to change, and can thereby compromise the resilience of desired ecosystem services. The international stalemate around action in response to climate change could arguably be interpreted in this way (Harris 2007).

BOX 10.1. **Summary of the different principles (modified from Biggs *et al.* 2012)**

P1. Maintain diversity and redundancy. Response diversity, in combination with functional redundancy, is particularly important for providing options to maintain ecosystem services in the face of disturbance and change. In general, ecosystem services produced by SES with high levels of diversity and redundancy tend to be more resilient than ecosystem services associated with low diversity and low redundancy systems. However, very high levels of diversity or redundancy come at the cost of increasing complexity and inefficiency, which may reduce the capacity for adaptation to slower, ongoing change. Operationalizing this principle involves recognizing the value of diversity and redundancy, incorporating it into SES governance and management, and monitoring change in relation to key ecosystem services.

P2. Manage connectivity. There is no simple relationship between connectivity and resilience of ecosystem services. Connectivity can enhance resilience by providing links to sources of ecosystem recovery after a disturbance or providing new information and building trust in social networks. However, if connectivity is too high a localized disturbance can spread throughout the system or knowledge can become overly homogenized. Operationalizing this principle involves analysing the social and ecological connectivity of the relevant SES, identifying important nodes or elements and optimizing connectivity patterns to facilitate restoration or minimize the risk of disturbances spreading.

P3. Manage slow variables and feedbacks. There is a well-developed theoretical basis for managing slow variables and feedbacks to maintain, restore or create new SES configurations or 'regimes' that underlie the production of desired ecosystem services. However, there are substantial practical difficulties in identifying the possible feedbacks and slow variables that underlie regime shifts and transformations, and their consequences for ecosystem services. Maintaining key regulating services as a proxy for important slow ecological variables may be one practical way forward. Likewise, building shadow networks and social capital may be particularly important to grasp windows of opportunity for

BOX 10.1. **Continued**

transformation. Where key feedbacks are known, practical measures should focus on monitoring changes in slow variables and feedbacks, developing governance structures that can respond to this information in a timely manner, strengthening feedbacks that maintain desired SES configurations, weakening feedbacks that trap SES in undesired regimes and addressing missing feedbacks between key SES drivers and changes in ecosystem services.

P4. Foster CAS thinking. Fostering CAS thinking may help researchers, policy-makers and ecosystem managers develop mental models that appreciate the properties of SES as CAS, and ultimately influence institutions and decisions around the governance and management of SES and ecosystem services. In particular, CAS thinking may increase the resilience of ecosystem services by emphasizing the need for more integrated approaches, the existence of diverse perspectives, the potential for non-linear change and the pervasiveness of uncertainty in the management of SES. However, empirical evidence for effects on the resilience of ecosystem services is limited. In practice, CAS understanding co-occurs and co-emerges with approaches that emphasize learning, experimentation and participation. Operationalizing this principle entails recognizing the barriers to cognitive change, acknowledging epistemological pluralism, investing in building an uncertainty-tolerant culture, using system frameworks, investigating potential non-linearities and thresholds, and matching institutions to CAS processes.

P5. Encourage learning. Learning about social–ecological dynamics through experimentation and monitoring is essential for enabling adaptation in response to changes in SES and ecosystem services. Learning at societal levels requires trust, and appropriate relationships and institutions to flourish. Applying this principle entails investing in social–ecological monitoring, providing opportunities for extended engagement, encouraging diverse participants, and effective facilitation and resources. However, the optimal ways in which learning might be facilitated specifically in the context of enhancing resilience of ecosystem services in SES is currently unclear and requires further research.

BOX 10.1. **Continued**

P6. Broaden participation. Participation is important for building trust and relationships, and for facilitating the learning and collective action needed to respond to change and disturbance in SES. However, a nuanced understanding is needed of who participates, under which conditions participation is appropriate and how participation takes place. Operationalizing this principle requires clarifying goals and expectations; involving the 'right' people, inspired and motivated leaders and facilitators; sensitivity to power; and sufficient resources and skills to enable effective participation.

P7. Promote polycentric governance systems. Polycentricity provides a governance structure that enables other key resilience-enhancing principles, especially learning and experimentation, participation, connectivity, and diversity and redundancy. Coordination amongst governance units, negotiation of trade-offs between users, and social capital and trust are essential for effective polycentric arrangements. There is currently a lack of understanding of how this principle should be operationalized in different contexts. Comparative case studies are likely to be very helpful in this regard.

Likewise, some degree of connectivity can enhance resilience of ecosystem services by providing connections to habitat refuges that can serve as sources of recovery after disturbances, as in the case of recolonization of disturbed coral reefs (P2 – Connectivity). However, very high levels of connectivity reduce the functional value of refuges as disturbances (e.g. disease) will tend to propagate across the entire system. We therefore find that, in general, intermediate levels of connectivity, be it ecological, economic or social, often offer the best prospects for maintaining resilience of ecosystem services. Lastly, there is substantial evidence that SES can shift, often abruptly, between different system 'configurations' with marked consequences for the set of ecosystem services provided by the system (P3 – Slow variables and feedbacks). Such shifts are associated with a change in the dominant feedback processes in an SES, and are typically triggered by gradual changes in slow variables, such as habitat connectivity or social norms. Managing slow variables and feedbacks to maintain, restore or create new SES configurations that produce desired sets of ecosystem services is therefore central to building resilience of these ecosystem services.

In terms of key governance features that are important for building resilience of ecosystem services, our review suggests that fostering CAS thinking among policy-makers and managers (P4 – CAS thinking) – particularly an appreciation of the interconnectedness of SES, the multiplicity of perspectives among ecosystem-service users and the potential for non-linear change and inherent uncertainty – can play a pivotal role. Although empirical evidence linking CAS thinking to management outcomes is limited, there is a considerable body of evidence regarding ways in which more linear, reductionist worldviews have shaped ecosystem-service governance institutions and management practices in ways that have eroded resilience of ecosystem services. Attempts to introduce CAS thinking may, however, compromise resilience when complexity is not effectively communicated, and can lead to a sense of bewilderment and decision paralysis.

In contrast, there is substantial evidence for the importance of investing in monitoring and learning to enable adaptation in ecosystem-service governance and decision-making in response to changes in ecosystem services (P5 – Learning). Effective learning requires trust, good facilitation and adequate resources. Learning can be undermined by failing to acknowledge asymmetrical power relations, the appropriate scale for learning activities and the human and financial costs involved. Participation is, in turn, central to building trust, and facilitating the learning and collective action needed to respond to changes in ecosystem services (P6 – Participation). However, a nuanced understanding is needed of who should participate and how participation takes place in order that it is effective. Finally, polycentricity provides a governance structure that enables many key resilience-enhancing principles, particularly learning and participation, diversity and redundancy, and connectivity (P7 – Polycentricity). Coordination amongst governance units, negotiation of trade-offs between different users, and trust are essential for effective polycentric arrangements. However, there are substantial issues associated with differential power among users in most governance models (discussed below).

We have discussed the seven principles individually in the preceding chapters for analytical reasons. However, they are clearly interlinked in substantive ways. These interlinkages can cause synergies as well as unintended or unanticipated (emergent) effects, as discussed in the following section.

10.3 INTERACTIONS AMONGST THE PRINCIPLES

As SES are highly interconnected systems, the properties and processes associated with the different principles do not become effective in isolation from each other. Applying any one principle in isolation will rarely lead to enhanced resilience of ecosystem services. For instance, polycentric governance (P7) and effective learning (P5) both depend on the social capital and trust developed through participation (P6), whereas connectivity (P2) may not enhance resilience in the absence of diversity (P1) among nodes.

Principles that build understanding of the complex, non-linear dynamics of an SES provide the knowledge base that governance and management can build on when preparing for and addressing change. This may include enhancing the response capacity of the SES by managing for diversity (P1) and connectivity (P2) or creating governance structures that allow for participation (P6) and learning (P5). A supportive SES and governance structure (P7) provides opportunities for operationalizing participation (P6) and creating response diversity and redundancy (P1). CAS thinking (P4) is essential to create the awareness and the mental models needed to inform new models of governance and management that can support these outcomes and address key feedbacks of SES (P3). Facilitation of collective action is essential for implementing the principles. In summary, our analysis of the various mechanisms through which each principle enhances the resilience of ecosystem services has revealed three key mechanisms:

i. Increasing understanding of critical SES components and processes (P3 – Slow variables and feedbacks, P4 – CAS thinking, P5 – Learning) as well as suitable management options (P5 – Learning, P6 – Participation, P7 – Polycentricity);
ii. Preparing the SES for unexpected events by creating awareness of their likelihood (P4 – CAS thinking), and providing alternative approaches and ways of dealing with emergent issues when suddenly needed (P1 – Diversity, P7 – Polycentricity); and
iii. Enhancing response capacity by providing a diversity of response options (P1 – Diversity), building the trust needed to make decisions and take action (P6 – Participation) and providing ways to make use of different responses at the right scale (P2 – Connectivity, P5 – Participation, P6 – Learning, P7 – Polycentricity).

These key mechanisms set the stage for various interactions between principles, which can be facilitating, synergistic or antagonistic (Fig. 10.1). Facilitation, that is, a situation where one principle needs another principle in order to be effective, is the most common form of interaction between the principles. A prominent example is learning (P5) which is facilitated by diversity (P1), connectivity (P2), feedbacks (P3), participation (P6) and polycentricity (P7). While learning can take place without these, its effectiveness in addressing complex problems and developing shared understanding and strategies to enhance resilience of ecosystem services is limited. Diversity of actor groups, perspectives and knowledge systems (P1) enhance learning by providing a broader knowledge base and by making the problem-solving process more inclusive, which can have positive effects on collective action. Connectivity between actors (P2) facilitates learning because of a higher level of trust and mutual understanding and a better exchange of information and knowledge, but it also includes the danger of homogenization of knowledge. Learning builds on new insights generated from information feedback from changes in ecosystem services; however, if these feedbacks have large time lags due to slow variables (P3) learning about important changes in ecosystem services and thus timely responses to changes thereof can be inhibited. Participation (P6) is a

REFLECTIONS ON BUILDING RESILIENCE 261

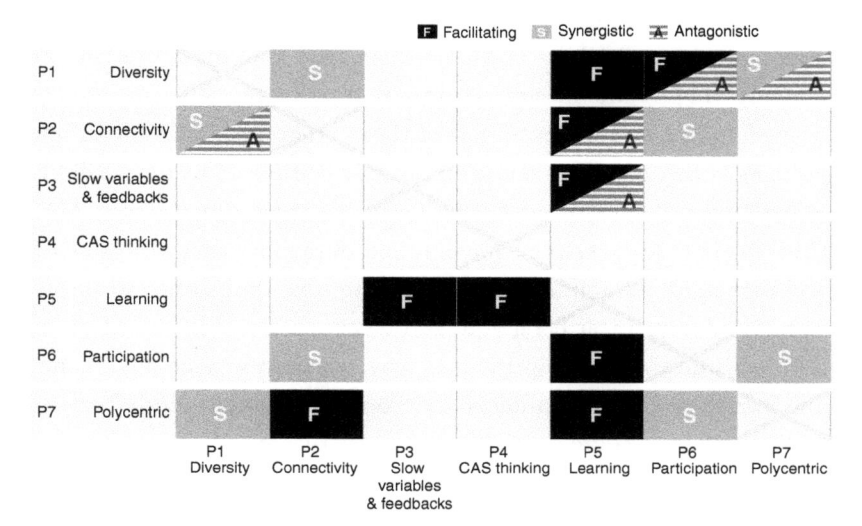

FIG. 10.1 Examples of interactions amongst principles. For facilitating and antagonistic relationships the principles in the rows act on principles in the column, i.e. the table needs to be read along the rows, e.g. diversity facilitates learning; connectivity interacts synergistically with participation. Note that CAS thinking facilitates all other principles and is thus not specifically marked here.

necessary condition for social learning because it creates the environment in which social interactions and learning can take place. Lastly, polycentric governance systems (P7) are more likely to enhance social learning because they provide connectivity and interaction possibilities between different governance actors that are needed for mutual exchange of experiences and learning and for bridging organizations that link knowledge across different levels and groups.

Polycentricity (P7) stands out as a principle that facilitates the function of several of the other principles (but does not automatically do so). Polycentric governance structures facilitate connectivity (P2) between actors by creating meaningful links between previously independent actor groups, and facilitate learning (P5). While learning (P5) is facilitated by a range of principles as noted above, it also facilitates other principles, particularly those associated with a better understanding of SES dynamics. Experimentation targeted at the effect of slow variables and feedbacks (P3) and their role in the dynamics of SES and the generation of ecosystem services can enhance understanding and management of these processes, if managers and policies allow. Experience with managing complex SES that is deliberated and reflected on in social learning processes can foster CAS thinking (P4), and enhance appreciation of the fact that SES are CAS and that management approaches need to take their inherent uncertainty and non-linear behaviour into account. Lastly, CAS thinking (P4) facilitates all other principles as ecosystem-service governance and management that builds on CAS understanding is more likely to be effective as it addresses CAS characteristics in a given context.

Two principles are synergistic when they mutually enhance each other. For instance, the capacity of an SES to respond to a disturbance may be enhanced if connectivity (P2) is at moderate levels in an SES that is also diverse (P1). Diversity provides response options that can become effective if there is connectivity between actors or parts of the ecosystems associated with the provision of specific ecosystem services. In a similar way polycentric governance (P7) may be more effective if the governance units are diverse groups (P1) providing more response options and perspectives for understanding and governing SES. Polycentricity is synergistic with participation (P6) because it creates arenas where actor groups can participate and introduce their knowledge and perspectives into SES and ecosystem-service governance. At the same time participation is crucial for effective polycentric governance because it creates the trust and social capital needed to make it effective. Participation (P6) and connectivity (P2) can interact synergistically to enhance the resilience of ecosystem services when the fact that actors in a participatory process are already connected elsewhere increases the likelihood of achieving collective action because there is a shared basis of trust and mutual understanding on which to build.

Finally, some principles can be antagonistic, where the abundance of one reduces the effectiveness of another. One example is the impact of diversity (P1) on participation (P6). While diversity is generally seen as working synergistically with other principles such as participation (see above), there can be cases where high diversity of actors and interests can lead to conflict that makes participation difficult and can render it politically ineffective due to the drowning of a particular perspective. A similar reasoning applies to the interaction of diversity (P1) and polycentricity (P7). Connectivity (P2) on the contrary can reduce diversity (P1) in SES, such as when knowledge becomes homogenized in social settings or when connectivity facilitates invasive species to spread widely in ecological systems. As a consequence of the homogenization of knowledge learning (P5) is also compromised. Finally, slow variables and feedbacks (P3) can prevent effective learning when time lags are large.

10.4 EVIDENCE FOR THE DIFFERENT PRINCIPLES

Our review points to substantial variation in empirical evidence supporting the different principles. Looking across the principles, the roles of connectivity (P2), slow variables and feedbacks (P3) and participation (P6) are fairly well understood, and there is substantial evidence for their importance. While there is also substantial evidence for the importance of diversity (P1) and polycentricity (P7), the most important mechanisms by which these principles act to enhance the resilience of ecosystem services are less well understood. In the case of fostering CAS thinking (P4) and learning (P5), both the evidence about the importance of these principles and the mechanisms by which they enhance the resilience of ecosystem services remain somewhat unclear.

For some of the principles, the lack of empirical evidence can be partly attributed to a lack of conceptual clarity. For instance, the large variety of definitions and ways of measuring learning (P5) in the context of ecosystem-service governance make it difficult to compare findings across cases. In other cases there are operational difficulties in measuring the impacts of the principles on resilience of ecosystem services, for instance in the case of connectivity (P2) or CAS thinking (P4). Lack of empirical evidence has been a common issue in the quantification of SES dynamics and processes by various authors (e.g. Walker and Meyers 2004; Ostrom *et al.* 2007). This is likely partly a result of an intense few decades of development around theoretical frameworks rather than empirical substantiation of those frameworks. Our review highlights the need at this stage to shift to a greater emphasis on comparative, empirical studies to further advance our understanding of the mechanisms underlying the different principles, and practical ways of defining and measuring the impact of the different principles.

The nature of SES as CAS, poses substantial difficulties to gathering empirical evidence to support the principles. The complex interactions in SES make it challenging to isolate a particular system property or principle (e.g. diversity) and establish its connection to the resilience of ecosystem services. Isolating the contribution of individual principles is very difficult, partly because they almost always act in tandem. More fundamentally, separating the different principles is more of an analytical construct than a reflection of individual, separable factors operating within an SES. In effect, in studying resilience-enhancing principles and their effects on complex, often multi-scalar SES, we confront what Young (2010) refers to as causal complexes in which many interacting, context-specific factors lead to particular outcomes and where similar outcomes can arise from very different combinations of factors. Furthermore, even if the effect of a particular principle is known, the fact that SES continually evolve and change over time implies that these causal links may change. At a practical level, the relevant system processes often happen over long timescales, which makes it difficult to assess the effect of a principle within the timeframe of a typical empirical study or management experiment. Furthermore, the indicators needed to monitor long-term, non-linear and variable change are generally not well developed and in some cases may require non-traditional methods and ways of thinking in their assessment (Moss *et al.* 2010; Halpern and Fujita 2013). These issues pose deep-seated challenges to untangling the effect of the different principles, and our knowledge may always be partial.

Besides these fundamental challenges to gathering evidence to support the principles presented in this book, the relatively recent focus on ecosystem services and resilience research means that many of the linkages we are interested in exploring in this book have received relatively limited research attention. Much of the evidence that does exist is confined to a few well-developed, local-scale case studies, and is often drawn from experience with adaptive governance, which is a broad approach to managing SES that encompasses multiple principles simultaneously. Comparable cases for studying the principles seldom exist let alone in the quantities needed to statistically separate the principles. The additional intricacy layered on by interactions among the principles makes the endeavour to parse effects even more arduous. Nevertheless, there are some notable recent attempts to synthesize data and knowledge to explain observed outcomes across case studies in fisheries, river-basin management and forestry using novel statistical analysis, qualitative comparative analysis (QCA) or qualitative approaches (e.g. Agrawal and Ostrom 2001; Basurto and Ostrom 2009; Gutiérrez *et al.* 2011; Huntjens *et al.* 2011; Cinner *et al.* 2012; Pahl-Wostl *et al.* 2012; SESMAD 2014).

10.5 IMPLICATIONS FOR MANAGEMENT AND GOVERNANCE OF SOCIAL–ECOLOGICAL SYSTEMS

The difficulties of gathering evidence for the effectiveness of the different principles in enhancing resilience, together with their multifaceted, multi-causal and interconnected nature, pose significant challenges for their operationalization (specification and implementation). Each of the chapters in this book highlighted a number of common shortcomings and problems that decision-makers face regarding the operationalizing and application of the principles. In this section we reflect on the general implications of these challenges for governance (i.e. the policy process including the rules on who decides on the objectives and the procedures to pursue them) and management (i.e. the actions to accomplish these objectives) and we highlight several notes of caution when considering the application of the principles.

First, it is critical to note that none of the principles is necessary or sufficient, or a panacea for environmental governance. Context matters, and whether a principle enhances the resilience of ecosystem services depends as much on the details of its application (e.g. who is involved) as on the given socio-economic, governance and biophysical situation. None of the principles is universally beneficial, and all require a nuanced understanding of how, when and where they apply, as well as how they interact with or depend on other principles. Whether a principle enhances the resilience of ecosystem services thus depends as much on the application of an individual principle as on finding the right combination of principles.

Second, as emphasized in Chapter 2, before applying any of the principles it is essential to reflect on what you want to build resilience of (in this case, which set of ecosystem services), and who benefits and loses by these choices. Simply building resilience of the ecosystem services currently provided by a landscape or region can often serve to further entrench and exacerbate existing inequalities and disparities among people in a region or across regions (Robards *et al.* 2011). The principles we have discussed for building resilience of ecosystem services do not weigh in on which ecosystem services to promote. In practice, managers must contend with trade-offs between the provision and resilience of various ecosystem services at the same scale as well as across scales both spatially (local vs. global ecosystem services, as well as at multiple intermediate scales) and temporally (intergenerational effects). This includes trade-offs between multiple groups in the selection of ecosystem services. As these trade-offs create winners and losers, power and politics play a key role in the selection and enhancement of ecosystem services both at any given scale as well as across multiple scales, and can create substantial barriers to implementation of the principles.

Applying the principles in ways that take various ecological and societal trade-offs into account often necessitates processes of social change that have to overcome differences in belief systems, gender roles, institutional inertia and historical legacies (Norström *et al.*

2014). Such changes can threaten the incentive structures people have learned to navigate, creating new uncertainty and anxiety; thereby reducing the power of some groups while elevating that of others. They also challenge existing institutional and governance arrangements, which are often fragmented in different sectors and administrative units, sometimes deliberately, and poorly reflect the fit of spatial and temporal scales of social–ecological interactions. For those gaining from an existing system, change may not be desirable. All of these issues point to the need for broad deliberation and awareness of the processes by which humans make political decisions at multiple scales (as facilitated by P6 – Participation), a contextualization of the choices managers confront and make, a push towards transparency and openness in the decision-making process and legitimacy as the central tenet of good governance.

Third, our capacity to predict and influence future developments of an SES or its responses to management actions is limited because of its self-organizing nature, the existence of non-linear social–ecological feedbacks, the inherent variability of many social–ecological processes and the reflexive nature of diverse actors and groups at multiple scales. These characteristics and the resulting irreducible uncertainties imply that we cannot manage (as in fully control) coupled SES for any particular outcome. This makes for a very difficult governance and institutional design problem and challenges what we mean by 'management strategies'. Conventional, widely used management strategies for uncertainty rely on exploiting large numbers of repeated outcomes where standard statistical tools apply (e.g. the central limit theorem). In an SES, however, we only get one realization of the system trajectory that we have to deal with, which makes building resilience even more critical. The principles build resilience through enhancing system structures and processes that provide for the capacity of actors to shape and adjust development trajectories of the SES in desirable directions, for instance in terms of ecosystem services and human well-being, and to promote novel ones if the existing trajectory is unsustainable. Consequently, applying the principles involves viewing them not as end goals but rather as processes or mechanisms for generating conditions that allow for resolving collective-action problems associated with multiple trade-offs, and to deal with the CAS nature of the SES. It also involves creating mechanisms to critically reflect and adapt along the way, rather than solely designing a policy to 'implement' a principle. To operationalize these ideas, there is perhaps a fundamental need for a shift in mindsets to more CAS-based approaches (Pahl-Wostl et al. 2011), acknowledging the interconnected and complex adaptive nature of SES and the fact that people are part of these systems (P4 – CAS thinking).

A synthesis across the different principles can highlight some opportunities and ways forward to address the considerable challenges highlighted above. Below we present five practical insights that have emerged by considering common issues actors face regarding the operationalization and application of the principles. Broadly speaking, these concepts often feature as hallmarks for successful governance of all types under the labels collaborative, adaptive and nested governance (McKinney and Johnson 2009). They address the two fundamental, overarching challenges in SES: (i) solving collective-action dilemmas and (ii) dealing with the non-linear, often unexpected, nature of CAS. The principles and strategies discussed below build on Ostrom's institutional design principles (Ostrom 1990) as well as literature on adaptive governance (Dietz et al. 2003; Folke et al. 2005). Ostrom's design principles provide elements for basic social structures that tend to promote capacity for collective action in local contexts. They include: (1) clearly defined social and ecological boundaries; (2) rules regarding the appropriation and provision of common resources that are adapted to local conditions; (3) collective-choice arrangements that allow most resource appropriators to participate in the decision-making process; (4) effective monitoring by monitors who are part of or accountable to the appropriators; (5) graduated sanctions for resource appropriators who violate rules; (6) mechanisms of conflict resolution that are cheap and of easy access; (7) self-determination of the community recognized by higher-level authorities; and (8) in the case of larger common-pool resources, organization in the form of multiple layers of nested enterprises. The practical ways forward which we suggest below connect directly to several of these design principles.

- **Clarify goals and develop and monitor relevant metrics for each principle.** In order to successfully enhance the resilience of SES and the ecosystem services they provide, society must first define and clarify its goals with respect to which set of ecosystem services to enhance (Chapter 2). Society then needs to consider how to do this (the governance) and the strategies with which to pursue these aims (the management). This includes the specification of each principle for a particular context, the resolution of trade-offs and decision-making challenges mentioned above as well as the setting of tangible goals with respect to the application of the principles. Each of the chapters on the principles discussed how to operationalize and apply the different principles, thereby providing suggestions on these goals and objectives on a general level. However, the main challenges arise when applying them in the context of specific cases and when taking their interactions with one another and across scales into account. Here, CAS thinking (P4), learning (P5), participation (P6) and polycentric governance (P7) become crucial to facilitate understanding, deliberation and collective action to clarify goals related to the principles and balance trade-offs.

    Once governance and management act towards developing features of the SES and its governance system as suggested by the principles there is a need to measure and monitor progress in reaching the set goals. Monitoring is also a critical prerequisite for continuous learning and adapting of goals and actions, which is important because of our limited understanding of the SES and because management activities, internal system dynamics or unexpected events can always result in unintended developments (P5 – Learning). While setting goals and defining metrics is needed for any implementation processes, it is far from easy to do this in the context of the multiple interacting processes in SES. Our review has shown that in many cases finding the right measures and indicators can be very challenging (e.g. there exist multiple measures of polycentricity (P7), connectivity (P2) and diversity (P1); and few clear measures of CAS thinking (P4)). In others, the relationship between the level of a principle and its capacity to enhance resilience is non-linear, i.e. more of the principle does not necessarily lead to more resilience (e.g. P1 – Diversity, P2 – Connectivity). The form of this relationship is often not fully understood. Without clearly articulated goals and the monitoring and gathering of specific metrics for evaluation of impacts – both baseline data and ongoing measurement – the information required for learning is often not collected or processed. As a result, sensible adaptation and effective modifications cannot be formulated.

- **Take an integrative approach that builds on multiple knowledge sources.** While linked or coupled SES have become an increasingly popular conceptualization in both academic and popular writing since the publication of Berkes *et al.* (1998), the current book attempts to take this a step further. Much of the literature on coupled systems still considers social systems and their ecological counterparts separately. As highlighted in Chapter 1, current thinking in the resilience field emphasizes that the importance is not in studying *both* social and ecological systems, but rather the consequences of interactions and feedbacks between ecological and social components, and the SES to which they give rise. For instance, managing feedbacks and slow variables in SES requires a focus not only within the ecological system, but across social and ecological systems, as it is these interactions that can be critical for shifting an SES into another regime, particularly in relation to governance and use of ecosystem services (P3 – Slow variables and feedbacks) (Lade *et al.* 2013). An integrative approach can work synergistically with CAS thinking (P4) and help shift management paradigms from one of controlling outcomes in the short term (e.g. quarterly financial reports, election cycles, etc.) and expecting fully explained causal relationships to a new focus on coping with change and uncertainty over longer timescales.

Developing an integrative approach in SES requires an understanding of the biophysical processes, use patterns, benefits and values underlying the trade-offs between ecosystem services and users across sectors and scales. Given the complex nature of SES these will always to some extent remain unknown. Understanding and management can, however, be greatly enhanced if these build on insights provided by different approaches and methodologies, multiple perspectives, multiple evidence and ways of generating knowledge that take social–ecological interactions into account. Our discussions of participation (P6) and learning (P5) point to ways in which co-production of knowledge by transdisciplinary groups, including representatives of knowledge systems such as Traditional Ecological

Knowledge (Berkes 1999; Tengö et al. 2014), can be facilitated. Understanding SES through research and societal learning processes can also greatly be fostered by the triangulation of multiple methodologies (Potetee et al. 2010).

- **Shift away from exclusively managing for efficiency towards planning for uncertainty and surprise**. Conventional management approaches are predominantly built on the management paradigm of managing for efficiency and controlling selected system variables to reduce uncertainty, such as building reservoirs to reduce the uncertainty of river runoff. Enhancing the resilience of ecosystem services on the contrary requires that SES properties such as diversity and redundancy (P1), connectivity (P2), learning (P5) and participation (P6) are fostered to enable polycentric management and governance (P7) to be adaptive and cope with uncertainty and surprise. One way of doing so is through changeable, collaborative initiatives such as adaptive co-management or integrative approaches, in which an adaptive approach to experimentation and knowledge acquisition (P5 – Learning) is combined with power-sharing and collective decision-making (P6 – Participation) (Armitage et al. 2009). However, structures and processes to enhance learning as well as polycentric governance arrangements to increase redundancy come at a cost due to the increased number of participants and need for coordination. This can be contrary to managing for efficiency, which often focuses on the singular goal of cost reduction and, as such, often eliminates redundancy and diversity, limits participation to increase speed of decision-making and may draw on simplified, static cause–effect relations.

  Management is also confronted with the difficulty of finding the right balance between having too much of a given principle and too little (alluding to the benefits and costs of increasing diversity and redundancy (P1), connectivity (P2), participation (P6) and polycentricity (P7)). In governance, we may view this as a balance in working towards appropriate levels of collaboration and nestedness. When discussing the individual principles similar ideas were raised concerning balancing the benefits versus the costs of marginally adding more of a principle (e.g. P2 – Connectivity, P5 – Participation).

- **Create spaces for spontaneous exploration**. The nature of SES does not allow decision-makers to 'force' any of the principles into effect by fiat. Rather, many of the principles can only build up through self-organizing processes that can at best be guided by the design of supportive SES structures.

Creating space for exploration is an important element to foster self-organization and the innovation needed to tackle novel problems or existing problems in novel ways. Bridging organizations that increase connectivity (P2) among normally isolated groups can increase the likelihood that exploration occurs between actor groups and that integration of knowledge systems and different understandings can take place (P5 – Learning, P6 – Participation). Such explorations can help foster CAS thinking (P4), as people open up to the possibility for surprise and innovation. Collaborative spaces for exploration can also help ensure that the results of such processes more easily make their way into decision-making because a greater swath of actors is aware of and benefiting from new insights (P5 – Learning) and ways of working together (P6 – Participation). Co-management institutions linking indigenous groups, government agencies and, sometimes, industry are a good example of such explorative spaces (e.g. Lefevre 2013).

While implementing mandatory new rules, particularly those that are novel or adaptive and reflect CAS thinking (P4), may be difficult under many governance regimes, opportunities usually exist for experimenting through the use of voluntary or informal rule systems. These informal rules may then become more formally established over a longer time period. Such approaches generally require clear sets of goals that build ownership, trust and social capital among key stakeholders, and frequently a leader with a vision and motivation to drive the process forward. Experience in the United States (and to some extent globally) with climate-change regulations has reflected such a bottom-up voluntary and adaptive approach to achieving goals. In some developed countries, sub-national administrative units have worked on their own volition to accomplish climate-related goals in a situation where there was an inability to strongly regulate emissions nationally (Schreurs 2008). Over time, national or global governance may find opportunities to embrace these local efforts as conditions change and radical ideas become more business as usual, towards a more encompassing and formalized polycentric system (P7) – even if only to capitalize on existing and less controversial momentum.

- **Build trust and social capital.** Implementation of many of the principles is connected with the need to create capacity for changing the structure and processes of an SES. Underlying this, however, there is a deeper need to foster relationships amongst people to facilitate collective action. We see this in the challenges of operationalizing connectivity between individuals as well as groups of people (P2 – Connectivity), fostering multiple perspectives and sources of knowledge (P1 – Diversity) and alternate mental models (P4 – CAS thinking), and ways to make them explicit through participatory processes (P6 – Participation). Connecting diverse groups of people for a common purpose and encouraging the resolution of collective-action dilemmas is greatly facilitated by trust amongst participants (Ostrom 1990). The need for trust is also evident in the inherent difficulties in attempts to increase collaboration amongst a broader set of stakeholders and increase participation in the process of governance (P6 – Participation). Social capital, as the value of strong social relationships, underlays the foundation for polycentric systems of governance (P7 – Polycentricity) in which multiple governance authorities interact and learn from each other (P5 – Learning).

Of course, building social capital is also not a panacea and it can in some settings create or strengthen feedbacks (P3) that can be very detrimental to change (e.g. Schlüter and Herrfahrdt-Pähle 2011), but ideally provides a democratic currency for navigating trade-offs. Trust and social capital provide a source to draw upon for negotiating inevitable misunderstandings, unexpected outcomes and unanticipated consequences. It can facilitate the sharing of knowledge and insights thus fostering learning (P5). However, social capital and trust among one set of actors (e.g. the disenfranchised) can also lead to revolution and change towards a different but sometimes more equitable and socially sustainable system.

10.6 FUTURE RESEARCH NEEDS

Each of the preceding chapters and the sections above have highlighted knowledge gaps concerning how each principle enhances the resilience of ecosystem services and how it interacts with others as well as challenges in measuring and operationalizing the principles for application in specific SES. In this last section we summarize research needs that are common across principles or relate to their interaction.

Improved conceptual clarity has been highlighted above as critical for establishing evidence for the functioning and impacts on the resilience of ecosystem services of each principle. This is particularly relevant for learning (P5) and CAS thinking (P4) where the lack of conceptual clarity has made it difficult to generate understanding of how the principles enhance the resilience of ecosystem services. Conceptual clarity is essential for operationalizing and measuring a principle and its effects in a particular SES and to compare evidence gathered across different SES. For the latter, and for developing a diagnostic approach, a precise and consistent delineation of key variables is necessary. Frameworks such as the conceptual ecosystem-services framework developed by the Millennium Ecosystem Assessment (MA 2005) or SES framework by Ostrom (2007) can provide useful starting points for developing the conceptual clarity and shared understanding of concepts needed for diagnostic and comparative, multi-scale studies of SES.

Improved methods for monitoring and measuring the principles are a second key gap. The interconnectedness between principles as well as multiple causalities makes their measurement far from straightforward. More research is needed to better understand how to measure a particular principle and develop metrics to evaluate processes and outcomes as well as implications for resilience (e.g. P1 – Diversity or P6 – Participation), particularly within the social system. This includes the need to identify indicators that serve as tools to monitor progress in implementing principles. Future research could for instance investigate opportunities provided by new information technologies as well as the combination of multiple methods for studying a principle. A stepped evidence-based approach, in which one gradually builds knowledge of a complex system while learning about what works under specific circumstances, may also be a useful way forward (Bohensky and Lynam 2005).

A third cross-cutting insight of our review is the need for a nuanced understanding of the functioning of each individual principle and their interactions as well as a nuanced approach towards their implementation at different scales. The relationship between the degree of presence of a certain principle and its effect on resilience is often non-linear, and more of a principle is not necessarily better (e.g. P1 – Diversity, P2 – Connectivity, P6 – Participation). The form of this relationship, i.e. the location of the breakpoint between too little and too much, warrants more research. We also need to better understand how the effectiveness of different principles varies under different social–ecological settings. What type of learning, participation or polycentricity works best under which conditions? Which aspects of a specific social–ecological context are particularly relevant for the functioning of a principle? And, as discussed above, which other principles need to be present in order for a principle to function effectively? These are all questions that need further research in order to develop an understanding that is transferable between SES but still takes relevant characteristics of a specific SES into account. Much resilience science to date has either been very general or very specific. To be useful, especially for addressing the pressing social–ecological problems society faces, we need a better understanding of the middle ground between these extremes: an understanding that enables sensitivity to context but is not entirely context-dependent.

As the section on evidence has highlighted assessing the effects of individual principles on enhancing the resilience of ecosystem services is particularly challenging because many of the principles work in tandem and often operate on long timescales. One way forward to address these issues are systematic cross-case comparisons and long-term case studies as envisaged for instance by the International Programme on Ecosystem Change and Society (PECS, Carpenter *et al.* 2012). Such studies can also shed light on the impact of combinations of principles for the resilience of ecosystem services under different conditions, as well as for piloting different approaches to their application. To some extent, the replication of case studies across space can substitute for the long time dimensions needed to understand changes in ecosystem services as factors such as diversity or learning are increased or reduced (Pickett 1989). However, these cross-case comparisons of SES are only at the beginning and face considerable challenges caused by the interdisciplinary nature of the data needed that often comes with different ways of naming and measuring variables, the paucity of data on social–ecological processes, the interconnected, dynamic and non-linear nature of SES as highlighted above and, lastly, the context-dependence of many processes in SES. Novel methods are currently under development that have the potential to tackle some of these issues. One example is QCA (Ragin 1987) that can help to tackle the need to take relevant contextual variables into account while generating insights that are valid across classes of cases and can deal with the scarcity of comparable in-depth case studies. Simulation modelling is another tool that can be useful for addressing the dynamics arising from social–ecological interactions under different conditions and thus provide for a more systematic exploration of the impacts of SES features related to the principles. Several modelling fields are moving towards incorporating social–ecological interactions and addressing resilience-related questions recently, and can substantially contribute to building this knowledge base (Schlüter *et al.* 2012).

While theoretical understanding and conceptual research on the individual principles has advanced somewhat, there is a need for more research on how to operationalize and implement the principles. To what extent can, and should, we design for them – and when we say 'we', who is that 'we'? And how do we best design for the principles? This question is particularly unclear for the application of some of the principles, such as diversity (P1) and connectivity (P2), in a social–ecological setting – e.g. what does diversity or connectivity mean in a social system, particularly aspects of diversity that may seem redundant at a specific point in space and time? When it comes to implementation, all principles that relate to the governance system acknowledge the role of power and leadership for shaping outcomes of, for instance, learning (P5) or participation (P6). However, we know little about how these factors actually affect implementation and how we can foster leadership and ensure equitable processes and outcomes. Much of this subject matter has been at the core of the work of political philosophers for millennia, and greater attention by resilience scholars to the philosophy of politics and governance is a fertile area for exploration that would address long-standing discussions over the merits and repercussions of different power distribution in society. This also relates to the need to better understand how to overcome institutional barriers and inertia in cases where the implementation of a principle calls for institutional change at the scale of implementation or at larger scales. In general, more research is needed to understand how we can mobilize understanding into action, so that outcomes from social learning actually make it into policy.

10.7 CONCLUSIONS

This book presents a first attempt at identifying a set of underlying principles for enhancing the resilience of ecosystem services in SES to unexpected shocks and ongoing change. We build on an extensive literature review, the input of leading resilience scholars and the synthesis of many SES case studies to identify seven underlying principles. We have found enough support for each of the principles, both theoretically and empirically, to draw conclusions about their relevance for enhancing the resilience of SES; however, the empirical evidence of many principles needs to be, and can be, enhanced. In this chapter we have synthesized some of the ways in which the principles interact, and considered the implications for governance and management as well as future research needs.

Crucially, none of the principles, individually or jointly, present a panacea for environmental and social sustainability. Each principle requires a nuanced and context-sensitive approach to their understanding and implementation, as the effect of each principle depends on (i) interactions with other principles, (ii) the way it has been implemented, (iii) its magnitude and (iv) the specific context of a given SES. The outcomes of each principle will additionally vary by the scale at which they are applied, which results in trade-offs not only between different ecosystem services but also between different users at different scales, such as the local and global scales. The repercussions of these trade-offs for the distribution of wealth and power, and the consequences of existing and new trade-offs, need to be carefully considered before applying the principles (Chapter 2).

Our book further highlights the multifaceted nature of each principle. Research has uncovered many of the mechanisms through which the proposed principles enhance the resilience of ecosystem services in SES, particularly at the theoretical level; however, many open questions remain. A better understanding of the interdependencies among principles within and across scales is a critical area for future research and cross-case comparisons of SES that apply novel methods are a promising avenue to do so. With increasing connectedness across scales in an increasingly human-influenced world the effects of these interactions could become even more pronounced. Linked to this there is a need to develop better approaches, methods and measures to establish evidence for the principles taking into account the challenges of multiple dimensions, multiple causalities and interactions between principles.

There is an urgent need for understanding how the principles can be jointly applied to foster transformative change, away from the unsustainable trajectories that many places around the world, and the planet overall, are on (Chapter 1). It appears that the mechanisms of the principles related to the underlying SES characteristics of the 'system to be governed' (P1–P3) are better known than those of the governance-system principles (P4–P7). We need more research to understand the types of learning (P5), participation (P6) and polycentricity (P7) that enhance the resilience of ecosystem services in different social–ecological contexts, and how they might enable transformations in SES. A shift in mindsets towards approaches that better recognize the features and behaviours of SES as CAS (P4 – CAS thinking) appears to be particularly fundamental in this regard.

As SES are characterized by self-organization, non-linear dynamics, inherent variability of social–ecological processes and diverse reflexive actors and groups at multiple scales our capacity to predict and steer an SES into a particular direction is limited. The development trajectory of a specific SES rather emerges from multiple interactions between people and their social and ecological environments. Given the unpredictabilities that this entails, resilience as an approach for dealing with change and uncertainty has a particular contribution to make. The seven principles we present have in our view theoretical and empirical evidence indicating their effectiveness in enhancing the resilience of ecosystem services, and are sufficiently well understood to be able to inform practical governance and management interventions to foster more sustainable SES trajectories. They do so by enhancing system structures that support collective-action processes to resolve trade-offs, support sustainable resource use and allow actors and governance to respond adaptively to new and unexpected challenges. They are, however, still an early attempt at identifying factors and processes relevant for the resilience of ecosystem services and the resilience of SES more generally. Other principles might be added or the existing ones revised or discarded, and our understanding of how and when and where they apply will grow with time. The future will tell which principles are most effective and useful under particular conditions and we invite everybody to join this endeavour and further test and develop these insights.

REFERENCES

Agrawal, A. and Ostrom, E. (2001). Collective action, property rights, and decentralization in resource use in India and Nepal. *Politics and Society*, 29, 485–514.

Armitage, D. R., Plummer, R., Berkes, F. *et al.* (2009). Adaptive co-management for social–ecological complexity. *Frontiers in Ecology and the Environment*, 7, 95–102.

Basurto, X. and Ostrom, E. (2009). Beyond the tragedy of the commons. *Economia delle fonti di energia e dell'ambiente*, 52, 35–60.

Berkes, F. and Folke, C., eds. (1998). *Linking Social and Ecological Systems: Management Practices and Social Mechanisms for Building Resilience*, Cambridge: Cambridge University Press.

Berkes, F. (1999). *Sacred Ecology: Traditional Ecological Knowledge and Resource Management*. Philadelphia, PA: Taylor & Francis.

Biggs, R., Schlüter, M., Biggs, D. *et al.* (2012). Towards principles for enhancing the resilience of ecosystem services. *Annual Review of Environment and Resources*, 37, 421–448.

Bohensky, E. and Lynam, T. (2005). Evaluating responses in complex adaptive systems: insights on water management from the Southern African Millennium Ecosystem Assessment (SAfMA). *Ecology and Society*, 10, 11.

Carpenter, S. R., Folke, C., Norström, A. *et al.* (2012). Program on Ecosystem Change and Society: an international research strategy for integrated social-ecological systems. *Current Opinion in Environmental Sustainability*, 4, 134–138

Cinner, J. E., McClanahan, T. R., MacNeil, M. A. *et al.* (2012). Comanagement of coral reef social-ecological systems. *Proceedings of the National Academy of Sciences USA*, 109, 5219–5222.

Dietz, T., Ostrom, E., Stern, P. C. (2003). The struggle to govern the commons. *Science*, 302, 1907–1912.

Folke, C., Hahn, T., Olsson, P., Norberg, J. (2005). Adaptive governance of social-ecological systems. *Annual Review of Environment and Resources*, 30, 441–473.

Gutiérrez, N. L., Hilborn, R., Defeo, O. (2011). Leadership, social capital and incentives promote successful fisheries. *Nature*, 470, 386–389.

Halpern, B. S. and Fujita, R. (2013). Assumptions, challenges, and future directions in cumulative impact analysis. *Ecosphere*, 4, 131.

Harris, P. G. (2007). Collective action on climate change: the logic of regime failure. *Natural Resources Journal*, 47. 195–224.

Huntjens, P., Pahl-Wostl, C., Rihoux, B. (2011). Adaptive water management and policy learning in a changing climate: a formal comparative analysis of eight water management regimes in Europe, Africa and Asia. *Environmental Policy and Governance*, 21, 145–163.

Lade, S., Tavoni, A., Levin, S. A., Schlüter, M. (2013). Regime shifts in a social-ecological system. *Journal of Theoretical Ecology*, 6, 359–372.

Lefevre, J. S. (2013). A pioneering effort in the design of process and law supporting integrated Arctic Ocean management. *Environmental Law Reporter*, 43, 10893–10908.

MA (2005). *Ecosystems and Human Well-Being: Synthesis*. Washington, DC: Island Press.

Martin, J. (2007). *The Meaning of the 21st Century: A Vital Blueprint for Ensuring Our Future*. New York, NY: Riverhead Books.

McKinney, M. and Johnson S. (2009). *Working Across Boundaries: People, Nature, and Regions*. Cambridge, MA: Lincoln Institute of Land Policy.

Moss, R. H., Edmonds, J. A., Hibbard, K. A. *et al.* (2010). The next generation of scenarios for climate change research and assessment. *Nature*, 463, 747–756.

Norström, A., Dannenberg, A., McCarney, G. et al. (2014). Three necessary conditions for establishing effective sustainable development goals in the Anthropocene. *Ecology and Society*, 19, doi:10.5751/ES-06602-190308.

Ostrom, E. (1990). *Governing the Commons. The Evolution of Institutions for Collective Action*. Cambridge, Cambridge University Press.

Ostrom, E. (2007). A diagnostic approach for going beyond panaceas. *Proceedings of the National Academy of Sciences USA*, 104, 15181–15187.

Ostrom, E., Janssen, M. A,. Anderies, J. M. (2007). Going beyond panaceas. *Proceedings of the National Academy of Sciences USA*, 104, 15176–15178.

Pahl-Wostl, C., Jeffrey, P., Isendahl, N., Brugnach, M. (2011). Maturing the new water management paradigm: progressing from aspiration to practice. *Water Resources Management*, 25, 837–856.

Pahl-Wostl, C., Lebel, L., Knieper, C., Nikitina, E. (2012). From applying panaceas to mastering complexity: toward adaptive water governance in river basins. *Environmental Science and Policy*, 23, 24–34.

Pickett, S. T. A. (1989). Space-for-time substitution as an alternative to long-term studies. In *Long-Term Studies in Ecology: Approaches and Alternatives*. New York, NY: Springer-Verlag, pp. 110–135.

Poteete, A. R., Janssen, M. A, Ostrom, E. (2010). *Working Together: Collective Action, the Commons, and Multiple Methods in Practice*. Princeton, NJ: Princeton University Press.

Ragin C. (1987). *The Comparative Method: Moving Beyond Qualitative and Quantitative Strategies*. Berkeley, CA: University of California Press.

Robards, M. D., Schoon, M. L., Meek, C. L., Engle, N. L. (2011). The importance of social drivers in the resilient provision of ecosystem services. *Global Environmental Change*, 21, 522–529.

Schlüter, M. and Herrfahrdt-Pähle, E. (2011). Exploring resilience and transformability of a river basin in the face of socioeconomic and ecological crisis: an example from the Amudarya river basin, Central Asia. *Ecology and Society*, 16, 32.

Schlüter, M., McAllister, R., Arlinghaus, R. et al. (2012). New horizons for managing the environment: a review of coupled social–ecological systems modeling. *Natural Resource Modeling*, 25, 219–272.

Schreurs, M. A. (2008). From the bottom up local and subnational climate change politics. *The Journal of Environment and Development*, 17, 343–355.

SESMAD (2014). Social–Ecological Systems Meta-Analysis Database: background and research methods. Available at http://sesmad.dartmouth.edu/.

Tengö, M., Brondizio, E. S., Elmqvist, T., Malmer, P., Spierenburg, M. (2014). Connecting diverse knowledge systems for enhanced ecosystem governance: the multiple evidence base approach. *AMBIO*, 43, 579–591.

Walker, B. and Meyers, J. A. (2004). Thresholds in ecological and social–ecological systems: a developing database. *Ecology and Society*, 9, 3.

Young, O. R. (2010). *Institutional Dynamics: Emergent Patterns in International Environmental Governance*. Cambridge, MA: MIT Press.

Index

accountability, 157, 219, 231, 234, 236, 238
adaptation, xx, 9, 18, 21, 59, 65, 158, 160, 175, 182, 205, 206, 255, 256, 258, 270
adaptive
  capacity, 20, 56, 147, 149
  management, 130, 161, 175, 180, 203, 204, 211
    Great Barrier Reef, 150–159
    governance, 175
    Kruger National Park, 130, 154, 159, 189
    learning, 175, 191, 192, 193
    monitoring, 180, 193
    natural resources, 148
    uncertainty, 143
Afghanistan, 122
African National Congress (ANC), 108
agency, 42, 44, 133, 156, 164, 203, 211
agroecosystems, 87
Alaska, 234
algae, 60, 115, 126
Amudarya River, 121, 122, 123, 124, 125
Androy, Madagascar, 91
antagonistic interactions, 63, 212, 260, 261
Antarctica, 108
Anthropocene, xix, xxii, 4, 23, 68
Apartheid, 107, 108, 136
Aral Sea, 121, 122, 124
Arizona, 239
Arctic, 16, 183, 185, 211, 217
Australia, 4, 85, 118, 149, 159, 163, 188, 205, 206, 210, 214, 238

bacterial communities, 63
balance, 21, 52, 53, 67, 219, 229, 271
  with nature, 36, 146
ball and cup, 116, 117
beaver, 60
beetle outbreak, 89
benthic fisheries, 158, 160, 164, 181

biodiversity, 12, 35, 36, 37, 39, 44, 51, 59, 64, 65, 86, 90, 91, 152, 154, 155, 185, 225, 237, 241, 242
  loss, 5
biosphere, xix, xxii, 1, 4, 5, 8
Botswana, 213
Brazil, 215
British Columbia, 172, 213, 214
British Common Law, 238
building resilience, xiii, xxii, 6, 26, 34, 35, 43, 159, 180, 185, 251, 254, 258, 266, 267
Bureau of Meteorology, Climatology and Geophysics (BMKG), 208

Canadian Arctic, 182, 185
capacity building, 216
carbon dioxide, 4
Caribbean, 60
Central Asia, 121, 122
Centre of Climate Change Response (CCCR), 208
CFCs, 5
Chile, 142, 158, 160, 164, 181, 213
Chiricahua Firescape planning, 240
Chisasibi First Nation of Cree, 238
citizenship, 214
Clayoquot Sound, 213
climate, 39, 125, 208
  change *see also* global warming, 4, 16, 58, 61, 97, 122, 125, 127, 128, 134, 152, 153, 154, 205, 207, 209, 211, 237, 242, 254, 272
  emissions, 44
  regulation, 13, 22, 57, 90, 236, 252
Cochise County, 240
cod fishery, 115, 187
collective action, 56, 87, 88, 95, 176, 177, 201, 202, 204, 206, 210, 218, 227, 237, 257, 258, 259, 260, 262, 268, 269, 279
  challenges, 242
  dilemmas, 17, 32, 227, 268, 273

283

resolution of, 17, 32, 273
trust, 98
co-management, 148, 173, 175, 177, 182, 183, 185, 203, 213, 229, 231, 271, 272
command-and-control approaches, 36, 106, 147, 166, 280
Commonwealth Scientific and Research Organisation (CSIRO), 205, 208
community-based conservation (CBC), 36
companion modelling, 44
compartmentalization, 88, 89
complex adaptive systems (CAS), xxi, 1, 6, 7, 107, 142, 143, 167, 251, 252, 256
complex interactions, 10, 264
complexity, xxii, 50, 57, 63, 64, 142, 147, 156, 158, 161, 165, 175, 176, 177, 242, 255, 258
conflict, 17, 32, 45, 58, 62, 65, 66, 186, 191, 203, 212, 215, 216, 227, 237, 239, 242, 263
  management, 215
  resolution, 216, 230, 238, 244, 268
connectivity, xix, 11, 57, 64, 80–93, 110, 134, 226, 229, 234, 254–263, 269, 271, 272, 276
conservation, 36–38, 39, 40, 57, 64, 71, 85, 86, 96, 150, 182, 212, 233, 235, 237, 239
  tillage, 129
consultation fatigue, 214
controlling conditions, 111
  outcomes, 270
  variables, 105, 107, 108, 110–118, 127, 128, 271
consensus, 20, 21, 150, 187, 205, 209, 215, 254
cooperation, 45, 61, 132, 160, 177
coral reefs, 5, 60, 83, 95, 128, 257
corridors, 64, 82, 86, 87, 96, 97, 233, 235
corruption, 213
cotton, 13, 122, 124
crime rates, 16
critical threshold, 5, 11, 108, 109, 114, 116, 118, 119, 133, 134, 143, 162
crop production, 15, 16, 70, 109, 120, 125
cross-scale, 11, 55, 89, 129, 152, 164, 177, 182, 183, 193, 227, 229, 231, 232, 238, 252, 266, 269, 278
CSIRO, Australia *see* Commonwealth Scientific and Research Organisation (CSIRO)

cultural ecosystem services, 13, 22, 90, 113
Cyclone Justin, 150

dampening
  feedback, 110, 113, 115
decision-making, 20, 34, 44, 131, 153, 165, 166, 174, 176, 179, 181, 185, 186, 188, 190, 203–210, 228, 234, 258, 267, 268, 271, 272
degradation, 2, 11, 47, 75, 108, 119, 131, 137, 169, 211, 214, 235, 237
deliberation, 7, 38, 42, 43, 192, 196, 228, 267, 269
Delphi method, xiii, 20, 21, 29
democracy, xix, 32, 43, 107, 213, 216
desertification, 119, 122, 224
developing countries, 44, 74, 78
disease, 2, 4, 5, 13, 54, 60, 68, 71, 81, 85, 257
disease epidemics, 89
disparity, 21, 52, 66, 67, 80
dispersal, 85, 87
  seed, 55, 92, 93
distribution, 7, 33, 35, 39, 41, 43, 92, 101, 157, 166, 276, 277
  networks, 95
disturbance *see also* shock, xxi, 2, 9, 22, 25, 33, 50, 51, 53, 56, 58, 63, 64, 65, 67, 68, 71, 80, 81, 83, 85, 89, 96, 97, 98, 107, 108, 111, 113, 114, 116, 126, 128, 134, 145, 148, 150, 153, 166, 175, 193, 201, 202, 227, 234, 251, 252, 254, 255, 257, 262
diversity, xiii, xiv, xxi, 7, 18, 24, 43, 46, 50, 71, 81, 85, 94, 95, 96, 98, 119, 154, 192, 202, 204, 209, 215, 226, 230, 234–236, 242, 254, 255, 257, 258–264, 269, 271, 273, 274, 275, 276
  ethnicity, 61
  functional, 86
  genetic, 86, 97
  response, 53, 55, 57, 60, 61, 65, 66, 71, 74, 134, 231, 233, 234, 241
dominant feedbacks, 11, 22, 111, 114, 116, 118, 257
drainage, 4, 121, 123, 125
drivers, 9, 106, 126, 129, 131, 133, 134, 147, 152, 154, 156, 159, 164, 217, 256
drylands, 119, 120, 188
Dust Bowl, 10, 120

early warning, 134
Earth system, xix, 4
ecological
  interactions, 98, 270
  networks, 66, 99
  system, xix, 8, 12, 14, 32, 98, 115, 263, 270
economic sanctions, 107
ecosystem services, xix, xxii, 1, 2, 3, 13, 32, 35, 36, 50, 51, 54, 59, 80, 81, 83, 89, 105, 106, 110, 120, 130, 142, 143, 148, 156, 174, 179, 183, 186, 204, 211, 227, 231, 235, 251, 252, 255
  bundle, 7, 16, 32, 34, 35, 36, 40, 46, 87, 105, 120, 241
  cultural, 14, 22, 90, 113, 163
  provisioning, 14, 22, 54, 59, 109
  regulating, 14, 20, 22, 106, 109, 118, 126, 130
  supporting, 15
educational outcomes, 16
efficiency, 63, 64, 65, 66, 271
El Niño oscillation, 150
emission reduction, 39
empirical evidence, xxii, 7, 19, 61, 66, 87, 165, 210, 253, 256, 258, 263, 264, 277, 279
environmental change, 33
erosion control, 87, 109, 118, 125
European colonialism, 38
eutrophication, 4, 126, 127, 131, 242
Everglades, 238
exploration, 147, 192, 228, 271, 272, 276
externalities, 129
extreme floods, 57

facilitation, 191, 174, 193, 208, 215, 216, 217, 256, 258, 259, 260
fast variables, 109, 127, 130
feedback, xiii, xiv, xxi, 7, 8, 10, 11, 13, 14, 20, 22, 25, 30, 41, 44, 45, 105–129, 131–135, 143, 145, 147, 212, 227, 254, 255, 257, 259–263, 267, 270, 273
  dampening, 110, 113, 115
  dominant, 11, 22, 111, 114, 116, 117, 257
  internal, 107, 110, 111, 113, 114
  negative, 110
  positive, 110
  reinforcing, 110, 113, 115, 121, 123, 132
fertilizers, 65
financial crises, 89

fire, 57, 81, 85, 106, 107, 110, 111, 113, 114, 118, 149, 154, 159, 164, 180, 240
fisheries, 11, 16, 54, 59, 66, 128, 129, 146, 149, 158, 160, 164, 181, 213, 229, 231, 232, 236, 243, 265
Fisheries Joint Management Commission, 185
fodder, 57, 65
food, 2, 14, 15, 16, 38, 53, 84, 87, 113, 236
  distribution networks, 95
  prices, 81
  production, 12, 63, 87
  security, 4, 70, 242
  sources, 71
  webs, 82, 83, 88, 98, 180
forests, 13, 17, 38, 55, 57, 89, 90, 97, 106, 111, 122, 123, 149, 178, 180, 188, 212, 214
forest savanna, 107, 113
fossil fuel, 4, 39
fragmentation, 6, 12, 86, 242
freshwater, 59, 109, 127, 131, 252
functional
  diversity, 52
  compensation, 54, 67
  redundancy, 50, 233, 234, 235, 241, 254, 255
fur seals, 40

Gabriola Island, Canada, 13, 19
Germany, 155
global
  biodiversity, 38, 39
  climate models, 188
  connectivity, 5, 81, 110
  greenhouse gas, 39
  population, 2
  warming see also climate change, 108, 187
Google Earth™, 194
Goulburn–Broken Catchment, 149, 188
governance, xxi, 10, 23, 33–34, 41, 43–46, 92, 93, 125, 127, 155, 157, 164, 177, 178, 179, 186, 187, 189, 210, 211, 213, 214, 227–236, 237–242, 251, 256, 257, 261–263, 273
  approaches, 158, 164

of resources, 61, 81
opportunities, 87
structures, 130, 236, 238, 241, 251, 252, 257, 259
systems, xxi, 7, 24, 55, 62, 65, 128, 226, 237, 241, 245, 254, 257, 261
Grain for Green programme, 130
Great Barrier Reef, 85, 142, 149–156, 159, 164, 181, 210, 239
Great Barrier Reef Marine Park Authority, 150
Great Plains, 10
green spaces, 16
greenhouse-gas emissions, 39
Greenland ice sheet, 5, 108
Gulf of California, 231, 232

harvesting, 110, 114, 129, 132, 181
Hasanuddin University (UNHAS), 205, 208
health, xix, 2, 10, 13, 14, 147
herbivorous fish, 60, 154
heterogeneity, 9, 56, 64
  spatial, 57
  social, 61
Hindukush mountains, 122
homogenization, 94, 98, 260, 263
honeybees, 68, 71
Horn of Africa, 115
human
  activities, 3, 4, 57, 132, 134
  rights, xix, 32, 42
  well-being, xxii, 2, 5, 6, 9, 11, 13, 14, 15, 23, 107, 125, 131, 132, 252, 267
human–environment interactions, 7
human–environment systems *see also* socio–ecological systems, 7
Hungary, 107, 155, 159, 192
hurricanes, 57
hysteresis, 118, 147, 162

identity, 4, 15, 214
Indian Ocean, 59
indigenous
  communities, 183, 214
  knowledge, 203
  rights, 214
  sovereignty, 214
Indonesia, 121, 204, 205, 206, 207
industrial era, 4
inequality, xix, 34

infant survival, 2
infilling, 4
inland water, 4
innovation, 50, 65, 129, 187, 215, 231, 272
institutional
  barrier, 143, 166, 277
  diversity, 226, 234
  settings, 213
interactions, 82, 5, 7, 9, 10, 11, 12, 15, 16, 46, 50, 57, 82, 96, 98, 99, 109, 145, 149, 152, 177, 179, 180, 183, 185, 186, 188, 229, 241, 251, 252, 253, 259, 260, 265, 267, 269, 270, 274, 277, 278
  antagonistic, 63, 260
  complex, 10, 264
  facilitating, 15, 260
  mutualistic, 98
  negative, 211, 242
  social, 178, 261, 275
  synergistic, 260
intergroup conflict, 17, 32
International Commission for the Conservation of Atlantic Tuna (ICCAT), 243
International Convention for the Regulation of Whaling, 40
International Programme on Ecosystem Change and Society, 275
intrinsic value, 15
invasive species, 4, 64, 263
Italy, 209

Kenyan reef fisheries, 54
key actors, 59, 60, 64, 119, 209, 242
keystone
  patches, 86, 96
  species, 59, 60, 64, 95
knowledge, 26, 50, 51, 58, 88, 95, 98, 127, 130, 131, 135, 143, 158, 162, 174, 175, 177, 178, 179, 182–187, 191, 192, 193, 204, 255, 259, 260, 263, 265, 270, 273, 274, 276
  experiential, 203, 204
  local, 58, 161, 206, 217, 234
  scientific, 19, 46, 58, 160, 187, 202, 232, 234
  traditional, 148, 158, 185, 187, 203, 234, 270
Kristianstad wetlands, 119, 181, 186
Kruger National Park, 130, 142, 154, 156, 159, 164, 189

lakes, 4, 11, 89, 115, 126
landscape patches, 52, 56, 81, 84
leadership, 12, 133, 189, 209, 213, 215, 216, 219, 235, 241, 276
learning, xxi, 22, 65, 88, 95, 145, 174, 207, 208, 215, 216, 226, 228, 232, 234, 256, 257, 258–263, 269, 270–271, 278
 transformative, 210
 social, 179, 12, 43, 94, 158, 162, 178, 191, 193, 212, 220, 241, 276
legitimacy, 35, 36, 43, 201, 202, 204, 209, 234, 236, 242, 267
life expectancy, 2
livelihoods, 51, 59, 66, 70, 115, 158
living with the river, 155, 159, 164
local knowledge, 161, 206, 217, 234
Long Beach Model Forest, 213

Madagascar, 90, 91, 93, 95
Maine, 231, 232
Makassar, Indonesia, 204, 205, 207, 208
maladaptation, 94
Malawi, 213
Malpai Borderlands, 240
Management and Exploitation Areas for Benthic Resources (MEABR)
Mandela, Nelson, 108
mangroves, 95
marine protected area (MPA), 85, 209
mechanization, 10
mental models, 22, 44, 47, 144–148, 149, 155, 158, 161, 164, 165, 166, 181, 186, 256, 259, 273
Mexican forest governance, 231
millennium development goals (MDGs), 205
Millennium Ecosystem Assessment (MA), 13, 162, 274
Minnesota, 192
'mock court', xiii, xiv, 19, 20, 21
modularity, 22, 88, 97, 226, 229, 230, 231, 233, 234, 235, 238, 241
monitoring, 22, 36, 43, 130, 153, 178–180, 188, 191, 201, 203, 210, 215, 217, 234, 241, 245, 258, 268, 269, 274
Monteregie connection, 97
Moscow, 124
mutualistic communities, 88

Namibia, 36, 37, 59, 215
National Water Act, South Africa, 236

natural disasters, 12, 57
natural resource management, 148
negative feedbacks, 110
nested institutions, 227
Netherlands, 155
networks, 65, 85, 95, 99, 164, 183, 187, 189, 192, 205, 212, 217, 240, 242, 255
 ecological, 66, 92
 policy, 229
 social, 12, 62, 81, 87, 94, 125, 178, 185, 191, 255
New Orleans, 121
New Zealand, 238
NeWater, 155
Newfoundland, 115
nodes, 60, 82, 84, 88, 92, 96, 255
non-linear behaviour, 1, 6, 21, 262
non-linear system dynamics, 9, 11, 63, 278
North American beaver (*Castor canadensis*), 60
North Pacific Fur Seal Convention, 40
nuclear proliferation, 5
Nunavut Wildlife Management Board, 184, 185
nutrient cycling, 5, 14, 57, 65, 118
nutrition, 2, 13, 39

ocean governance, 242, 243
organic farming, 65
Ostrom's institutional design principles, 268
overexploitation, 11, 88, 121, 132
ozone hole, 5, 187

palm-oil plantations, 38
Pamir mountains, 122
Pareto frontier, 42
parrotfish, 95, 128
participation, xiii, xxi, 7, 36, 43, 65, 87, 180, 191, 193, 201–208, 234, 256, 257, 263, 273, 275, 278
participative methodology, 215
participatory monitoring, 189, 209, 210, 217
pasture rotation, 41
path dependency, xx, 166
pathology of resource management, 148
payments for ecosystem services (PES), 130
perspectives, 7, 23, 33, 41, 58, 88, 90, 147, 156, 161, 165, 179, 192, 202, 209, 214, 258, 260, 262, 270, 273
 diversity, 65, 191

pest outbreaks, 89
  regulation, 94
pesticides, 121
pests, 13, 81
Philippines, 210
pine beetle, 89
planetary boundaries, 28, 135
Poland, 213
politicization, 41, 46
politics, 32, 45, 146, 190, 237, 266
pollination, 15, 16, 65, 71, 87
  services, 68, 95
pollution, 4, 152
  control, 57, 188
polycentric governance systems, 7, 21, 226
polycentricity, xxi, 7, 10, 25, 43, 55, 65, 164, 185, 218, 227–244, 254, 257, 258–263, 269, 271, 273, 275, 278
portfolio theory, 56
poverty, xix, 2, 36, 39, 44, 120, 129
poverty traps, 39, 44
power, xix, xxii, 17, 24, 32, 36, 41, 43, 52, 62, 143, 144, 162, 165, 166, 174, 185, 187, 191, 193, 201, 202, 203, 204, 212, 213, 215, 216, 219, 227, 238, 257, 258, 266, 276, 277
  differentials, 34, 46, 216
  dynamics, 32
  grid, 97
  inequalities, 32, 67
  inequities, 203
property rights, 40, 238
provisioning ecosystem services, 13, 15, 40, 54, 59, 109

Quebec, xxiii, 97

racial discrimination, 107
rainfall patterns, 4, 5, 108
rainwater harvesting, 129
recolonization, 83, 84
recreation, 2, 11, 14, 15, 16, 22, 87, 113, 149, 181
Reducing Emissions from Deforestation and Forest Degradation (REDD), 44
redundancy, xiv, xxi, 7, 8, 20, 50, 56, 70, 71, 226, 230, 231, 233, 234, 235, 236, 241, 254, 255, 257, 258, 259, 271

refuges, 57, 85, 257
regime shifts, 11, 13, 22, 85, 115, 116, 118, 119, 122, 126, 131–135, 154, 252, 255
regulating services, 13, 40, 87, 118, 238, 255
Representative Areas Program (RAP), 150
representativeness, 219
Resilience Alliance (RA), xvii, xxi, 19
resilience, xvi, xix, xxii, 1, 5–10, 12–18, 20–24, 26, 32–35, 40, 42–46, 50, 51, 80, 81, 83, 85–99, 106, 108, 110, 115, 116, 118, 119, 131, 142, 158, 161, 189, 194, 212, 213, 218, 226, 245, 251–257, 270, 274
  approach, 22
  of ecosystem services, 174, 19, 23, 25, 26, 32, 125, 142, 143, 145, 148, 149, 152, 156, 157, 163, 165, 178–186, 193, 194, 201, 204, 214, 219, 231, 232, 235, 237, 238, 241, 246, 262, 263, 264, 266, 271, 273
Resilience Alliance Young Scholars (RAYS), 12, 19
resilience workbooks, 162
resource
  management, 9, 56, 58, 62, 146, 148, 155, 161, 213, 236
  production, 94
  use, 38, 40, 92, 162, 279
response diversity, 23, 50, 54, 55, 57, 60, 61, 65, 66, 67, 71, 134, 231, 233, 234, 235, 241, 255
rice, 121
Richtersveld Cultural and Botanical Landscape, 38
Richtersveld National Park, 36, 37
Richtersveld Transfrontier Park, 36
rigidity traps, 46
roving bandits, 129
rules, 18, 38, 40, 84, 126, 176, 226, 227, 231, 234, 265, 268, 272

Sahel, 115, 119
salinization, 4, 121, 122, 123
savannas, 106, 111, 112, 114, 118
scales, xix, xx, xxii, 4, 5, 8, 9–12, 16, 17, 23, 33, 46, 68, 71, 84, 129, 135, 143, 153, 164, 165, 177, 182, 183, 193, 226, 227, 231, 234, 235, 241, 245, 269, 270, 274, 277

ecological, 203
global, 135, 252, 277
multiple, 95, 162, 176, 227, 229, 236, 266, 267, 278
spatial, 51, 145, 188, 227
temporal, xxii, 62, 81, 266
scenario planning, 152, 153, 159, 161, 162, 163, 165, 192
scientific knowledge, 202, 19, 46, 58, 160, 187, 232, 234
scientization, 41, 46
Second World War, 2, 3
self-organization, 21, 272, 278
sense-making, 209
Seri fisheries, 231, 232
severe acute respiratory syndrome (SARS), 5
shadow network, 119, 155, 156, 159, 240, 255
shocks *see also* disturbance, 5, 6, 7, 9, 10, 17, 18, 22, 23, 25, 66, 68, 110, 128, 180, 201, 230, 277
sink–source dynamics, 85
slow variable, 23, 105, 107, 109–115, 116, 120, 127, 128, 130, 131, 133
social
  capital, 156, 189, 212, 213, 238, 241, 255, 257, 259, 262, 272, 273
  learning, 12, 43, 94, 158, 162, 178, 182, 183, 186, 190, 191, 192, 193, 212, 216, 260, 261, 276
  networks, 12, 60, 61, 81, 87, 88, 92, 93, 94, 98, 125, 174, 185, 191, 240, 255
social–ecological systems (SES), xii, 5, 8, 11, 12, 13, 15, 32, 33, 50, 56, 81, 84, 105, 142, 143, 174, 175, 176, 201, 202, 227, 251, 252, 265, 270
  governance, 24, 41, 65, 133, 237, 254, 255
  management, 23, 24, 63, 130, 145, 146, 192
social–ecological
  memory, 58
  transformation, 119, 120
societal goals, 17, 34
socio-political stability, 12
soil conservation, 41
soil erosion, 10, 16
South Africa, xxiii, xxiv, 36, 59, 107, 130, 135, 149, 154, 159, 161, 189
South African National Park (SANParks), xxiii, 36, 135, 154

South Sulawesi Province, 205, 206
Soviet Union, 124, 125
spatial insurance hypothesis, 86
species diversity, 57
  interaction, 82
  richness, 57, 64
stability domain, 11, 13, 157
stakeholder, 61, 66, 108, 148, 152, 154, 159, 162, 164, 177, 187, 190, 201, 202, 203, 205, 206, 208, 209, 211, 212, 214, 215, 217, 272, 273
  engagement, 152, 206
  participation, 203, 206, 218
stewardship, xxii, 7, 211, 214
stormwater management, 65
strategic adaptive management, 130, 154, 159, 189
surprise *see also* shock, disturbance, 50, 68, 142, 145, 147, 162, 175, 271, 272
sustainability, 5, 6, 12, 23, 36, 43, 44, 132, 185, 227, 277
sustainability science, xx, xxii, 5, 7
Sustainable Urban Development (SUD), 205
Sweden, 119, 186

Tajikistan, 122
Tanzania, 129, 137, 221
technology, 15, 40, 78, 146
athreshold *see* critical threshold
thresholds of potential concern (TPC), 130, 135, 154, 159, 162, 167
timescales, 23, 109, 130, 188, 264
tipping points *see also* critical threshold, xxi, 5, 6, 135
Tisza River, 106, 140, 142, 155, 156, 157, 158, 159, 172, 199, 224
trade-offs, xxii, 7, 16, 17, 24, 32–39, 41–43, 45, 46, 48, 49, 89, 139, 145, 152, 158, 180, 236, 237, 245, 246, 257, 258, 266, 268–270, 273, 277, 279
traditional ecological knowledge, 148, 167, 171, 172, 185, 187, 195, 197, 198, 203, 234, 270, 279
transaction costs, 46, 62, 184, 235, 236, 237
transformation, xii, xvi, xx, 12, 16, 20, 28, 29, 48, 73, 74, 106, 119, 120, 125, 129, 132, 133, 136, 137, 138, 149, 155, 158, 159, 169, 178, 195, 255

transformational change, 12
transformative change, learning, 133, 181, 278
traps, 11, 122, 193
  poverty, 39, 44
  rigidity, 46
tropical forests, 38
trust, 25, 84, 88, 98, 160, 179, 184, 185, 189, 199, 201, 202, 204, 214, 215, 216, 219, 238, 240, 241, 255, 256, 257, 258–260, 262, 272, 273
Tugai forests, 122
Turan lowlands, 122
Turkmenistan, 122

uncertainty, xxi, 1, 12, 50, 62, 68, 123, 142, 143, 145, 146, 147, 152, 155, 157, 161–164, 165, 168, 172, 175, 176, 180, 183, 187, 194, 199, 236, 256, 258, 262, 267, 270, 271, 279
UNESCO World Heritage status, 38
Upper San Pedro Partnership, 240
urban water management, 222
  planning, 204, 205
urchins, 60
US Dust Bowl, 10
Uzbekistan, 122, 125

values, 15

variables
  controlling *see* controlling conditions
  fast, 109, 127, 130
  slow, 23, 25, 105–115, 116, 120, 126, 127, 130, 131, 133
variety, 21, 52, 53, 55, 57, 60, 108, 109, 206
vegetation corridors, 82
volcanic eruptions, 57
volunteers, 203, 218

water
  provision, 87
  quality, 87, 130
  system innovations, 28, 129
  table, 118, 121, 122, 123
  use, 12, 122, 125
well-being, 252, *see also* human well-being
West Africa, 115, 164
wicked problem, 255
Wilamette Valley, Oregon, 237
windows of opportunity, xx, 119, 133, 255
worldviews, 39, 61, 109, 144, 148, 158, 169, 178, 182, 185, 187, 191, 193, 258

Yellowstone-to-Yukon project, 86, 97, 103
Yunnan, China, 209